GARDENS
THAT CARE FOR THEMSELVES

Tam Mossman

GARDENS
THAT CARE
FOR THEMSELVES

How to Grow Neater, Healthier Plants
and Cut Your Outdoor Chores in Half

Drawings by Dann Jacobus

DOUBLEDAY & COMPANY, INC.
GARDEN CITY, NEW YORK
1978

Library of Congress Cataloging in Publication Data

Mossman, Tam.
Gardens that care for themselves.

Includes index.
1. Landscape gardening. I. Title.
SB473.M74   712
ISBN: 0-385-11171-1
Library of Congress Catalog Card Number 77–76256

This book is for my father

CONTENTS

INTRODUCTION

WHY YOUR PROPERTY DEMANDS ENDLESS WORK

Eight years ago, I bought a house in a neighborhood laid out by developers some twenty years before. Next door lived an elderly Scandinavian who had landscaped his subdivision from the beginning, ringing his property's perimeter with a magnificent privacy hedge of trees and shrubs. He kept their foliage scrupulously pruned and neat, raked bare the earth beneath them, and clipped back his pines and flowering shrubs each spring and again in autumn.

But by the time I moved in, his entire ménage was slowly, inexorably getting out of hand. His once-small spruces and pines had overgrown the shrubs planted between them; his viburnums, forsythia, and mock orange were now in almost full shade, unkempt and sprawling, blooming with only a fraction of their original splendor. Each year, the white pines he'd planted as a low hedge sprouted with at least a foot of new growth. He now needed to climb a stepladder to clip their bristling tops. But even so, they had begun shading their own lower branches. And, deprived of light, these eye-level, privacy-giving twigs were dropping their needles and dying back, making the "hedge" transparent.

His lawn, once green and lush, had become hard-packed under the feet of visitors and the press of lawn furniture. Twice a week, he mowed his grass and carted away the clippings—thus removing a good percentage of the subsoil's few remaining nutrients. But now, the lawn required extra water and fertilizer to maintain its handsome appearance. However, a narrow strip of grass between his privacy hedge and the street was beyond the reach of his mower's electric cord, and so he had to mow it with a separate reel mower—that, unfortunately, was unable to decimate the tough sedges and ragweed that were colonizing themselves in the dry soil.

When I bought my place, I also planted some white pines—but dwarf ones that soon grew into the low, billowy shapes that he needed shears to maintain. My front yard needed a privacy hedge too, but instead of deciduous shrubs like forsythia, I used rhododendrons and evergreen azaleas. They naturally grew into neat, compact shapes, but tolerated shade well enough that even as they grew large, their lower branches remained lush and attractive. Being evergreen, these shrubs provided seclusion during the winter as well, when my neighbor's deciduous hedge was largely a translucent assortment of bare branches.

Just as he did, I had a strip of lawn bordering the street, but I immediately ripped up the grass and replaced it with pachysandra. Within a year, I no longer had to mow. Nor rake, either: the pachysandra swallowed up the deluge of autumn leaves from an enormous pin oak. That fall, I interplanted the pachysandra with large daffodil bulbs, and the next spring, that neat border became an ever-increasing display of yellow flowers while my neighbor's grass strip was just beginning to choke itself with sprouting weeds and wild grasses.

Meanwhile, I hauled away his grass clippings (thus saving him a trip to the town dump) and used them as mulch on the bare earth underneath my own shrubs and perennials. Within a few months, my soil had begun to improve, and the plants were far healthier, filling in many of the originally empty gaps. Even though I was putting into my garden only about a third of the work he did, my property continued to improve itself without much assistance, growing more attractive and neater each year. The older it gets, in fact, the *less* work it requires.

Not long ago, my neighbor's doctor advised him that his regimen of garden maintenance had become simply too strenuous. He was forced to sell the house and grounds he loved and move to a condominium. When a new owner bought the property, he was appalled at the estimate a local nursery gave him for "renovating" the overgrown plantings. But now, at my new neighbor's invitation, I'm using my own techniques on that ailing privacy hedge between his land and mine, making rather easy changes of pruning and planting that are rejuvenating it and transforming it into a "free form" hedge that needs no upkeep at all.

If so many of our established gardens grow to be time-consuming eyesores, it's largely because gardeners are too optimistic about what they can accomplish singlehandedly. And to understand this excessive ambition, it helps to recall how the Western tradition of gardening began.

Tourists who visit Anne Hathaway's cottage in Stratford-on-Avon today can see a reproduction of the cheerfully robust, sprawling "peasant" gardens such as were planted by Shakespeare's in-laws in the sixteenth century. Those rankly growing herbs and perennial flowers needed little care or attention. The upper classes demanded a bit more neatness, of course; but even so, most medieval and Renaissance gardens were fairly modest affairs, constrained by walls and piazzas. But then came the Baroque Era—a time of opulence and unrivaled extravagance—and the creation of a garden whose memory has haunted Western horticulture ever since.

The Château of Versailles was begun by Louis XIII—a withdrawn, unhappy King who discouraged visitors by building his modest hunting lodge in a tract of unpleasantly swampy forest. The sheer wildness of the spot was an affront to his son, Louis XIV, who thrived on pomp and public spectacle. He soon enclosed his father's original château in a vast complex of wings and apartments. And outside the walls, virtually nothing was left in its natural state. The land was leveled, drained, and replanted with the most rigorous discipline.

The gardens of Versailles, as originally designed by André Le Nôtre, have been precisely restored. If you visit the palace today and gaze out the windows at the *Grande Parterre,* only the colors of the leaves and flowers suggest that what you're viewing is actually living vegetation. An avenue of full-sized horse chestnuts has been pruned into an enormous hedge. Amid a sea of pebbled mulches, potted orange trees are severely cropped into enormous lollipops. Grass is trimmed to within literally an inch of its life. Annuals and perennials are laid out with a mathematical rigidity in which a stray leaf is *lèse majesté* and the presence of weeds unthinkable.

It's hard to underestimate Versailles' enormous influence. Virtually every monarch of Europe tried to emulate the palace in one way or another—sometimes plagiarizing it directly, as in Vienna's Schönbrunn. Where an archaic castle resisted architectural expansion, gardeners made the building more imposing by cutting down surrounding trees, just as many homeowners today try to make their split-levels more elegant by framing them with a wide sweep of lawn.

Not all green thumbs had blue blood, of course, but up through the nineteenth century, botanical pioneers and garden-builders were usually wealthy. Tulips were first grown and hybridized by the wealthy Dutch merchant class; a new line of hybrid azaleas arose on the Rothschilds' Exbury Estate in England; today's arboretums began as either private preserves or well-funded horticultural clubs. If these gardens are impressive, it's because they were deliberately intended to be! Even as late as the 1920s, most wealthy Americans wanted to stun their visitors with the legions of gardeners they could command, rather than with their taste or botanical knowledge.

Nowadays, however, even a lawn service can run up astonishing monthly bills. Now that most suburban properties measure half an acre or less, it would seem to make sense that gardens should be cultivated in a less taxing and expensive way. Yet the cherished ideal of how a garden is "supposed to look" has not changed: everyone wants plenty of lawn and flowers—at any cost—and a bare, "neat" look under and around growing plants. These standards are not only costly to maintain, but often they actually work against nature—with disastrous results.

For one thing, the soil of most gardens is entering a serious decline. In uncultivated land, infertile subsoil often lies within six inches of the surface. Above it is a fairly thin layer of black, crumbly soil that seems unimportant because there's so little of it. But it's this thin humus layer that keeps plants alive. Composed of decayed leaves and old wood, it is rich in nutrients, fungi, and bacteria.

The roots of many perennials and shrubs are quite shallow, so that they can take advantage of this thin layer. Of course, many larger trees and perennials have roots that plunge straight down into the subsoil. But they too are benefiting from the nourishing humus above. Rainwater washes nutrients out of the humus layer, and though *itself* infertile, the subsoil beneath humus usually has a good amount of these nutrients passing through it. A plant's deeper roots provide a "backstop" for any nourishment their higher roots may have missed.

In your own garden, however, this vital humus layer is probably absent. If the builder didn't cart it away to sell as "topsoil," the bulldozers probably buried it in deep pockets where only an accidental root can reach it. Even if your humus layer was carefully preserved and replaced, it's hardly permanent. Rainwater will continue to leach nutrients into the subsoil. Unless new vegetable matter is *constantly* added and allowed to decay, even healthy humus will begin to degenerate into barren, lifeless clay.

Take a look under most "approved" shrubs and atop most "neat" flowerbeds, and you'll see bare earth—a sign of sterility in nature. Raking the ground bare this way also makes it dry out much faster. This draws subsurface water to the surface, and, when the water evaporates, soluble salts and minerals that your plants *don't* need are deposited near the top of the soil. This explains the hard crust that usually forms atop a bare-earth vegetable garden around midsummer. The surface "soil" will usually crack and crumble into large chunks, while only a few inches down, the soil will usually be much more loose and friable.

In the old days, soil could be carted in from the nearby woods to revitalize an exhausted garden. But today, this is wildly expensive. The missing chemical nutrients can be replaced with commercial fertilizers, but this is only a temporary remedy. When you remove weeds, grass clippings, and fallen leaves, your topsoil has no way of replenishing itself *structurally*. And in the end, it will take mechanical aeration and massive doses of fertilizer to make such soil support plant life at all.

You can also court disaster by choosing the wrong plants. For example, I guarantee that any healthy Lombardy poplar will either ruin your lawn with bumpy surface roots, heave your asphalt driveway, clog your sewer pipe, or tear loose your telephone wires some stormy night. Norway maple, sycamore, sweet gum, and pin oak are among the most widely used shade trees, but each assures you a lifetime of messy fallen detritus and a dead lawn underneath. Of the many hundreds of juniper varieties sold as "landscape" plants, only a half dozen keep their trim shape when mature. The rest form a dry, prickly bundle of shapeless growth. Two particularly highly touted groundcovers—crown vetch, and goutweed (*Aegopodium*)—can ruin a garden, spreading so rampantly that they smother everything in their path.

Why are such awful plants used so frequently? Simply because, in general, they're all the average nursery bothers to stock.

Jim's Nursery is a convenient stop on my way home from work. Last August, I transplanted a few seedling dogwoods from where they had sprouted inconveniently. I kept enough soil around their roots so they never felt the transfer, but I really had more than I wanted. So I stopped to ask Jim (a red-haired Scotsman with an incongruous Georgia accent) if he wanted some free dogwood seedlings. "Can't move 'em this time of year," he warned me. "They'll wilt immediately, and you'll lose every one of them."

In Jim's greenhouse, I once noticed a cattleya orchid (basically an "air plant") dying after being potted in *soil.* Another time, Jim assured me I could plant one of his rhododendrons without removing the bag around its roots, since the bag was sure to decay within the year. The bag happened to be of *plastic,* but far be it from me to tell a man how to do his job.

To be fair, it's hard for a nursery proprietor to get to know plants as well as his customers do. To make any profit at all, Jim must turn over a vast amount of stock. This means buying nearly full-grown plants from a wholesale grower and then—hopefully—selling them all before autumn. Jim simply can't afford to care for sickly plants. If they die after the customer gets them home, Jim must replace them at his own cost—so his stock invariably emphasizes the real steel-driving unkillables of the plant world: hemlock, andromeda, taxus, juniper, pin oak, Norway maple, and "ready-made" grafted fruit trees. All can withstand astonishing abuse. But aside from brute strength, these species have little to offer in terms of real beauty, and gardeners who buy them don't give them credit for the fiercely competitive organisms they really are. True, they may seem rather docile because your soil is wretched. But when even moderately healthy, they will need constant clipping to maintain a pleasant appearance.

The question, basically, is whether you want to cover your land quickly with undisciplined "take-over" plants, or have the patience to introduce more refined species that will maintain their original, neat appearance. In succeeding chapters, I include "Kill Lists" of plants that you shouldn't grow under *any* circumstances. For each of these unruly specimens, there is *always* a far more satisfactory substitute that is usually more attractive, while requiring far less attention. Moreover, it's always possible to effect the transition gradually, encouraging desirable species at the expense of "Kill List" ones so that you never have to put up with gaps and empty spots.

There's no single secret to my gardening methods, aside from a wholesale rejection of mindless tradition. I grew up on an old four-acre estate that had been coddled by caretakers and professional gardeners. It was one vast lawn, with only a few old diseased trees that had been misplanted in the first place. So over the years, my father and I kept our eyes peeled for plants that would cut down on a featureless expanse of grass that meant practically nonstop mowing.

Even then, there were a number of no-maintenance gardening books on the market. But unfortunately their directions don't work —I know because we tried them. Contrary to every book I've read, pachysandra does *better* in full sun. Only a few catalogs mention the reblooming strains of iris that give flowers *both* spring and fall. The author of one tome for "reluctant" gardeners took a course at a botanical garden, yet a great deal of her information is either misleading, incomplete, or just plain wrong. For example, she praises box elders and says they grow "only in the Western states." The ones across the street from me here in New Jersey grow like weeds, and I have found that box elder is one of the *worst* trees to plant if you hope for any grass or shrubbery to survive underneath.

In short, no book or course offered what we were trying to accomplish. And so, we had to strike off on our own, simply observing and experimenting to learn what books and articles failed to mention. Over the past twenty years, my father and I have planted, propagated, pruned, bonsaied, and cut down (when unsatisfactory) over 200 species and varieties of trees alone. Meanwhile, I've been on my own hunt for acceptable grass substitutes. After trials with some two dozen candidates, I have finally discovered two or three that really work. I've built a wildflower garden from scratch atop new clay, constructed over 300 feet of brick and rock paths, and observed the shortcomings, needs, and advantages of over 400 species of wild and cultivated perennials.

I've also designed and planted two Miniature Landscapes—entire countrysides in miniature, with normal-sized rocks serving as hills and mountains, planted with *naturally* miniature species and varieties of full-size plants. Between them, these two gardens cover less than 100 square feet, but feature over 75 different miniature exotics and groundcovers including the world's smallest violet, with leaves the size of a baby's thumbnail.

Much of the traditional advice, I've found, simply doesn't apply.

When a tree expert visited my father's land, he noticed a lush, healthy *Sciadopitys verticillata* (a fairly rare Japanese evergreen with no common name) growing in full sun. "That tree should be in shade, you know," the man explained. "But yours is doing better than the ones I've seen in shade. Maybe you better leave it."

Now whenever *any* garden book tells me what to do without explaining why, I deliberately do it differently—to see the results. In the process, I've learned any number of things that horticultural authors seem to think too unimportant to mention. No source will tell you that the leaves of tulip tree and mulberry break down within three weeks of hitting the ground, but that pin oak leaves can still be intact after three *years*. No writer points out that often the low, sagging branches of old azaleas often take root naturally. If cut, they become virtually "instant" bushes that transplant with no shock at all. No garden encyclopedia admits that spiderwort, which is horridly difficult to transplant, will root in a few weeks from stem cuttings.

The very first chapters of this book tell you how to recognize pitfalls that, sooner or later, are going to cost you days of extra work and unforeseen expenses in the hundreds of dollars. All of my advice centers on how to solve these problems permanently, or—even better—do things right in the first place so that you'll never have to do them again.

Of course, some solutions are easy—chop down that Lombardy poplar, and get a sledgehammer ready to mash the watersprouts that will begin arising throughout your lawn. But other changes—such as planting a red maple to the south of your house, where it will cast cool shade in high summer—take longer. You should know about the literally self-pruning shadblow or sarvice tree, but it'll take time to grow tall enough to flower. Similarly, it will take you some years to achieve a "double decker" privacy hedge of rhododendrons and flowering fruit trees—or the long-term mulching that will assure you can grow exotic wildflowers like pipsissewa and partridgeberry.

Some tasks, in short, need to be done before others, so each of the following chapters appears in order of priority—first things first, so that you can tackle them as soon as possible. But once you've pachysandraed a slope too steep for mowing, or laid a mortarless brick path, or planted a tupelo where it will look handsome for the next hundred years, the job is *done,* finished; and requires little or no further upkeep. My directions combine minimum work with maximum results, so even while your long-term projects are under way, you can begin *enjoying* your place.

Throughout this book, I'm concentrating on particularly desirable plants that have done very well for me. If you find one of your favorites missing, it's because I haven't had a chance to observe it personally and would rather not mislead you with guesswork—mine or anyone else's. But I believe I *have* covered every common plant with bad habits, so that any remaining "unknowns" are less likely to cause you trouble. By the time you're halfway through this book, you'll have a good idea of how to tell if any stranger is welcome or not.

Nor can I claim that my methods will give overnight results. But then, I've never seen an "instant" garden that wasn't either ruinously expensive or didn't demand increasing repair and revision over the years. You have to start correcting your worst obstacles one by one, methodically and stubbornly, until the individual improvements finally start pulling together and your property is working *with* you. Only then can you devote time to the joyous projects that most gardeners never have the time to begin: wildflowers, extensive rock gardens, even a Miniature Landscape.

No satisfactory property is *ever* maintenance-free, but by putting your efforts into my system, you should enjoy increasingly greater rewards—and fewer boring chores and expensive failures. You may even find yourself devoting more time to gardening than before. The difference is that you'll *want* to.

GARDENS
THAT CARE FOR THEMSELVES

🌷 PART ONE 🌷

LANDSCAPING
FROM THE GROUND UP

1

LEVELING YOUR LAWN. RETAINING WALLS AND STONE STAIRS

A friend of mine spent several years turning his infertile back yard into lush, tree-studded grass. But the lawn he created followed his property's original steep grade. Thus when he wanted to install a small swimming pool, the entire slope had to be terraced. The bulldozers stripped off his trees and grass and left him with heaps of the same bare earth he'd faced before.

An upstate account executive finally ripped out the wild briers and weeds that had congested a steep bank beside his driveway. He planted it anew with taxus, junipers, and sedum. But these plants' roots were too shallow to hold the freshly bared bank against erosion. Each thunderstorm brought a slide of mud down onto his macadam. Finally he began building the retaining wall he should have constructed in the first place, only to find that his new plantings were in the way. They all had to be dug up again, replanted temporarily elsewhere, and moved back when the job was finished.

Relatives of mine decided to replace their "rustic" hop-skip-and-jump front walk with a path easier for their young children to navigate. A new flagstone path was sunk even with the surface of their lawn and ran directly and conveniently to the street. But before laying in that new path, they had to import three tons of topsoil to fill up depressions, chop down a thirty-year-old magnolia that had grown too large to transplant, and relocate almost a thousand spring-flowering bulbs.

The point should be obvious: too many gardeners still begin major plantings long before the soil—the most basic consideration of the local landscape—has been arranged to their complete satisfaction.

Part of the problem is a result of the population boom. Back during the 1920s and '30s, when open land was more abundantly available, builders automatically selected fairly level ground for new homes. But because today's developers need to make every plot count, houses are often built on grades better suited to mountain goats. The fairly recent evolution of the split-level house is one architectural attempt to mitigate this problem. But the surrounding land usually is left to slope as much as it did originally, which makes it that much less enjoyable.

For idle outdoor life, there's no ground surface that can beat a nice *flat* lawn. A gentle grade may still be okay for sunbathing or picnics but murder if you want to play baseball or badminton. Food arranged on a picnic table slides continually down to one end. Iced tea glasses tip over when set on the grass. So the more your lawn surface departs from the horizontal ideal, the less you'll be able to do on it.

It will also be that much harder to maintain. Sloping grass dries out too quickly and is hard to fertilize or reseed evenly. On slopes, a person walks not on his sole but on the ball or heel of the foot, so the soil beneath packs down more rapidly. As a lawnmower encounters a major change of grade, it becomes much harder to control, and its blades tend to scalp. But if you're willing to put in a bit of effort *now,* you can fix this problem once and for all. The basic technique is guaranteed, because it's been used for centuries.

Rice—a staple of much of the world's population—grows only in standing water. It would seem that if any plant needed absolutely flat country for cultivation, rice would be it. Yet in Indochina and the Philippines, rice is grown on the most precipitous mountainsides, which farmers have carved into a series of level terraces.

Obviously, a series of narrow rice paddies is no place to play lawn tennis. But theoretically, as long as you build your eventual retaining walls high enough, you can have a flat expanse of practically any width. (See Figure 1.) Basic geometry assures you that the soil you remove from A will almost perfectly fill up B, so that you won't have to cart in too much extra.

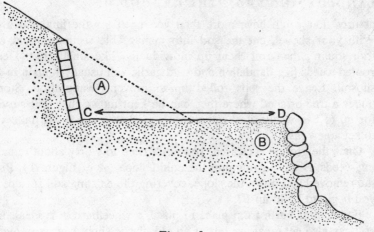

Figure 1

The only trick is to make the horizontal distance *C–D* as long as possible, although that may mean raising the retaining walls at top and bottom to extravagant heights. If you have a very steep slope, the leveled area will have to be narrow. But the wider it is, the better for cookouts, touch football, or Frisbee.

I admit this may seem like a radical change. But an accessible lawn or flower bed that suits *your* taste will pay off for as long as you own your property. And it needn't take all that much work. Many lawns that slope only gently can be leveled in a day or two, and the retaining walls are so low they can be mistaken for edgings.

How to Go About It

A bulldozer is quickest, of course, but the soil packed down in its tracks will need to be dug up later and loosened. If you use a shovel, the blade should be wide to hold as much soil as possible. But make sure the end is tapered. A squared-off spade or shovel is harder to drive into the hard subsoil you're likely to encounter.

Before you actually start digging, remove any existing grass. Otherwise, the clumps of sod mixed with the soil will make later stages of the work much more difficult. If your lawn is at all decent, you can try to preserve as much of it as you can—and again, geometry assures that you'll have more than you need for the final flat area. With your shovel, cut the sod into manageable sections about one foot square, then roll them up individually, like small rugs. Deep-rooted weeds like dandelion and wild garlic will usually remain in the subsoil. Leave the sods rolled up to prevent evaporation. Stored under a tree or shed where they can be kept moist, they will survive for up to two weeks, and can greatly speed the time it will take you to get a new lawn surface started.

Once the ground is cleared, you don't need to worry about remaining weeds. Begin digging into the uphill slope (*A* of Figure 1). Push the removed soil down the slope, covering the existing soil surface as you begin to build up *B*.

For hauling earth from place to place, a wheelbarrow is ideal. But you can also get great use out of an old plastic shower curtain. *Never* throw out one of these handy items; it makes an ideal tarpaulin for dragging soil and bundling up leaves. Even when worn full of holes, it will come in handy for a number of uses I'll describe in later chapters.

If you turn up sizable rocks, you'll need to pry them loose. (Never use a shovel to pry loose a heavy rock; it's too easy to break off the handle.) But the standard cast-iron crowbars are extraordinarily heavy, and I've switched to a hefty length of 1½″ galvanized steel pipe culled from the local junkyard. Simply place the end of your would-be crowbar in some immovable corner, and give a shove. If it bends, it's too light. Proceed to the next heavier size. The larger ones are remarkably strong but, being hollow, are vastly lighter than any crowbar. And when you're temporarily through with them, they plunk into the soil quite easily without tipping under their own weight.

As you come across rocks wider than two or three inches, toss them to one side. You're *hoping* for ones over a foot across, since they're what you'll need to construct the first of your two retaining walls.

The cut you make at the top of *A* should be straight across—and at right angles to the slope. A string held between two posts will help you cut a straight line. As you dig deeper, though, the cut should not be vertical but should slant outward toward its eventual base *C*. The taller face *A* becomes, the more *C* should protrude to help support the weight of the soil behind it.

How far you spread your soil downhill depends on how deep you're willing to dig down into this top slope. If your original slope was constant, *B* will more or less equal *A*. So a good rule is to stop when bank *A* approaches four feet tall.

The loose earth to be dumped into *B* will be impossible to firm and pack if not held in place. That enormous flattened mound of dirt will wash on down the slope—unless it's stopped and held in place. So even before leveling the soil any further, you must construct a retaining wall to prevent erosion.

RETAINING WALLS

For several reasons, I'm against concrete. First, it's difficult to pour it in an almost vertical form, as is called for here. You'd have to dig down below the foot of *B*, level the bottom of the trench, introduce a foundation layer of small stones, build wooden molds, and then mix and pour vast amounts of cement, leveling its surface carefully before it sets. Blocks of concrete or cinder block are easier, but become really filthy and unattractive over the years. Paint them, and the paint soon blisters and flakes off, giving a mangy effect between patch-ups. And there's no way to adjust such a wall six inches in or out without major exacavations.

I'm also against railroad ties or old telephone poles, because they aren't as permanent as claimed. Creosoted wood takes on an increasingly sullen appearance as it weathers and, since creosote is a poison, it inhibits the growth of nearby plants. If you must use wood to shore up a bank temporarily, use untreated beams and set them back a few inches, so that a later facing can be built right over them.

The ideal—and most formal—retaining wall is a regular fitted stone wall of the sort built in colonial times as fences to mark property lines and restrain cattle. Such a wall is basically free-standing, and so can be built at the lower limit of your new terrace even *before* you begin the soil excavation. All you have to do is dig into the ground where you want it to stand, so that the bottom rocks rest on a strip of level soil. Later rocks should be fitted slightly inward, so that the entire wall leans back slightly toward the top (Figure 2).

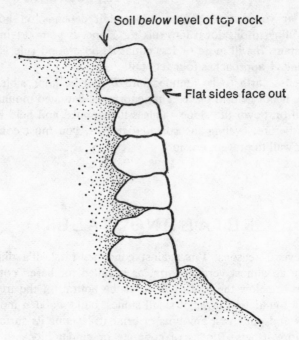

Soil *below* level of top rock

← Flat sides face out

Figure 2

A fitted stone wall should be of gneiss, limestone, shale, or granite
—which break to form angular rocks with fairly straight edges. That
kind may have been carted away for building in earlier times, or simply be missing in the first place. In my area, most gardeners have little else but quantities of rounded, glacier-tumbled rocks with no flat
edges. Extremely awkward to fit one atop another, they usually begin
tumbling down again after a few seasons of frost.

However, this is true only if the stones are fitted *atop* each other.
If you're building a retaining wall where one side is solid dirt, you
can still use rounded rocks in a structure I call the Poor Man's Stone
Wall.

I invented it out of necessity. The ground beside my driveway
slopes so steeply that some kind of retaining wall was a must. The
original owner had made a good try at fitting the local stones one
upon the other, but by the time I moved in, his entire heap was bulg-
ing at its many seams and threatening to avalanche whenever I
parked the car.

One chilly spring day I dismantled the entire stone wall. Then—as you must do—I chose the very largest rocks and placed them where I wanted the bottom of my new wall to be (in my case, right at the edge of the blacktop). To hold these stones securely in place, I tipped them back against the bank and filled any remaining spaces behind them with loose dirt. Then when the filled-in dirt was even with the top of any two rocks, I placed a single smaller rock behind and between them—its bottom set in the added soil, not *on* the fore-going rocks. I added layer after layer, filling in soil behind each before beginning a new one, until the entire bank was covered with layers of rocks, each dovetailed against the one just in front of it (Figure 3).

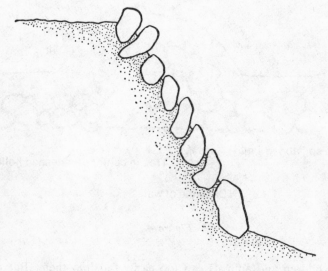

Figure 3

The best rocks for this use are *relatively* flat on both sides, so that they can be stacked rather closely together. The result is not as seemly as a regular stone wall, but it has other advantages. For one thing, gravity is on your side. Because the individual stones are sup-ported by soil, not by each other, they can settle or shift individually without throwing the entire structure out of whack. Should any part of your wall sink or collapse, it's easy to fix that section without tearing the whole thing apart. And any creeping groundcover planted at the top of the wall will soon tunnel under the rocks, emerging from the soil pockets in between, so that the entire structure becomes effectively camouflaged.

The Poor Man's Stone Wall can also be made concave, freeing an enormous amount of soil that can then be used elsewhere. Just carve a wide semicircular vertical trench in the bank you're going to cover. Faced off with rocks, the resulting niche lends interest to otherwise blah terrain. If its bottom is flattened off, it can even be planted with a shrub or small tree (Figure 4). I'm basically against tree wells be-

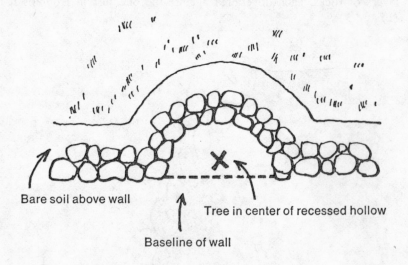

Bare soil above wall

Baseline of wall

Tree in center of recessed hollow

Figure 4

cause children and animals can too easily fall into them. But since this well is open-faced, it can't act as a pit-trap.

As with a more formal fitted wall, I'd advise you to begin your Poor Man's Stone Wall as soon as you have enough large rocks for the first layer. Because these stones won't be flat at the bottom, they need to be sunk a bit deeper in the existing soil to avoid later tipping. Again, the stones should *not* be vertical, but settled back against the dirt behind them—and thus braced against the weight that might otherwise push them forward and down the slope.

Keep building your lower retaining wall as you dig the soil to pack behind it. You should stop digging at A when its bottom, C, and the top of the lower retaining wall at D come within about six horizontal inches of each other, as determined by a level. Especially if you've removed a lot of rocks, the soil in B will still pack down quite a bit, but you can always find extra soil later to top it off. Better to stop prematurely so that you don't overexcavate A and start a slope going in the opposite direction.

To determine true horizontal, use a bubble level atop a long plank stretching from C to D. If you don't have a bubble level, an ice-cube tray will work well in a pinch. Higher water at any side of the tray will show you that that end's too low. The cube dividers not only make visual measurement easier but keep the water from sloshing around.

The downhill retaining wall can be uneven at its base—in fact, if your slope is uneven, it *has* to be. But the top has to be relatively level, because that's where the retaining wall will meet the new lawn. The top layer of stones should extend from three to six inches *above* the level of the grass, so don't be afraid to build it too high. But the line of the soil in front of it (as well as the line of soil along the base of A) must be as level as possible. So even before you begin serious leveling, add the final top layer of stones to the lower retainer. Then, move a six-foot plank with a bubble level or ice-cube tray on it along the edge of D, a few inches at a time. Where dips and bumps turn up, adjust the soil (and move the top stones if necessary). Then move the plank and level to C and do the same. These lines, if perfect, can then serve as the guide for the rest of the lawn surface.

At this point, you should have a fairly level surface at C and D, but with a peak of soil at the middle. Now attack that center peak, spreading most of it toward D. (You can always add extra soil at C, but D needs to be a very delicate compromise between soil and retaining wall, so tackle it first.)

Once you have a series of smallish mounds that no longer respond to a shovel, it's time for an iron rake. Use the tines to spread the soil and remove tree roots and remaining pebbles. For more precise flattening, turn the rake over and use the flat back.

Now, using the D line as a guide, start moving your soil evenly back toward C. Turn your plank at right angles to the line of C and D so that you make sure your soil doesn't slope sideways. Your soil may still need shifting, of course, but at least now you'll see exactly where. *If it isn't right, go back and correct it!* A little extra fuss at this stage means vastly more satisfying results later on.

You should now have a fairly level surface of soil, but it won't be packed down yet. Your feet will sink into it about an inch or so, and your latest raking will have turned up a fresh crop of roots and pebbles. Now switch to a bamboo rake. Its tines are light enough to roll up roots and gravel without moving the soil appreciably, as would a metal rake. (If a bamboo rake handle breaks, never discard the rake part. I've found that soil-finishing is actually easier with a broken rake, whose short handle you can hold in one hand as you would a paintbrush.) You aren't ready for tamping and grass yet, however. Chances are that the dirt you carved out of *A* was mainly clayish subsoil that will never support a good lawn.

Have you ever noticed how tufts of grass that seed their way into cracks in the driveway usually look healthier than the grass you're *trying* to grow? Chances are it's because the cracks in your asphalt have filled up with humus. That's the same kind of soil your lawn needs—rich, moist, and deep.

Many lawn manuals emphasize that raw clay should be *mixed* with leafmold and humus, but I can't agree. The organic matter lightens the clay briefly, but drinks up subsoil minerals like a sponge. Soon the minerals, plus the compacting of feet, will leave the soil nearly as dense as it was before. Machines that aerate the soil by punching tiny holes will let more air and water enter, but they actually compact the soil even further.

It's fairly pointless, then, to try to improve this existing soil. Simply consider this stuff subsoil—which it is—and build on *top* of it.

A good lawn should have at least two inches of porous, highly fertile humus. Even if your soil looks good according to the pointers in Chapter 4, spread a few loads of topsoil or humus atop your current soil surface to an *un*tamped depth of at least three inches. (This will raise the overall level by a couple of inches, but this is why you built your downhill retaining wall a few inches higher in the first place.) With the subsoil already flattened, smoothing the humus will be a cinch.

Before you rake out your humus, mix in one or two 10-pound bags of crushed limestone to sweeten it. Although most plants enjoy a soil that's slightly on the acid side, grass is an exception. The Department of Agriculture once seeded an experimental plot with grass seed, then treated half of it with lime. In their published photograph, the limed grass is lush and fairly healthy-looking, while the untreated acreage behind it looks like a Tiajuana parking lot.

But don't tamp yet! Once you know the approximate final level of your lawn-to-be, it's time to construct your uphill retaining wall.

Uphill Retaining Walls

The uphill face of *A*, of course, has been created by your digging *down*. That's why you have to wait until its base—that is, your new lawn level, including topsoil—has been precisely determined before building a retainer for it. First off, its base *must* be even and straight, because you'll want to mow along it later. So use the long-plank technique to shave down bulges and identify hollows that need to be filled.

If you like, you can face this slope too with a Poor Man's Stone Wall. But remember that because this wall goes *uphill* from where you'll be sitting, you'll be looking at it more often. Therefore, it makes sense to have it look as neat as possible. If *A* is over four feet, a Poor Man's Stone Wall may be a bit scruffy.

What material you use should largely be determined by the wall's height and whether its top has to be level with yet another terrace of lawn or garden. A formal fitted stone wall over six feet can give you the feel of being in a prison courtyard. But if the wall is low—under two feet—bricks are neat in appearance and vastly easier to adjust if the lawn at their base ever tends to settle.

See Chapter 3 for more brick specifics. But for a wall, lay the bricks at a slight angle to the slope (Figure 5). Use odd numbers of staggered layers—3, 5, or 7 give a better look than 2, 4, or 6. The top of any brick wall can match the top of the bank *exactly* if you fudge a bit by burying the bottom row the proper depth below lawn level.

Brick walls higher than seven rows look a bit institutional, so you can always build a Poor Man's Stone Wall to hold the soil *above* that. When a groundcover gets perfectly established, the rocks can be removed. You can also construct a couple of permanent Poor Man's Stone Walls, each only one stone tall, giving you narrow but deeper

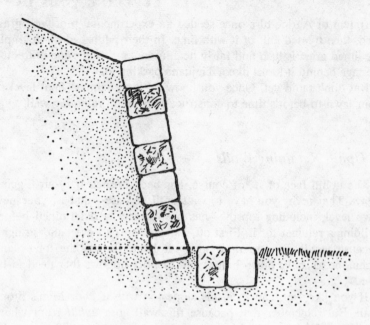

Figure 5

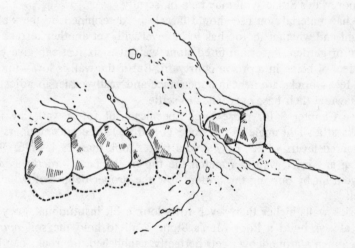

Figure 6

beds in which to plant bulbs and perennials. Bury the foot of each rock at the proper individual depth to make them all come out even on top (Figure 6). You can achieve a more natural look by removing one rock from the series and letting a slope of soil take its place. (Such rugged terrain should be planted in groundcovers and shrubs *only;* save Rockeries and Miniature Landscapes for more accessible, erosion-free locations.)

For the most part, the downhill retaining wall is going to be viewed from above, so you don't have to be quite as careful with it. But don't make the mistake of letting it go wild. Grass and weed roots can dig their way into a Poor Man's Stone Wall in ways that will mean excruciating weeding later. Start covering it with a dependable groundcover *now,* as per instructions in Chapter 9. Ideally, both this and the uphill retainer wall should serve as buffer zones that trap any airborne weed seeds that would otherwise make their way into the grass. A fairly high groundcover will provide a tiny windbreak, enough to make weeding an easier job in years to come.

STAIRS

It's odd how the owner of my property went to great pains to build a terraced lawn without considering how anyone was to get down to it. In place of an upper retaining wall, he had used an ivy-covered slope. The two paths through it were at either side of the property, making for a meaningless detour. So while you are planning these two retaining walls, remember that at least one of them will have to include a flight of steps so that people can reach the lawn *conveniently.*

Since this staircase will be getting a great deal of traffic, safety is a must. Curving, meandering steps are good only on a sunlit Rockery, where your visibility is excellent and you want to pause along the way. But steps for getting places should choose the quickest, most accessible route.

Figure 7 shows the basic components of any staircase. Note that the steps are continuous, so that you don't have to worry about grass or weeds growing up in the gaps.

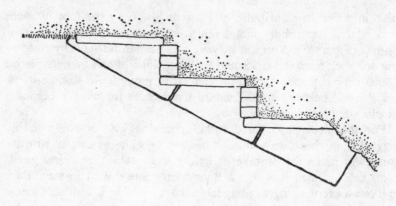

Figure 7

Unless your property abounds with *very* flat and angular stones that can be fitted with real precision, I'd advise you to get your stair materials from a local quarry or stoneyard. For the flat portion of each step, you'll need flagstones—preferably slate; for the risers and side guards, bluestone slabs.

Remember that quarries often cut their flags in slightly varying sizes. Since your steps' sides have to be strictly parallel, you'll be in trouble if you've built them halfway to the top, only to find that your supplier no longer has precut flags of that dimension. So get *all* the "step" stones you think you'll need at the same time. The approximate dimensions of each should be at least two feet by one, but exact size doesn't matter as long as they all match.

Since the stairs will be straight as an escalator, it makes sense that the bank in which they're fitted should also be a uniform grade. If it isn't, take the time now to clear a smooth six-foot-wide ramp. It'll make your later work vastly easier.

Whether the stairs are to go up or down from the lawn, always begin construction at the *bottom* of the slope. Start with a flag (or two across, as I did). The guards—vertical pieces of flagstone with the irregular sides buried—have their tops at the level of the soil bank into which the horizontal steps will be sunk. They're vital to keep this side soil from oozing onto the stairs and to keep soil under the risers from oozing *out*.

Build the first riser directly in back of the first ground-level flagstone. How tall should each riser be? A minimum of six inches, but you may have to adjust this riser height if you find your steps falling above or below the slope of the surrounding bank. (A steeper slope will take taller risers between flags, and if you've ever walked up a flight of those *endlessly* gentle steps leading to a library or museum, you'll know that steeper steps are preferable.) With a *very* steep incline, you'll want to bury the back of each step just under the next riser above it (see Figure 7).

Once each riser is complete, set the guards on either side, and then fill the "box" you've created to overflowing with loose dirt. Set a flagstone atop it, and it will pack down automatically. If the guards begin to angle outward under the pressure of the compacted soil between them, brace them with heavy stones or with short stakes hammered beside them into the soil on either side. Later they'll be held in place by the extra humus you'll be adding to the slope as per instructions in Chapter 4.

From here on up, the work is repetitious but satisfying. Unless you need to raise the stairs' angle by beginning a riser on the heel of a step, the next riser should always begin *exactly* behind the already-laid flagstone, making the work perfectly accurate. The only problems you'll have are from odd-shaped riser stones that fail to match up, or from sudden bulges and dips in the surrounding soil. But always keep the top edges of the guards the same distance *above* the corners of each step, or your supporting soil will start oozing out.

When you reach the top, you may find that the final step doesn't match up with the actual soil level. But this is really no problem. If the top step is too high, extend it into a small platform by placing other flagstones around it. If the top stair is too low, cut a level rectangle back into the surrounding soil. Around the top step, construct a "box" of flagstone guards (Figure 8)—this way, the new soil level itself serves as the final step to your staircase.

If you are going to mortar your stairs, do it only *after* you've completed the whole shebang, so that last-minute errors can be ironed out. But my stairs have gone six years without any cement or repair except an occasional transfusion of clay beneath a tipping flagstone. (The cause is almost always a tunneling mouse, rather than erosion.)

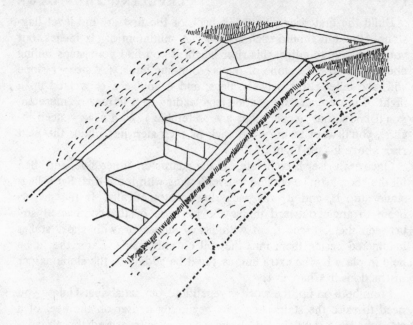

Figure 8

It would seem that your work's over, but not quite. Unless your garage or tool shed directly adjoins this leveled terrace, you're going to have to move a lawnmower there and back again after the grass comes up. Bumping a lawnmower down a flight of stairs is hard on the machine, and harder still on you if you try to carry it. But any artificial ramp of concrete or flagstone will be slippery for the feet, and somewhat unsightly.

In short, you will also need a grass path leading up or down to this new terrace. (I said before that grass is not good for slopes. However, if a grassy slope is trod upon only once or twice a week, it will survive—and serve as the perfect route for your lawnmower.) To keep visitors from using it, tuck it off to one side of your slope. If the grade isn't too steep, it can go straight down. Make the path half again as wide as the widest lawnmower you suspect you'll ever own. This way, the grass on it can be mowed automatically—half as you descend, and half when you come back up.

2

GRASS
AND WHERE NOT TO GROW IT

There's nothing better than grass for children, dogs, and people to walk and play on. But grass is also the most time-consuming plant you'll ever cultivate. One reason why grass entails so much work, of course, is that you have to mow it. But the mowing, in turn, drastically alters the grass's growth habit.

In the wild, most species of grass mature at two feet tall, while most suburban lawns are trimmed down to two or three inches. Most recent hybrid lawn grasses have blades that arise at a low angle to the soil, rather than straight up, which lets them keep a greater leaf surface after they're mowed. But even so, no other garden plant is expected to thrive with only a fraction of its potential leaf area.

Still, this constant clipping makes grass use its remaining vigor to best advantage. You've probably seen an apple tree throw out long watersprouts shortly after a severe pruning. This surge of new growth is triggered when a plant's foliage-to-roots ratio falls below 1-to-1. The same thing occurs with grass. But your lawn will look lush and attractive only if you carefully *maintain* its foliage-to-roots imbalance. Trimming the foliage is no problem; the trick is to encourage the roots, whose normal vigor depends directly on nourishment from the leaves!

Most gardeners don't realize how deep grass roots can really go. The sods you removed from your original sloping lawn—like the ones you can buy in garden centers—are deceptive. Although the sods themselves look healthy enough, they seem to have roots only an inch or so long. Actually, these are simply the *tops* of their roots. When sods were pulled up, the longer feeder roots broke off in the subsoil. When the sods are replaced, a new crop of feeder roots must grow to replace the old—and can delve as deeply as six inches.

Whether you should use (or reuse) sods at all depends, first of all, on their quality. If your old lawn wasn't particularly healthy, or if the sods your nursery offers have been trucked in from a warmer part of the country, the results can be disappointing. Sods have more leaves than they do roots—in other words, the proper imbalance of roots to leaves has been reversed, sapping the sods' vitality. Most of the original soil has fallen away from a sod; and its remaining roots will be rather dry and stiff, like the bristles of a toothbrush. This makes it particularly hard for them to introduce themselves into a new soil layer. The only way to make stiff roots and hard ground meet is by force, which is why professional landscapers use a great deal of tamping—and water, to get the subsoil as mushy and receptive as possible. But the heat of midsummer can dry out the soil so quickly that new feeder roots never have a chance to develop. Even with proper watering, new sods can often be scalded by hot sun into a prolonged slump.

Obviously, freezing temperatures are no good either, because the sods will heave loose before their roots can penetrate. My observation is that sods apply well only in early spring and late autumn, when naturally cooler temperatures give them the best advantage. However, you can employ grass *seed* at practically any season except the dead of winter.

Most lawn grass seed comes in mixtures, which is a sound idea. The mixes in your local store will be especially blended for the climate of your area, but each lawn has its own unique micro-environments of shade, soil, temperature, and moisture. Each hybrid grass strain has a *slightly* different cultural requirement, and the grass itself has to be the final judge of where it will grow best.

When buying grass seed mix, therefore, opt for the widest possible variety of different seeds. Even buying two competing blends (with different ingredients) is a good idea. This is a basic principle that applies to other plants as well: if you want to get a piece of ground covered up, introduce several different strains of similar habit and let them fight it out. The losers will at least help hold down the soil while the winners take over.

All grass seed comes with full planting instructions, so the only tips I'm giving here are ones that supplement or contradict the official line. For one thing, lawn experts suggest you seed in late fall or early spring. True, temperature and rainfall at those seasons are ideal for grass seed germination. But you can raise a lawn at *your* convenience as long as you provide enough moisture.

Even if you're seeding at the proper season, never tamp the ground *thoroughly* before you seed. Of course, seed needs a fairly compact medium in which to root. But if rollers flatten the soil to pool-table hardness, the seeds cannot penetrate the soil and have to lie atop it, vulnerable to wind and birds. My method is to tamp the soil part way, *then* seed and resume tamping. The seeds' hard coating keeps the seeds from being crushed, and this additional agitation distributes them more evenly. Best of all, it buries a good many of them just under the soil surface where germination can occur far more efficiently.

If you don't have a tamper, use a fairly heavy flagstone, dropped repeatedly from waist height. After seeding, add a light layer of grass clippings—just enough to cover the soil—and then finish tamping. This gives the soil surface a bit of shade and holds it against erosion, taking the place of the springy surface-holding roots that aren't yet there.

Even in midsummer, you can count on a certain amount of dew during the night, which is why nighttime watering is somewhat superfluous. The trick is to get moisture into the soil that will last through the hot mornings and afternoons. Let a sprinkler play for fifteen minutes each morning before ten o'clock. At 3 P.M., with two hours of strong daylight still to go, give the new grass another fifteen-minute soak.

The only problem with midsummer seeding is that weeds germinate along with the grass. Some studies have estimated that every acre of soil contains several *tons* of weed seeds. Many are buried down to a foot deep where they can lie dormant for decades, until chance—or your shovel—brings them to the surface. (After one of my father's neighbors built a swimming pool, the piles of soil she removed sprouted lavishly with jimsonweed—a plant that hadn't grown there in living memory.) Thus, just as your new grass shoots are breaking the ground, they will be joined by a host of broadleaf weeds.

Don't worry! Weeds delve their roots far deeper and more quickly than grass, so there's no immediate competition for nourishment. In fact, the taller weeds' leaves will also provide some shade, giving the grass an even better chance to establish itself.

In the meantime, of course, your new lawn will look positively rotten. But weeding isn't the answer, since each weed will pull up the still weakly rooted grass next to it. Just be patient: before the summer is over, you will mow your new lawn at least twice, and this will solve the problem. When cut back repeatedly, most weeds will give up. Those that still survive will have their flowering stalks amputated, and thus won't go to seed and reproduce themselves. So let them go for now: their days are numbered.

When you *should* mow for the first time is a tricky question. Standard advice tells you the first cut should come when the grass reaches four inches. That's fine if the soil has been packed down very hard by rollers, but yours shouldn't be. Light humus always has a tendency to fluff itself a bit under summer sun, and I find that a lawnmower often leaves deep wheelruts in a new lawn.

If you notice that your foot sinks slightly into the new lawn surface, postpone your first mow until the grass reaches six inches; by then it'll have more side roots to hold the soil steady. Always water a new lawn *lightly* before cutting, or your rotary lawnmower may act like a small wind machine, blasting clouds of dry dust from between the new grass sprouts.

I'm not saying that the result of a midsummer seeding will be fit for Arnold Palmer. But after about six weeks, the grass will be thoroughly established and ready to walk on. A few bare patches may still remain—a usual occurrence with any seeding—but if you mulch them with grass clippings, the surrounding lawn will spread to cover them more quickly.

Brick Edging

Lawns should be edged for several reasons: any plot of grass looks better when precisely limited. Moreover, if your grass grows right up against a retaining wall, it'll be out of range of your mower blades. This means going back with a hand clipper—a needless chore. It's much easier to establish a "no plant's land," along the border of the lawn—a narrow strip where your lawnmower's wheels can fit so that its blades straddle the edge of the lawn itself.

Many gardeners use a strip of bare soil instead of an edging, but grass will constantly invade vacant soil, and the turf has to be trimmed back several times a year in order to keep it neat. Aluminum edging will halt the spread of the grass, but eventually the bare soil beyond it erodes. When your lawnmower wheel dips into this ditch, it scalps the lawn's border.

To contain the grass and provide a level support for the mower's wheels, the best solution I've found is a brick edging that can be installed in a day and lasts for years.

You must wait until the grass has grown a fairly thick turf of roots, because they're what will be holding the bricks in place. For *any* lawn edging, you'll want a double line of bricks, as in Figure 9,

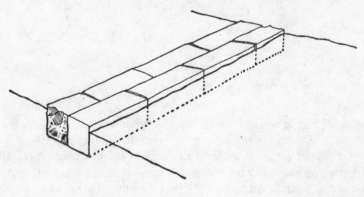

Figure 9

placed on edge, as shown. If you lay them flat side down, the individual bricks will tilt up too easily under the weight of a mower's wheel, with disastrous results to the blades. Also, grass runners can creep underneath flat bricks to colonize whatever soil lies beyond them. But edge-on bricks are deep enough to stop grass cold, and afford far greater stability. A double row of brick gives you about four inches of flat surface on which to steer your mower's outside wheel. Be sure to stagger the bricks as shown. Not only does it look better, but the entire assembly is more stable if joints do not match up.

The brick edging should fit exactly against the uphill retaining wall. But when you edge the top of the lower retaining wall, *don't* set the bricks at the very brink. Even if visitors don't trip off the edge, their weight will cause undue pressure on the bank. The bricks, with little to support them on their far side, will begin angling outward and need constant refitting. So move the edging back about 18″ from the top of the stone wall (Figure 10). The narrow gap between brick and stone will be ideal for a Low or Pachysandra Garden.

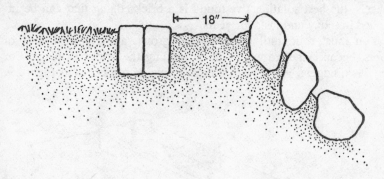

Figure 10

Brick edging is a good test of whether your lawn is really as level as it looks. Of course bricks can be made to follow a gentle slope, but you should set them as level as possible so that they reveal any small rises or slumps. You can add more soil later where necessary. Meanwhile, your lawnmower will be following the bricks—not the lawn—as its guide for a flatter, more uniform cut.

Care of Established Lawns

Commercial fertilizers are like vitamins—good as a diet supplement, but no substitute for the "main course" of fertile humus you should have used in the first place. But in spring, a sprinkle of lime (especially if trees near the lawn are evergreens or oaks) and dry, pulverized manure will help boost a lawn into good root production.

Water-soluble fertilizers eventually leach out in the rain, so a fresh dose is appropriate in autumn. This traditional spring-and-fall fertilizer regimen may seem arbitrary until you realize these are the seasons when grass grows most rapidly. As a rule, any plant should be fertilized only when in active growth and able to use the nourishment.

Mowing, by itself, can make a poor lawn look great. For years I used a reel mower because it was quiet, nonpolluting, and inexpensive. It also did a very poor job. My lawn is interspersed with a vigorous fescue that grows much taller and quicker than the surrounding grass, and the reel mower usually crushed its stalks rather than cut them. The reel mower had only two wheels, making it overly sensitive to bumps and low spots, resulting in an uneven cut. Worse, the model I'd bought accumulated circlets of dead grass between the axle and the wheels; and literally stalled whenever a small twig got jammed between the blades and the bottom cutting plate.

When I finally bought a power model, the advantages were immediately obvious. Because it has four wheels, a rotary doesn't jog over uneven ground. Even healthy weeds are decimated, and the final effect is incredibly neat and "crewcut," regardless of the texture or quality of the grass itself. The rotary also breaks up stiff twigs, dead leaves, and other debris, which a reel mower can't.

Unless you have a *great* deal of lawn, however, I'd advise against any model that moves forward under its own power. A self-propelled job eats up extra gasoline and hurries along so quickly that you can't turn it aside to get every last blade. Awkward to maneuver safely in small corners or along a curved border, it will climb right over small trees, as my father found when his choice *oculis draconis* pine was turned into a splatter of wood chips. A push-model rotary, on the other hand, mows just as well on a "backstroke," is far more accurate, and doesn't demand quick reflexes.

Many gardeners rake up their grass clippings, or pick them up automatically in a bag or cage attached to their mowers. This supposedly avoids the buildup of a mat of dead "thatch" that will invite disease and strangle the living plants. But if you remove clippings, you're taking away a great many nutrients as well as the natural mulch grass needs to maintain a deep, rich turf. Eventually, this practice results in a dry, compacted lawn that requires inordinate amounts of fertilizer.

Before the invention of the lawnmower, gardeners' scythes did leave long clippings that needed raking. But a rotary lawnmower cuts its clippings into tiny pieces that soon shrivel and sift down easily between the living blades. Thus, the objection that grass clippings don't look "neat" is valid only if you're maintaining a putting green. For this reason, I removed the wire "cage" from my mower and reversed the handle so that the clippings are shot out to the *front*. This way, the same clippings are usually run over more than once and minced even finer than usual, so that they quickly break down, supplying the lawn with vital nourishment.

Mats of dead clippings occur only where clippings can't break down properly—that is, atop dry or heavily-trodden areas where the underlying soil is too hard to admit them. The surrounding grass will be doing poorly chiefly because of these adverse conditions, not because of the "thatch" itself. Sparse patches in a lawn may also be the result of disease or insects but again, such pests are more likely to attack grass that's unhealthy in the first place. Therefore, extra water, lime, and nitrogen-rich fertilizer should be enough to improve the grass *and* hasten the clippings' decay.

If grass persistently avoids any single spot, simply raking it up and reseeding it won't help. You should dig down to find what the problem is. Most likely you'll discover a pocket of hard clay, or an outcrop of bedrock—in which case, see Chapter 14 on how to make use of it. But if you don't want a Rockery, just bare the hummock of stone and sledgehammer it down. Don't stop until you've knocked it down to about six inches below current lawn level. Fill up any previously infertile hole with *pure* humus cut with lime, and keep tamping it down until its surface rises about a quarter-inch *above* the surrounding soil. (Decay will pull it back into line automatically.) Then reseed and treat like a new lawn.

For places where the soil isn't bad, I cover thin spots with an inch of fresh humus—extending it right over the ailing grass and up to where healthy, vigorous turf begins—and then seed it. This way, the healthy lawn begins to invade the new soil by the time the seeds are up, and the new patch blends in much better. It may seem unorthodox to spread new humus right atop your lawn, but it's also extremely effective. Grass *is* easily smothered, but only by heavy, impenetrable materials. Fresh, friable humus is one of the most permeable of all soils, and your lawn will sprout through it with pleasure. As a top dressing, it's much more nutritious than commercial topsoil, let alone peat moss.

Your one caution should be that the lumps of humus aren't too large. Just buy some quarter-inch steel mesh and mount it on a rectangle of scrap wood, such as an old window frame. Prop up this screen at a 45° angle so that pebbles and other hefty debris roll down it easily. Underneath, spread one of your old plastic shower curtains. Then rub handfuls of compost against the mesh. Whatever falls through the screen will be light enough to sift into your lawn. Add a bit of lime and whatever chemical fertilizer you have on hand, then just broadcast this mixture over your grass.

A spreader isn't necessary unless your area is enormous; spreading it by hand lets you concentrate on the bald, thin places. If your lawn is small, it probably receives a higher number of footprints per square foot, and should get a bit extra. Pile it at least an inch thick over any depressed areas; if you're in a rush for new grass, seed it. Then water lightly to help pack it down. Further rain will carry this light, spongy material down to the grass's roots where it provides slightly more room for them to forage.

You'll be raising your lawn level minutely, but that's the whole idea. Repeat this treatment every year or so. The humus will crumble further under the pressure of feet and mower wheels and enrich the surface soil from brown to a rich black. You'll see your grass thickening up and competing with weeds as never before.

Midsummer watering is probably the best single route to a luxuriant lawn. Immediately *after* mowing is when it'll do the most good: the grass leaves have been cut and will lose some extra sap until their wounds cauterize. Their potential for photosynthesis has been decreased; their roots are suddenly exposed to more heat and light. Water helps pack down the clippings and helps the surviving plants bounce back. But unless you live in a hot climate where daily watering is imperative, I'd advise against an automatic below-ground sprinkler system. It's expensive and awkward to install, and in cold climates must be drained each autumn to avoid freezing. The nozzles invariably get blocked by soil or grass clippings, and even if working perfectly, they distribute water *too* evenly—a lawn needs more water in some sections, less in others. Worse still, they make your lawn a semipermanent fixture; you can't plant trees or even dig down for spot renovation without fear of hitting a pipe.

Weeds

Every so often, an article appears suggesting a "natural" lawn—in which low plants other than grass are allowed to flourish. Personally, I don't mind if veronica or moneywort invade a lawn, because their bright, tiny flowers are quite attractive, and the plants don't smother the grass. But I wouldn't care to *introduce* them either—they're more attractive in a Low Garden, and when out of bloom, give a lawn a spotty, uneven look. The only nongrass plant I encourage in a lawn is white clover (not to be confused with the tall, gangly red clover). Some lawn purists object to it, but since clover bears nodules of nitrogen-fixing bacteria along its roots, it definitely helps improve the subsoil. And its small, tidy flowers appear regularly throughout the summer.

All weeds (including clover) are automatically controlled by mowing. Thus, the only ones you need worry about are those that keep a normally low profile, beneath the reach of your mower blades. But most creeping and clump-type plants such as chickweed and plantain are easily removed with a trowel. If you can't pull them easily, it means your soil's too hard in that spot; the grass needs a top dressing or even replacement with fresh humus.

Two lawn pests require extra work, however. One is the wild garlic or wild onion. Its small bulbs multiply amazingly, and over the years a single plant will spread into a thick clump several inches across. Wild garlic is mostly dormant during the summer, so the best time to get rid of it is in March, when the rubbery, onion-scented leaves come boiling out of the soil ahead of the grass. Because the leaves break off, single bulbs usually have to be dug up, but larger clumps are easily pulled up by hand. The bulbs are quite hard to kill, though, so *don't* beat a clump against the ground to jolt the soil loose from its roots—you'll likely be scattering small bulblets that will root and form new colonies in years to come. Either leave the clumps to dry, soil and all, on top of a stone or path, or drown them in a bucket of water.

The real menace to any lawn is the dandelion. If you've ever pulled up sods, you'll see why it's so tenacious. As the grass pulls loose, the dandelion's long taproot stays firmly rooted in the subsoil, from which new leaves will soon arise. This weed is particularly well adapted to lawns because its leaves are arranged in a flat rosette, low enough to avoid lawnmower blades. Moreover, its yellow flowers don't depend on insects for pollination. The flowers automatically go to seed via parthenogenesis (the botanical equivalent of virgin birth). And once they do, the stems elongate by as much as seven times. This is why you can mow a lawn of blooming dandelions on Saturday, scattering yellow heads in your wake, and return the next Tuesday to find a crop of fuzzy puffballs waving above the neatly trimmed surface of the grass. These are the low flowers you missed, which have since shot up to broadcast their seeds. This "unnatural" selection only ensures the evolution of low-flowering strains of dandelion even better suited to a lawn environment.

The dandelion's carrotlike root breaks easily and regenerates if not entirely removed, so even the most careful digging is often fruitless. Moreover, it's too easy to miss the tiny seedlings that usually cluster under and around full-sized plants. This is one instance where I advise a broadleaf weedkiller—use one of the foaming sprays that poisons the plant simply by touching the leaf. However, dandelions' probing taproots do a fine job of hoisting nutrients up from the subsoil and any of these weeds that you dig should be added to the compost heap.

Once you have rid your lawn of dandelions, you must keep them from wafting back again. All too often, your upwind neighbor's lawn is alive with dandelions whose wind-borne seeds will quickly recolonize your grass. In this case, the only remedy is a sturdy evergreen hedge to break the wind and allow the seeds to settle short of your lawn's border. A buffer zone of pachysandra or tall perennials is added insurance. But in any case, avoid an unbroken lawn between properties unless your neighbor maintains his lawn as carefully as you do.

You'll know that you're growing a good lawn when it's seemingly just as green as the grass on the other side of the fence. In reality, your own lawn will then be the healthier one—because given two identical lawns, the grass at a distance will *always* seem greener. It's the same principle that makes a venetian blind look whiter when it's closed. We see distant grass from the side, so that our eyes view the countless blades all crowded together with no apparent spaces in between. But looking at the grass under our feet, we see *through* the blades and down to the soil beneath.

Seen from above, even a healthy lawn may appear a fairly dull green. But sit down on it—thus changing your angle of view—and the color of the grass only a few feet away will intensify. So in other words, if your lawn looks equal to your neighbor's, it's actually *better*. I'm proud to say my lawn *does* look better than my neighbor's, which means it's actually several light years out in front.

The most serious lawn problem of all, however, is having too much grass in the first place.

Mowing services can tell you they do their work in two shifts. The actual grass cutting—running a machine back and forth over the center of the lawn—takes seldom more than a half hour. It's the "trimming" or "edging" of grass that's tucked under trees, beneath walls, and on steep grades that consumes the rest of the morning.

Besides excessive and awkward mowing, a wide variety of seemingly unrelated problems arise because it is easier to sow grass seed than to landscape a place properly. When I first bought my house, water seeped into the basement every single time it rained. I didn't have the cash to waterproof the foundation, and so postponed that job. But meanwhile I decided my terraced back-yard lawn was all I really needed, and began converting the fragile grass in my front yard into a Pachysandra Garden. Even *before* this new garden was fully established, I noticed that the basement was flooding less frequently and when it did, was admitting less water. It seems farfetched, but the elimination of extra lawn turned out to be the reason.

My front yard, you see, slopes *down* from the street to my front door. The original front lawn—also sloping—was built atop clay subsoil. Rainfall quickly saturated the thin layer of grass and then ran downhill until it reached my basement walls. But atop that clay lawn I introduced humus, mulch, and new plants with longer roots. They began to act like a giant sponge, trapping more rainwater and holding it until it could be evaporated or transpired. Result: not just a more inviting front yard, but less mold and water damage indoors.

Think back to the last lawn you saw (in a picture or in real life) that really impressed you. I'm willing to bet it was an open, uninterrupted expanse where mowing machines could graze at top speed without detours into corners and crannies. The ideal lawn should have clearly defined edges. It's okay to have small "islands" of trees, perennials, or shrubs within a lawn's perimeter, but not isolated islands of lawn scattered over your entire property, or strips of grass oozing out of bounds and under trees where the lawnmower finds them hard to reach. The following is a partial checklist of places where grass is seldom justified:

- On any slope too narrow to level out, where the grade is steep enough that a glass of water spills when set down.
- Around or atop massive rock outcrops.
- Along access routes to the house where foot traffic is unusually heavy.
- Under fences, shrubs, and low trees where you have to stoop and push the mower with one hand.
- Wherever you have to go back and hand-trim grass that escaped the mower.
- In strips between a privacy hedge or fence and the road or sidewalk.
- Right atop a high retaining wall, where the mower risks tumbling off the edge.
- In any corner where dry leaves are regularly piled by the wind.
- In any spot where water collects in summer, ice in winter.
- On high, dry ground where the lawn's doing poorly to begin with.

Are those sites ever used for romping or lounging? Where your feet can't go comfortably, it isn't a lawn, it's just *grass*. But after you've spent several years mowing those inaccessible, awkward places, the work seems habitual. You may feel that if you've already gone to all that trouble, why change now? But once you get your "chief" lawn leveled, vigorous, and revitalized, it's easier to recognize those other places where you really don't need it at all—where the space would be far more attractive if converted to one or more of the other garden environments discussed later in this book.

Whatever your new plans for those spots, the first step in any case is getting rid of the existing grass, which means getting rid of it *all*—eradicating the roots completely. My method is to wait for a dry day. I then cut sods into manageable sections—about one foot square—and roll them up.

Even healthy, deep-rooted turf comes up easily. Pile these sods to one side. Then when you've collected a good stack, pick up a sod in each hand and beat their root-sides together to dislodge as much trapped dirt as possible. When the dribble of soil particles slows down, discard them and pick up a new pair. This way, you return as much humus as possible to your bare ground.

Some gardeners claim you can kill unwanted sods by turning them face down or cutting them into small pieces for mulch. But this seldom stops the more vigorous strains of grass. Grass rhizomes usually grow sideways to begin with, so they simply take a 90° turn and keep growing. Besides, chopped-up grass roots are remarkably slow to decay and can linger atop the ground for years, presenting a severe obstacle to bulbs and perennials.

To kill sods dependably, get a watertight oil drum or plastic garbage can. Place it in an out-of-the-way corner of your yard, preferably where it's downwind. Dump in your sods and fill to the top with water. (Don't add water first, because the sods will take up most of the room and the water will simply overflow.)

The reason you placed this "silt bin," as I call it, out of nose range will soon be apparent. At first, sods drown and produce a slightly acid smell. (A silt bin is also the only sure way to kill off the bulbs of wild garlic, which otherwise survive for months after uprooting and resprout as soon as they touch anything that resembles soil.) But when left for a month or more, they soften into a vile brackish gook topped by enormous green bubbles and an oily slick (possibly from traces of oil dropped from your lawn mower). The smell is a cross between undiluted ammonia and a stockyard in August, and will draw flies unless the bin is kept covered.

Kept in a silt bin until the end of the summer, the decaying roots will release the rest of their trapped soil, giving you a gallon or so of fertile silt that makes a fine top dressing for the lawn. The roots themselves won't have broken down completely, but they'll be weak and pliable enough to use for compost or rough mulch.

3

PATHS OF STONE OR BRICK

Grass will accept a lot of abuse, but it won't survive where people are constantly trooping back and forth. Haven't you noticed places where the grass is worn down to hard-packed soil, where shrubs regularly get brushed against and broken, where the corner of a flowerbed gets trampled? These sites already *are* paths, and need some kind of paving to define them as such.

Remember that a path serves to *restrict* pedestrians to a narrower avenue. If your access routes are ill-defined, it's easy to channel errant feet onto a single track so that plants on either side can grow unmolested. The result is *more* garden space, not less. You can also use paths to invite visitors into corners and byways that they might otherwise overlook. But for now, concentrate on where they're *already* walking. Legend has it that the slate paths of Yale University's Old Campus were laid after observing the tracks that students left in the snow, trudging in straight lines to and from classes. "Paths should be where people walk," is true for the first paths you build—to *follow* human feet.

Many nineteenth-century houses with vast expanses of "approach" lawn twisted their front paths into curves, or made them diverge to enclose a statue or fountain. Modern landscapers still insist that straight paths are boring. But being the shortest distance between two points, they're also the most practical—especially in the case of the thoroughfare that connects your front door to the street or driveway. This front walk will eventually be used by deliverymen carrying heavy breakables, by impatient children, by guests who may not be sure-footed. Thus, it's pointless to *create* curves in a path for hurried everyday use. It usually will have a few, regardless: uneven ground, existing plantings, and even the irregularity of the paving materials will introduce some twists and angles. But these *natural* eccentricities will look far more logical and proper than any fancy swerves you mapped out in advance.

As well as straight, your front walk should be utterly safe. Thus if winter ice is a problem, bricks are out. Unless *very* carefully fitted, their seams make them difficult to clear of snow.

Not only does concrete look humdrum for a front walk, but it reflects too much light to melt off hard-packed ice. But even after a heavy snow, light filters down to the surface of asphalt, so that the bottom layer of snow is part slush when you go to shovel it. Therefore, blacktop—in other words, an extension of your driveway—is perfect for a front walk. With water-base sealers applied every three years or so, it can be kept looking glossy as a seal's back without losing any of its traction in slippery weather. Remember, though, that in an established front yard, the heavy rollers and scorching hot tar may damage plants nearby.

If you don't want asphalt, the material for your front walk should still be as dark as possible. Even when air temperature hovers well below freezing, these surfaces absorb enough heat from the low winter sun to melt themselves off. (In my front yard, for example, the light-colored brick paths often remain snow-covered for days, but the slate front walk usually clears itself within twenty-four hours.) Granite or bluestone holds up better than slate—but for any major path, avoid round or eccentric steppingstones in favor of rectangles or squares of flagstone, laid end-to-end. These flags should not touch, but be placed close enough so that no grass has a chance to invade from either side. And unlike other paths listed later, your front path should be no higher than the surrounding grass or flowerbeds. This way, anyone who steps off by mistake won't turn an ankle.

If your front yard slopes, it's better not to level it, or you'll wind up with a retaining wall requiring fairly steep steps. Better to leave the land as is. If occasional risers are needed to keep the flags ascending along with the slope, these risers will be supporting heavy pressure. It makes sense to fill them with concrete, using a thicker-than-average flag for the top of the step. But don't cement the riser to any other flags but this top one—this way, bits of your front walk can be replaced if need be without chiseling loose the entire assembly.

Aside from this front walk, your other paths can be less formal. For those worn-down avenues across the lawn, the best answer is to inlay a series of round bluestone circles. You can set them up to six inches apart, and let grass grow in between. With the stone sunk at ground level, you can mow over both stone and grass at the same time. Just be sure that the circles themselves are wide enough so that you step on *them* more than you do on the regenerating grass—too many "stepping" stones are too small for anyone not wearing ballet shoes.

Though best for flat terrain, flags can also be used for very gentle slopes with a constant angle of decline. But they're utterly wrong for where the ground changes abruptly. If you want to pave a hump or turn a sloping corner, flat stones cannot adapt to these uneven surfaces.

I have this problem at the corner of my house. Right outside the kitchen is a fairly level concrete slab that's the only logical out-of-sight site for the garbage cans. Right beside them, the previous owner had planted some choice mountain laurels and azaleas; and between them, he'd laid a few flagstones to indicate the proper route to the garbagemen. But the flagstones were rather puny for hurried men in work boots. Worse, the ground in which they were set slants sharply uphill before leveling off in lawn—and the route itself makes a 135° turn. The flags tended to slip and wobble, especially in wet weather, so to avoid slipping, the garbagemen wisely *avoided* them, stumbling through the shrubs whose mulch at least afforded a good foothold!

I was about to cut down on my lawn area anyway and, so as to give the shrubs a chance, decided to build a sturdy, safe, and unmistakable path. The slope was too low for steps, but too abrupt for asphalt. The only material I found that could adapt *neatly* to such an uneven surface was brick. The present brick path conforms to that twisted rise, curving in a tight turn away from the house and then straightening out for the long run to the street.

If you try to lay bricks on end on a slope, they'll tip under pressure. For this reason, I had to lay them flat. The initial bricks were

sunk right into the existing clay subsoil, even with the cement platform, though later ones went right atop the de-turfed lawn. Each row
is two and a half bricks wide, laid *across* the slope I was covering.
For appearance's sake, I staggered the rows so that the half brick fell
on the opposite side each time.

To keep these flat bricks from budging outward—and to define the
path even more unmistakably—I edged it with two lines of bricks on
edge, each running right along each side of the path proper. (The
basic design appears in Figure 11.) Since the side-upright bricks
stand taller than the flat ones in the middle, this path's borders show
up even under a fairly heavy snow. There's never the least confusion
as to where to step.

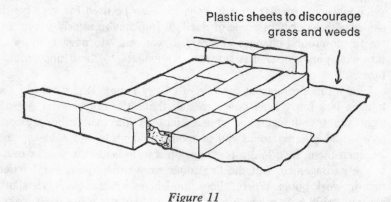

Figure 11

The only tricky part comes in breaking bricks into the "halves"
you'll need for the end of each horizontal row. If you have only a
short path and thus only a few halves to manufacture, you can usually get a good break by supporting a brick between two others. A
sharp hammer blow on the unsupported midsection will usually split
it. But the work is vastly easier and more accurate if you invest in a
rock pick or mason's hammer, one face of which is narrowed to a
chisel. Lay the brick on flat soil with the chisel's line at right angles
to the brick's length, and strike it sharply in the middle.

Even so, a great many older bricks will shatter or break unevenly.
Larger fragments can be trimmed down to half size if you hold them

in one hand and, with a hammer, strike glancing blows *away* from you at the broken end, so that chips don't rebound in your face (Figure 12). But be sure to save your brick fragments; they have an important use I'll get to in Chapter 4.

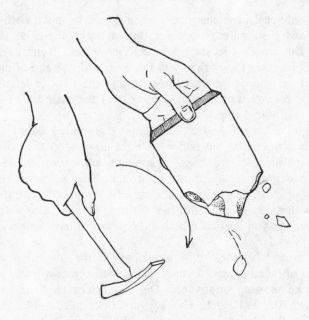

Figure 12

After building the path to the garbagemen's utmost requirements, I liked the effect so much that I decided to extend the path—in a narrower one and a half brick width—through the Pachysandra and Low Gardens I was planting at the time.

In a meandering path, the charms of used brick are more evident. Some are already curved thanks to faulty firing, so you can make a straight path describe a gentle curve where necessary. Any one pallet usually contains bricks from a number of different yards, so their colors cover a variety of warm pastels. Often one side will have the manufacturer's name embossed on it, and when a row is faced upright, they make a delightful catalog! One of my deep red bricks is labeled—appropriately—ROSE, but HUTTON, W & G, CURRY, XXX, MAYONE, and other Irish names whisper up at me as I walk along. My personal favorite is marked ZZZ; I hope anyone constructing a path to a shady hammock is lucky enough to come across one.

The only real problems came when I had to make both the flat bricks *and* their on-edge borders turn at right angles at the same places. But usually I let the bricks lay themselves. Eventually, the far margin of a row of flat bricks will fall even with the end of an edging brick. By extending the next three rows to the right or left (or even by laying a new set of rows at right angles) the path can be made to form its right-angle jog.

Except for where they crossed sloping ground, I didn't set these bricks into the earth, but laid them right down atop the existing soil —with plastic garment bags underneath, of course, to discourage weeds and grass from sprouting through. This saves an enormous amount of time. The edge bricks may be tippy at first, but bracing them with banks of new, fertile soil on either side, also assures that any plantings you introduce beside the path will have an easy time of it.

One great advantage to a raised path is that the wind naturally clears it of fallen leaves. A raised brick path across a lawn, however, will make mowing impossible. Dig the bricks so their surface is even with the soil level. The edging bricks need to be dug even deeper, so that the entire surface is level (Figure 13).

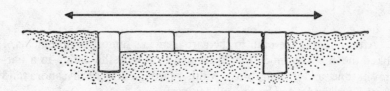

Figure 13

As I went, I discovered the paths had unexpected visual effects. Viewed strictly by themselves, my front-yard plantings might look cluttered, but the brick paths provide a frame and a sense of spacing and order.

The final result consumed six tons. Even if I discounted the broken, the deformed, and the crumblies, that's practically three thousand bricks. For a more informal brick path that turns corners without jogs (and without any half bricks to slow you down), you might consider the zigzag or herringbone pattern shown in Figure 14.

Figure 14

While such a path *looks* geometrically precise, it's easy to make it curve to left or right by adding bricks to one side or the other, as per the shaded areas. By building out on *both* sides, the path can be made to fan out or part to pass around existing trees. Bricks can be zigged either flat or on edge, but in either case, they should be buried even with the surrounding soil. The pattern is a bit busy for long walks, however, and serves best as a short access route to nooks and crannies.

Once your brick path is down, pour builder's sand atop it and sweep it into the cracks with a broom. A few light rains will wash in the grains you miss. If you notice any brick tilting or sinking lower than its neighbors, lift it up and add sand underneath the low end. You may also want to spread dry cement over the path and wash it down with a hose. The result won't be actual concrete, but the sand will clump together firmly, eliminating a great deal of later settling. Yet the semi-mortar will still be fragile enough to make later repairs easy.

And repairs *will* be needed! Bricks are porous, and on cold winter mornings you'll notice that certain ones bear a rime of white frost. These bricks have sopped up subsurface moisture that has frozen when it hits the air. Some spongy ones often crumble from the pressure of interior ice; others will crack or split for no obvious reason. But such failures seldom afflict more than two or three bricks per hundred, and replacement is no chore.

Brick paths look best when roughly parallel, as mine are. However, you'll still want to step from one to another. I tested small "stepping squares" of brick, but found them awkward and unsightly. Finally I decided on circles of bluestone. They're dark enough not to clash with the brick, and aren't obvious from a distance. The only problem is raising them up to the level of the paths they connect. I've used several methods, but the easiest is to use drowned grass sods from the Silt Bin (see Chapter 2), along with chips of wood or bark.

. Since dead grass roots take a very long time to decay, they make ideal pads to support and stabilize individual steppingstones. Start by arranging three turfs underneath each circle. Then replace the flag, and step lightly on its various corners. A new piece of turf, or handful of chips, should go beneath any point that wobbles. This may take a few minutes of lifting and rearrangement, but the finished result will stand up for years. The stone keeps the organic materials beneath relatively dry so that they break down very slowly. But when they do, the stone will settle uniformly.

Once you have paved the paths where visitors *do* walk, you can concentrate on paving the places where you'd *like* them to, providing handy access to any of the thickly planted gardens described later. (It makes little sense to raise a stand of rare trilliums if you can't approach them closely enough to appreciate them.)

The "Japanese" Steppingstone Path

Used brick is expensive in large quantities, and for a Wild Garden or Rockery, you may want a more rustic look. Chances are you'll have plenty of free material right at hand. Any part of the country that's been visited by glaciers, rivers, ancient seabeds, or heavy erosion is usually a minefield of rocks. Certainly New Jersey is; even after I'd erected my Poor Man's Stone Walls, I had a great number of others left over. Most were too roundish for PMSW use, but too

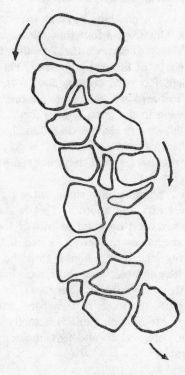

Figure 15

numerous to hide and too heavy to lug to the dump. But when I came upon some photographs of a Japanese tea garden and its lane of natural steppingstones, I began looking at my own boulders with new appreciation.

No matter how round a rock, it usually has at least one side that's flatter than the others. By declaring that side "up" and digging a hole deep enough to accommodate the rest, you can set out a rock path of really remarkable charm.

Basically, this reduces a three-dimensional jigsaw puzzle to two dimensions, so that all you need consider is the shape of the exposed faces. (Figure 15).

The Japanese deliberately arrange steppingstones in single file to slow down visitors and give them a chance to absorb the beauty of the garden. But Westerners sometimes want to get quickly from one spot to another. Accordingly I began constructing my own path at a width of two small rocks or one big one, with each separated by only an inch or so of soil. This way, a foot that misses one stone usually falls on the next. It's easy to arrange them so that the shape of one rock "answers" the shape of the one adjacent. That is, straight sides should face each other. Rounded corners should face the outside of turns in the path (see arrows). A bulge on one rock should be matched by a depression in the next, and so forth. Roughly triangular stones should point in the general direction the path is leading. The resulting meanders of such a path are largely dictated by the shapes of the stones themselves, and they manage to form their own delightful calligraphy.

The only real trick is planting each stone at the right depth, so that their tops are all level with one another. This is a cinch with small rocks, which can be arranged by hand in pits of loose soil. But for sinking really giant specimens properly, I often have to stand atop the crowbar supporting the rock while I shift the soil beneath it. Even with repeated fussing over larger boulders, I find it no trouble to lay ten feet or better of path in an afternoon. And for grades and slopes, you can "terrace" the rocks so they form natural steps (Figure 16). The uneven base of each stone is actually an asset, making the rock steadier when stepped on and leaving no open pockets that harbor mice and slugs.

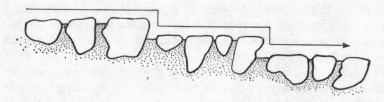

Figure 16

This is fairly sweaty work, which is why I do such work in late winter. Before spring comes, the ground has heaved, and the rocks are settled in so that they need only slight adjustment before the surrounding soil can be planted.

The Cobblestone Path

Obviously, there are places where a slightly more sure-footed path is called for. For instance, I have a steep, shady bankside where brick or flagstone would be too formal. Yet a steppingstone path would invite a broken leg. While considering this site, I still had a great many rocks too small for steppingstones—all under six inches across. So I began packing them together in an absolutely flat ramp, with as few gaps as possible.

I have to admit that a cobblestone path takes forever. You must fit and refit the stones to get them—and the path's edge—just right. Because they're lightweight, you have to prevent their rolling underfoot by packing their seams with clayish subsoil. Add smaller pebbles to fill in holes and irregularities. But withal, this is the perfect way to use up those small, annoyingly common rocks that any digging usually turns up. Eventually, your own feet will pound the clay into a hard matrix that holds the rocks firmly. Such a path provides superb traction, and is probably the best paving solution for small, cramped yards and tiny "mini-patios" beneath sundials and birdbaths.

I can't overemphasize how any path helps define the space around it. Originally dictated by your existing plantings and contours, a path immediately suggests ideas for further improvements. That corner cries out for a clump of spring jonquils; that hollow demands a spreading fern. A turning point in the path practically begs for a small, upright tree just beyond it to justify the swerve. This is why your paths and patios should be laid before too many of your other permanent plantings are in: stone and brick can be beautified by vegetation far more easily than the other way around.

4

SOIL RENOVATION:
THE ETERNAL NECESSITY

After the proper sites have been leveled, edged, and paved, it's time to find out how much improvement the surrounding soil needs before you can begin effective planting.

Many horticultural guides advise you to have your soil tested to determine if it's acid or alkaline, rich or poor in specific nutrients. But the pH and fertility of soil vary enormously in built-over areas. For example, if your builder buried left-over concrete in a corner of the yard, that area will test out as alkaline, while a tract a few feet away where oak leaves fall may be markedly acid.

Decay of plant matter *automatically* creates soil that's slightly on the acid side. But since most plants enjoy a slightly acid soil, further correction is seldom needed. Your soil will not be *excessively* acid unless there are pines and oaks overhead. Even so, acidity is easy to control, simply by adding or withholding crushed limestone.

Heavily alkaline soil *throughout* your property occurs only as a result of underlying geological conditions. Near the White Cliffs of Dover, for instance, underlying chalk bedrock makes the soil far too sweet for azaleas and rhododendrons. If you live in the Southwest where the subsoil is heavily impregnated with alkaline minerals, you'll have a similar problem. But the real question is how long it will take you to transmute your soil into something better. Therefore, I feel most soil testing is a waste of time and money—especially since the three basic soil types are quite obvious to the naked eye. Just drive a spade into the ground and turn up a clod of soil.

Clayish Soil is often brightly colored—reddish, beige, slate gray—and lighter in hue than the soil above it. In some areas, clayish soil is a deep brown, masquerading as good soil. But the clue is the way it stays clumped together, whether wet or dry. Moist clay often sticks to the shovel blade and must be knocked loose; when dry, clay lightens perceptibly in color but remains packed in sizable clods. (Other kinds of soil tend to fall apart when dry.) Heavy clay coats rocks and garden tools with a thin tint that won't wash off easily, even after repeated rain.

Sandy Soil, usually found in the South and West, is composed largely (or entirely) of small grains that readily fall apart. Water drains through it immediately, never puddling. Rubbed between the fingers, the soil feels roughly abrasive. Bits of organic matter mixed in appear distinctly darker than the sand, often making it look "dirty."

Loam or **Humus,** found mostly toward the surface, is composed of decayed vegetable matter. It is spongy and light; the shovel penetrates it very easily. It is usually dark in color. If finely decomposed, it will be almost black and sticks to the shovel and your hands in tiny granules that easily dust loose.

This humus is what your plants need to grow. But as I explained before, such humus—also called "topsoil"—has usually been carted or eroded away. You must constantly replenish it atop your existing sand or clay subsoil in order to convert your property into fertile ground.

With sand, this is fairly easy. Sand is a good basis for any garden soil because a plant's roots can penetrate it deeply and easily. But because sand is so heavy, it doesn't readily admit organic material. Rather than breaking down, dead leaves and twigs tend to lie atop the surface in mummified form. In Florida and Southern California, for example, the soil surface often accumulates an ankle-deep layer of brush and debris that gardeners usually rake away in disgust. If these plant materials were buried, they would help alleviate the need for constant watering—necessary not so much because of the heat, but because pure sand drains away water so rapidly.

Clay is a different story, however. Its extremely fine particles tend to infiltrate humus, effectively "fossilizing" it. Mixing clay with humus ruins the humus far more than it improves the clay. So the trick is to build your humus in a separate layer *atop* the subsoil.

In the wild, this occurs naturally. Most of the wildflowers of the Northeast grow lavishly in forests whose trees are rooted in clay subsoil. A layer of humus only a few inches deep is sufficient for trilliums, ferns, and the most delicate ladyslippers. New humus is being constantly built up on—not mixed with—the subsoil by the steady decay of fallen leaves, twigs, and branches.

Where a tropical climate hastens decay, new soil accumulates so rapidly that some plants like the vanda orchids of Hawaii sprout new roots along the stem to take advantage of new debris. But even in the tropics, if humus is not constantly replaced, it soon erodes and leaches away. When farmers in Latin Amerca burn rainforests to clear the land for crops, the rich humus supports bumper crops for a few seasons. But right underneath it is sterile clay. So when the topsoil erodes away, the land becomes useless for further agriculture. The acreage is abandoned, and it takes the "jungle" many years to reclaim soil robbed of its organic components.

All plants need a steady diet of new organic matter, for as long as you intend to grow them. But this doesn't mean simply mulching. Unless you *already* have a good six inches of loose friable humus atop your subsoil, you must make up for lost time.

Compost Heaps

Except in a few places like the Wild Garden (Chapter 12), it's unsightly to have dead leaves and twigs lying on the ground. Therefore, it's best to cart them off to some single site where they can rot neatly and rapidly. Such a pile—better known as a compost heap—is an absolute must, no matter how small your property.

The question is not *if* but *where*. By now, your lawns, edgings, and paths will have determined your main living and strolling areas, and you should be able to figure where a compost heap will be the least conspicuous. You needn't take *too* much care in selecting a site, because there's no reason a compost heap has to be permanent. If it is, a great deal of nourishment will be washed down into the subsoil before the new humus is ready for digging. So I'd advise that your first compost heap be a strictly temporary one, perhaps built directly atop a bed you later intend to use for flowers or vegetables. When this heap breaks down, it will blanket the subsoil with a layer of humus that can then be raked and planted; and any nutrients that wash into the subsoil will be available for the new plants' more deeply probing roots.

You can build a quicker-rotting heap if you remember that the presence of limestone speeds decay. This is dramatized in the Yucatán, where the jungle repeatedly overwhelms archeologists' efforts to clear the Mayan temples. These ruins are largely built of limestone, so that anything that falls on them is quickly converted to humus that seeds can root in. Up north, the same principle explains why shaded marble tombstones are often covered with moss while granite monuments remain relatively clean. Similarly, dry leaves that fall atop a concrete patio will rot faster than ones that land on regular soil because of the extra lime in cement. So today, I sow a thick layer of crushed limestone before building my temporary heaps. (You can also use an inch-thick layer of crumbled concrete, as long as you're willing to screen the compost later to eliminate these chunks.)

To break down effectively, however, any heap should be allowed to stay put for at least a year. Organic gardeners have worked up standard recipes for a fast-rotting heap—alternate layers of leaves, grass clippings, and manure; all regularly watered and/or covered with a tarpaulin of black plastic to retain heat. Some even add nitrogen-rich bone meal and a ready-made mix of decay-promoting bacteria. But since all compost will decay *eventually,* you needn't give your heap too much tender loving care.

The basic idea is to mix as many *different* components as possible, to assure that the resulting humus has the broadest possible spectrum of minerals. In actual practice, 90 percent of the volume of any compost heap is composed of fallen leaves, so try to collect leaves from as many different species as possible. If you have mostly oaks, for example, and your neighbor has maples and sycamores, it's worth borrowing his autumn rakings.

Unfortunately, untreated leaves decay rather slowly. Maple leaves tend to pack together in stacks, like the pages of a wet book. This excludes the air that decay bacteria need to do their thing, and the pile will last for years. On the other hand, oak leaves curl and stiffen, becoming so springy that they leave too *many* air spaces in between, and the pile remains loose and dry. All leaves will decay much faster if you cut them up into smaller chunks, producing a mixture that's more uniform and quicker to pack down.

Mulching machines can reduce drifts of leaves to a small, heavy pile of half-inch confetti. These gizmos are expensive, though, and seldom see use except for a few weeks each October. Unless your property features a number of good-size trees and you simply must reduce that glut of leaves by assembly-line methods, an ordinary rotary lawnmower will do almost as good a job.

Lawns need extra mowing in autumn, when grass begins growing faster again. But with a rotary, there's no need to rake up the fallen leaves before you mow. In fact, I rake extra leaves *onto* the lawn just before mowing. Then I begin cutting the lawn in a concentric spiral from the outside in. My mower—with its handles reversed and the cage off—spews its leaves and grass clippings toward the lawn's center.

Normally, a rotary shoots out leaves that are only slightly nicked, still more or less in one piece. But my mowing plan means that leaves get run over again and again. By the time they've been spewed to the center of the lawn, they're pretty well ripped apart and—best of all—mixed with grass clippings that greatly speed their decay.

If any leaves have escaped the blades, rake them into a coherent heap. Then rear the mower back on its hind wheels and gently lower it down onto the pile, rearing it back up again if it threatens to stall. (Arrange your pile and mower so that the resulting chaff won't spew out of bounds.) Then, with a bamboo rake, collect the results onto a plastic shower curtain and haul it away. These mulched-up leaves take up far less space than whole ones and, being small and easily packed, won't scatter about in winter gales.

It's silly to invest in any of those compost bins or drums that are regularly advertised. They're expensive, unusually unsightly, and simply too small for the vast volumes of material that you'll want to reduce. Instead, build your leaves into an open-air circular mound, as high as possible. (This way, any heat it builds up will take longer to dissipate.) Now flatten the top and make a slight depression so that the whole resembles a lazy volcano (Figure 17). This helps collect the rainwater the heap needs to remain internally moist.

After leaves, grass clippings are your compost heap's most important component. It's easy to see why: if you collect fresh clippings in a plastic trash bag, the grass will start to decay within minutes. Leave it a few hours, and the bag's center will be literally steaming with bacterial heat, often beginning to melt the enclosing plastic. Anything that decays this fast will hasten the decomposition of anything nearby.

Unfortunately, the relatively few clippings raked up with your

Figure 17

mulched leaves won't be enough to start this reaction. You'll need to add extra clippings to the pile during spring and summer. But since your *lawn* also needs grass clippings to keep healthy, I don't advise you to put a bag or cage back on your mower. Lawn services will often let you have the grass clippings they'd otherwise have to haul away; and it's not hard to locate a neighbor who hasn't yet read this book and who still bags his clippings. He must either transport them to the dump or leave them on the corner where they sink under their own hot weight, squishy and unsightly. Said neighbor will usually jump at your offer to haul the bags away.

For best results, dig a small pit in the center of your compost heap and dump clippings in it. This way, their heat will radiate out to the surrounding pile. The clippings themselves will sink down within a week, reducing to a rich grayish gook that continues decomposing everything underneath it.

Most sources tell you not to compost twigs or branches. Their main argument is that wood decays more slowly than leaves, and is still in firm condition when your heap is ready for harvest. This *is* true of large branches over an inch thick. But any new growth— wood that has emerged from a bud since spring—has not yet hardened off, and decays rapidly. So do the dead twigs that fall from larger trees. They've had a chance to become infused with dry rot, which is why they broke off and fell to begin with. In a heap, they'll soon break down completely and add bulk to the resulting compost.

Since a compost heap sinks as it decomposes, you can constantly add new materials. But if you want all the components to break down at more or less the same time, what you add should be more rottable than what's already there. If you began your heap with chopped leaves and twigs, follow with quick-rotting stuff like lawn weeds, grass clippings, and green leaves.

Adding dry manure (to replace nitrogen used up by decay bacteria) and turning the heap's materials upside down, so that its top layer is buried, will help speed decomposition. But even when left to its own devices, a heap's bottom layer will degenerate in about a year into a loose mass of friable—if still recognizable—leaves and twigs. You can use them as mulch immediately or let them break down for one more winter. By then, they'll have become rich, loose humus that's perfect for any use.

On even a small property, unfortunately, normal pruning of trees and shrubs results in countless older twigs, limbs, and branches that a compost heap can't accommodate. But the minerals locked in this "brush" can still be returned to your soil by other routes. The ideal answer is to rent or borrow a chipping machine that can reduce even sizeable logs to attractive, durable mulch. Certainly most branches and limbs will fit in the fireplace: cut them into eighteen-inch lengths and burn them. In late winter, add their ashes to compost heaps, lawns, and flowerbeds; scattering ashes atop the snow helps you assure an even distribution (Do *not* distribute the ashes from backyard barbecues. The briquets sold in supermarkets are made of ground charcoal mixed with a clayish substance that gives them their shape. When these fat little pillows burn, the charcoal is consumed and only the infertile clayish binder remains.)

Still, without a chipper, you're going to wind up with vast quantities of twigs and branches too small for the fireplace and too thick for regular composting. Rather than create a brushpile—which looks untidy and becomes a home for mice and chipmunks—I've figured a way to put these long-term decayables to immediate use.

Mini-Heaps

I've always thought it silly to haul prunables off to the farthest corner of the yard, only to haul them back again after they've decayed. Probably you already have seen many spots—especially beside raised paths and behind retaining walls—where you could use a bit more humus. Why not begin permanent mini-heaps at the very places where you want to raise the ground level?

A retaining wall above my lawn, for example, is only three bricks high. When I built it, it wasn't "retaining" anything because the original grade sloped down to the lawn. The wall was free-standing. Behind it I wanted a flowerbed about a foot deep, but hadn't nearly enough humus to fill it in. Instead, I simply began packing twigs and branches right behind the length of the wall. For now, they support the bricks, but after they decay in a few years, they'll provide deep, rich soil for a wonderful Pachysandra Garden. Such "local" compost heaps make for really effortless landscaping. Since they never need moving, they can absorb even the most slow-rotting of your garden leftovers.

Rotting wood in small doses is a good thing in itself, since it provides nourishment for the larva of the firefly. From mid-June to late July, the twilight is punctuated with flying males making U-shaped dips, lighting up their abdomens as they come out of the dive. The flightless females waiting on the ground answer them with a more prolonged and softer, almost forlorn glow. Fireflies are beetles, and most beetles' grubs need decaying plant material, preferably heavy, in which to feed.

Start a mini-heap by laying your branches and twigs right atop the existing subsoil. You don't want them to form a loose, airy heap, so cut or break off all side branches. Then lay these sticks parallel to one another, just as if you were fitting spilled matches back into a box (Figure 18). The thickest, hardest-to-rot branches should go at

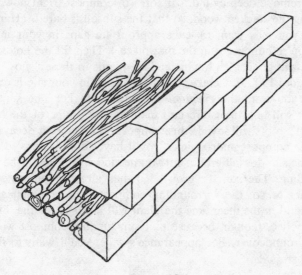

Figure 18

the bottom. This way, faster-rotting material you add later will sink down into the gaps below, keeping the stack of wood wholly camouflaged. If any twigs are brittle, break them into short sections, since increasing their surface area will speed decay. Then lay them in the cracks between larger branches, so to pack as much wood into that space as you can.

Such an arrangement can use up a really unbelievable number of branches; if you don't have enough, just wait for your next pruning job. But stop building when the branches and twigs are about eight inches high. Now it's time for leaves (even whole ones are okay), drowned turfs, spare grass clippings, or what-have-you. This top layer will decay before the wood, of course, settling the pile so you can add even more waste material within a few months. Eventually, the wood too will decay and settle, but by then you'll have added enough new compost to take up the slack. Thus the top of the heap remains at almost exactly the same level—a very important advantage, as I'm about to explain.

If you haven't heard of mini-heaps before this, it's probably because most gardeners prefer to have *one* unsightly heap in a corner than half a dozen little ones in plain view. The trick is to camouflage these mini-heaps so they don't betray their true nature. You can mask your heaps the same way you would plots of bare earth—plant them!

First remove deep cylindrical cores of compost, right down to and including the stacked wood, so that the subsoil is bared. (Hard work, this, so you may want to leave appropriate gaps in your mini-heap when you're building it in the first place.) Then fill the holes right to the top with good, rich humus and set plants in these "silos" of good soil (Figure 19). Just make sure that the soil in your silo is exactly as high as you want the *eventual* soil surface to be. The surrounding compost will hold moisture and maintain the shape of the silo, and the plant's roots will invade this compost even before it decays.

As the compost matrix sinks, you'll have to add more so that the top of the silo doesn't erode, but you needn't worry about the plant itself settling. The soil it's growing in has already compacted. After five years or so, the surrounding compost will be practically pure humus, and in the meantime the plant will never know the difference. *You'll* notice, though, because that surrounding compost won't support a groundcover. For appearance's sake, you'll want to finish off

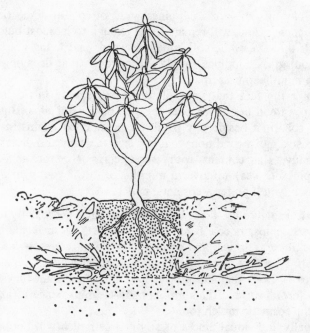

Figure 19

the unplanted surface of the mini-heap. The answer is a mulch, either functional or cosmetic.

Functional mulches are basically vegetable matter—grass clippings, dead leaves, broken-up twigs, or wood chips. They'll eventually decay into soil. To make them look good while they do so, use only one type of mulch over any given area. That is, your mulch should be *all* grass clippings, or *all* leaves, or *all* wood chips—minced up as fine as possible. The finely shredded leaves that emerge from a mulching machine look like some factory product, and pruned wood that's been through a chipper (which you can rent or hire from tree surgeons) is beautifully decimated.

Long before the Department of Agriculture declared grass clippings to be the best all-around mulch, canny gardeners had used them unofficially for years. As you already know, grass heats up if piled deeper than five or six inches. But when spread no more than an inch thick and allowed to dry—you can tell when the green color starts to bleach out—grass clippings will not rot for some time. A layer two inches thick will remain loose enough to let most bulbs and perennials through, while still impeding weeds and living grass. And in addition, grass clippings supply the nitrogen that decaying wood deep in a mini-heap uses up.

To mask the fact that your plantings are simply inlaid in your mini-heap, extend the mulch over the side of the soil silos. But leave bare the soil right beside any trunk or stem. Piled against a plant, mulch creates moist conditions that can lead to decay and disease.

Personally, I'm content with wood chips (or for acid-loving shrubs, pine needles) to cover a mini-heap. But if you want a more formal look, you'll prefer a cosmetic mulch.

Cosmetic mulches are those sold (often in bags) specifically to look good—bark chips, cocoa bean hulls, pebbles, crushed marble or limestone, natural gravel, and so on. They do look great—for a few months. But because a cosmetic mulch is so elegant to begin with, any leaves or twigs that fall atop it look far worse than they would on a less formal surface. This means hand-cleaning, since a rake will remove the cosmetic mulch too.

Eventually, individual pieces of any pebble mulch will bounce out into lawns or flowerbed where they stand out glaringly. Weeds and grass find their way through. And the heavier stone mulches invariably begin sinking into the soil. You then have to pick them out one by one, rerake the surface, and start again.

Happily, you can eliminate all these headaches and *still* have the advantages of a functional mulch. First, cover the entire area you want to neaten up with two to three inches of grass or dead leaves. They don't have to be homogenous or even finely minced, as long as they're *flat*. Now here's where your old plastic shower curtains come in. Lay them down over the functional mulch, arranging their sides so that they overlap each other, with no gaps in between. If you haven't enough spare shower curtains, get a heavy plastic tarpaulin from the hardware store. Cover the *entire* area to be mulched with this plastic. Then with a large nail, punch holes through the plastic every six inches or so.

Spread your cosmetic mulch heavily enough to hide the plastic foundation and you're done. This way, the functional mulch is down there out of sight, enriching the soil or mini-heap beneath. The holes or seams you punched in the plastic let water pass through. But your expensive pebbles—or bark chips, or whatever—are held up atop the plastic. They can't sink out of sight or make contact with the soil. When they collect leaves and twigs and start looking scruffy, simply haul up the plastic at one corner. Roll the mulch off to one side where it can be screened or raked. Then be sure to add some more functional mulch before replacing the plastic.

Even so, it's not a good idea to use bright, glossy stone mulches beneath any plant with exceptionally small foliage. The leaves of most deciduous trees, too wide to get stuck between pebbles, are easily removed. But an azalea, hemlock, or juniper will drop leaves or needles just tiny enough to stick between pebbles—and large enough to show up. The mulch beneath such a plant won't look good for more than a month at a time.

Washouts and How to Correct Them

A mini-compost heap or heavy mulch will usually halt routine erosion. But at the bottom of sloping land, rainwater can often collect into furious torrents, washing out unprotected soil to a depth of six inches or more. This problem is especially damaging beside a steep driveway or parking lot, since eventually the undermined asphalt starts to crack and break up. But here's where your used-brick fragments come in.

If the water hasn't already done it for you, excavate your washout site to a depth of about a foot. Pour eight inches of brick fragments into the trench. Their sharp angles and weight will hold them together even under fairly heavy runoff. Then mix in a good quantity of heavy subsoil, washing it down so that it settles in between the bricklets.

Now the crucial step—dig a series of clumps of *very* well-rooted pachysandra. Set them down atop your brick-and-clay foundation, and pour in more subsoil atop them, finally weighting them down with more brick fragments and small sharp rocks. Water and fertilize that pachysandra as if it cost fifty dollars a sprig, and cross your fingers.

When the next flood occurs, the pachysandra will probably be engulfed. The water will rush through its stems, carrying off dry twigs, dead leaves, and any surface soil that may have sifted in. But chances are that the current won't penetrate the pachysandra's tightly tangled root system—and because of the weighty rocks and brick chunks, the water can't *float* it loose either. Any soil that's washed out will be minimal, and easily replaced after the rain stops.

Should the pachysandra give way, the underlying brick chunks will stay put as the second line of defense. But as time passes, the pachysandra's runners will delve deeply among those brick chunks, binding the whole trench together. Its stems will grow thickly enough to trap floating debris, so that each flood begins *adding* more organic material than it washes away.

Kitchen Compost

You may be missing out on a free, plentiful, and enormously useful source of compost—vegetable table scraps. However, any but the most dedicated organic gardener balks at carting each evening's lettuce leaves and potato peelings down to the heap where they belong. And worse than the inconvenience is the appearance: dead weeds and leaves tend to blend in with the surrounding landscape, but add eggshells, coffee grounds, corncobs, and orange peels, and you'll have what looks like a full-fledged garbage dump. On the other hand, what if you only had to step outside the back door, and the nasty stuff was out of sight?

Buy *two* small plastic garbage cans of the exact same size; one or both should have a tight-fitting lid. Fill one can about six inches deep with small rocks, pebbles, or sand so that cats and raccoons can't possibly tip it over. Then fit the second can into the "socket" formed by the weighted one. As long as the lid on the top can clamps down securely, no foraging animal will be able to get at its contents.

Next, buy a small plastic container, preferably with a lid, and keep it handy on the kitchen counter beside the chopping board. Into it goes each day's vegetable refuse, starting with the breakfast orange peels. After you've washed the supper dishes, take the container outside and dump it into the Kitchen Compost can, conveniently located right beside the door. Within a week, most fresh scraps will erupt with molds and mildews whose colors will astound you. Corncobs turn a bumpy pink; orange peels swiftly acquire a blue nap. Protected by the lid from drying sun and wind, the fibers of ordinary mildew can reach lengths of an inch or more. Yet the smell is not at all "garbagey," just slightly sour and not entirely unpleasant. (Unless you add meat or bones to the bin, you aren't likely to get that distinctive garbage-dump reek.) The contents may not be a pleasant sight, but that's what the lid is for.

If you use a lot of citrus rinds—squeezed lemons, grapefruit halves, orange rinds—your Kitchen Compost will be a bit acid and slow to break down unless you add crushed limestone. A handful of dry manure helps; otherwise, the bin needs no further attention. It even supplies its own moisture: when you lift the lid each evening, you'll see the inside beaded with condensation that naturally drips back into the can.

Should the Kitchen Compost start breeding flies—not likely if you keep the lid on tightly—fill the can with water until the topmost garbage can be pushed beneath the surface. Stir the contents every few days so that surviving maggots and pupae are drowned. The water will absorb a great many nutrients, and so can be poured or siphoned off later for use as a superb liquid fertilizer. (One warning, though: leftover onions in the Compost will make the water smell like something that died of halitosis.)

In general, though, Kitchen Compost decomposes faster when it is not submerged. The bin is ready for "harvest" whenever the contents have finally reached within an inch of the rim. At the bottom of the can will be stringy, half-decayed mush that makes a fine addition to your "temporary" compost heap: simply dig a hole in the pit and bury the bin's entire contents, as you would grass clippings. The minerals and trace elements in vegetable refuse will greatly increase your compost's nutritional "vocabulary," resulting in humus that will support larger, healthier plants. Meanwhile, you'll be reducing the volume of your garbage considerably.

One last *caveat* for cat-owners: some brands of kitty litter advertise their product as "recyclable" and claim that it can be spread on the garden after the cat's through with it. This is a drastic oversimplification: the only biodegradable litters are those made of cedar chips or of pellets of compressed alfalfa. *All* other litters are absorbent clay pellets that will *not* break down when used as mulch and will, in fact, ruin any underlying humus. And even if the litter itself is organic, the raw nitrates of cat droppings are too strong for most plants. Any soiled organic litter (and dry feces from a standard litter box) should be added to the regular compost heap where they can decay into safely usable form.

5

CANOPY TREES

When I was ten years old, my father and I transplanted a young American chestnut we found in the woods. It was soon killed by chestnut blight, but not before our interest had spread to other native and foreign species. We bought them from nurseries or catalogs, collected them as seedlings from forests and roadsides, and accumulated a shelf of reference books to identify them. But while most of our specimen plantings thrived, few looked right where we originally planted them. Some were transplanted as many as five times, others were trimmed mercilessly. A good number had to be cut down entirely because they had grown too large.

It took me another ten years to realize that selecting a healthy tree isn't enough; you must first consider its visual *function*. Scores of books have been written on American trees alone, but all ignore the question of how a tree serves as a strictly architectural element in a cultivated landscape.

First off, forget the term "shade tree." Obviously, any tree casts shade. When a landscaper speaks of a shade tree, he means a species like maple, oak, hemlock, and beech that grows to at least fifty feet, with branches that angle out at least fifteen feet from the trunk and a growth rate that's swift enough to show results in a few years. When grown in the wild, most of them will outstrip the competition. Because of their rapid growth and prolific seedlings, they often form the topmost, or canopy level, of a mature forest. Thus, it's more accurate to use the term "Canopy Trees" to describe those species that will easily outlive your grandchildren, developing into giants that brook no competition under their branches.

If your property's been under cultivation for more than five years, you'll probably have several trees of appreciable size already on their way. If you don't already know what species they are, borrow one of the many tree identification guidebooks from your local library. But for some reason, these descriptive horticultural guides list only a tree's *good* qualities.

In a letter to the editor of *Horticulture* (September 1975) George W. Brailean of Detroit put the problem succinctly:

> Regarding (your) article on the horse chestnut . . . how about a note on whether the nuts are edible? How about its use as a lumber tree? How about the way the nasty things clog up gutters, or the way grass refuses to grow under them? . . .

In reality, horse chestnut is a mild offender. If your property hosts any of the species listed below, they should be cut down as soon as possible. This may sound drastic—especially if they've attained respectable size—but like a sloping lawn, these particular Canopy Trees can make your property unpleasant and often downright dangerous.

Kill List Canopy Trees

Most of the following exert a killing shade that effectively scuttles any grass or perennials you try to grow underneath. Besides casting a deep shadow, Kill List trees are so dense that light rain falling on their leaves often evaporates before it can drip to the ground. But such trees have extremely efficient feeder roots that drink up moisture within their own leafy perimeter, and so any plants underneath are left dark and dry. And because many of these trees grow so fast, their wood is highly brittle and quick to decay: after a hard wind, your property will be littered with twigs and small branches.

And perhaps with sterner stuff. One blustery night, the two-foot-thick trunk of my father's huge Lombardy poplar broke loose in a gale and took the nearby telephone wires with it. Needless to say, the tree was chopped down—as yours should be. Even if you like the following monsters' looks, each can be replaced with an acceptable look-alike.

Acer platanoides (Norway maple) is the most widely offered "shade" tree, but does its job too well. Old trees cast a positively twilight gloom, and the soil next to the trunk is almost invariably dry and bare. Its thick, shallow roots invade lawns and flowerbeds, often forming thick matted tangles that no other roots can penetrate. Young trees are fairly upright, but older specimens lean and gangle like demented apple trees, growing low, thick horizontal branches up to thirty feet long. Norways' new growth also hosts aphids all summer, so that cars or guests underneath are subjected to a slow rain of honeydew.

Used to colder climates in Europe, Norway is the last maple to drop its leaves in late October. But they're slow to decay. More than routine raking is needed to keep them from forming a soggy blanket that smothers grass and perennials. To make things worse, these trees are incredibly prolific: better than 90 percent of *all* tree seedlings that appear on my property are offspring of a single upwind Norway. The same drawbacks afflict Norway cultivars, such as 'Schwedler' or 'Crimson King' maple.

Acer pseudoplatanus (sycamore maple), sometimes offered as a substitute for Norway, is said to do well only around coastal areas. Mature trees are squat and broad, throwing killing shade. The leaves of some specimens are a startling raspberry purple on the underside, but what you'll see chiefly is the muddy dark green top surface. For some reason, sycamore maple's bark is always a dark sooty gray. (This is true even of trees growing away from heavy air pollution; sycamore maple either picks up extra grit or grows its own.)

Acceptable look-alikes: sugar or silver maple.

Ailanthus altissima (tree-of-heaven, "Tree that grows in Brooklyn") was introduced from China as a possible food tree for silkworm moths. The moths didn't care for it, and neither do most gardeners. The compound leaves, up to four feet long, emit a vile musky odor when crushed. In winter, they fall to reveal utterly twigless, sticklike branches. The wood does not burn well, however, and the smoke has been said to cause rashes.

Ailanthus is sometimes offered by mail as a "tropical wonder tree" that will provide shade "in a few short years." Indeed, the tree grows up to ten feet a year, often producing multiple trunks. But only in an inner city does this sumac look-alike become desirable, growing lushly out of cracks in the street and subway gratings. The shallow roots are highly invasive, sprouting new shoots wherever they break ground and often blanketing entire railway embankments.

Probably ailanthus insists on quick reproduction because each individual tree is so short-lived. After it attains about forty to fifty feet, growth usually slows. Branches begin dying back. But even when you cut it down, your battle won't be over. Fast new shoots will emerge from the stump, and ailanthus can be incredibly persistent. For five years, I have kept chopping off a seedling that has wedged itself deep in the cracks of a stone wall. By the time it grows out far enough for me to hack loose, it has photosynthesized enough energy for yet another try.

Acceptable look-alike: black walnut.

Populus nigra 'Italica' (Lombardy poplar) is one tree you absolutely must dispose of if it's anywhere near your house or driveway. This widely touted tree is usually offered in quantity so that homeowners can line their property with a series of fast-growing columnar trees. But like most poplars, 'Italica' demands water. The rains of spring often coax it into enthusiastic, prodigious new growth, but when August droughts arrive, the tree finds itself overextended. Leaves—then twigs and entire branches—will shrivel and die back.

Even if you supply enormous quantities of water, the extremely shallow roots will still journey out in a search of more. Soon the lawn nearby will look as if you'd buried a number of gnarled shillelaghs just under the surface. And find water they will! Poplar roots are notorious for detecting far-off water sources, and if they can't find a natural spring, they'll settle for the nearest water pipe.

My father once planted two Lombardies at the rear corners of his house. Exactly five years later, when the trees had grown thirty feet tall, the toilets inside suddenly backed up *en masse*. Excavating the blocked sewer pipe entailed tearing up the lawn and digging a trench six feet deep. One of the Lombardy's roots had penetrated the supposedly watertight seal between two sections of terra-cotta pipe. Inside was a six-foot mane of roots growing "downstream" and packing the pipe as tightly as cotton batting.

Any Lombardy lucky enough to find such a water source will grow splendidly. But like ailanthus, its roots soon begin sprouting. Lombardies will also arise through concrete and blacktop, where the rapidly swelling underground burls make releveling impossible. But even if a Lombardy doesn't incur ruinous plumbing and surfacing bills, this tree, like ailanthus, is short-lived. Larger branches often become infected with fungus or die back on their own, calling for constant pruning. One day, suddenly, the top half of the tree will die back. When dry, the wood is extremely brittle, and if you don't have the tree taken down promptly, the next windstorm can send it into your roof or electrical cables.

Acceptable look-alikes: any fastigiate form of beech, black locust, or linden.

Quercus palustris (pin oak) is probably the most tolerant of oaks, but also the least desirable. In spring, the tree drops vast quantities of catkins that clog gutters and litter streets and driveways. The young leaves are unusually liable to inchworms, which late in May descend on silken cords to reach the ground where they pupate. Not nearly as fast-growing as some other species, pin oak tends to throw long, sweeping branches that need pruning if anyone is to walk comfortably underneath—and even under ideal growing conditions, pin oak branches are full of dead twigs that fall constantly.

In fall comes another messy shower, this one of acorns. Then, while other oaks put on dramatic foliage displays, pin oak's leaves usually turn the color of a brown paper bag—and again, an inordinate quantity wind up caught in the gutters. Since they curl slightly after falling, they litter the ground in deep, springy drifts—and even when they pack down, pin oak leaves are as unrottable as any you can find.

Acceptable look-alikes: any other native American oak species.

Salix babylonica (weeping willow) looks good at a distance, and that's where you ought to keep it. The tree is vigorous and fast-growing, but needs abundant water and full sun to become shapely. In the meantime, it behaves a bit like a Lombardy: surface roots emerge in the lawn; older twigs and branches are constantly dying back and falling to the ground. Without yearly pruning (or more accurately, cleaning out), a willow soon becomes a thin canopy of weeping leaves over a snaggle of dead branches. The pendant crown of an older tree camouflages this unsightly interior, but the fall of dead twigs still makes large weeping willows poor trees to sit underneath.

Willows in general are prone to fungus diseases that afflict their leaves and branches, and larger specimens can throw a killing shade. I'd avoid the entire genus unless you can plant them on a riverbank where water will float away the detritus.

Acceptable look-alike: weeping Japanese cherry (Chapter 6).

A Kill List tree can be reprieved on grounds of old age. For example, my father's property once hosted an incredibly old ailanthus with a three-foot girth at the base. Even assuming this species' rapid growth, it must have begun its weedy career well before the turn of the century. It had apparently outgrown its own bad habits: when it finally died in its sleep one winter and was taken down, no new sprouts arose from the roots.

I am still saddled with a pin oak that litters my driveway and gutters, but it's a venerable giant of at least two hundred years, with a stately look that no tree under thirty could match. I figure it's earned its right to remain there, but I do make sure that its seedlings are quickly rooted out.

The "Think Twice" List

The following trees, also widely offered in nurseries and by mail, fall short of my Kill List only because they can be improved by pruning. But before planting them or allowing young saplings to survive, consider their various disadvantages:

Acer negundo (box elder) is one of the few maples with compound leaves. Exotic and attractive, the foliage admits rain and decays rapidly. The tree grows very quickly, but mature trees take on a low, spreading form that resists high-pruning and produces a killing shade.

Box elder is also ruthlessly prolific. Seedlings arise with all the vigor of Norways, throwing far sturdier roots. (You should uproot seedlings as soon as you notice them. Larger saplings will demand a machete.)

Aesculus hippocastanum (horse chestnut) bears utterly lovely candelabra-like sprays of flowers in late May. But the tree grows very slowly. Unless planted where its unambitious roots can reach plentiful moisture, its enormous compound leaves begin browning at the edges in July. By August, many trees are completely denuded. The heavy fall of handsome (but inedible) chestnuts is an asset only if you're about twelve years old; the burrs are a nuisance. If you like the flowers and exotic leaves, my own recommendation is to substitute the buckeye, a smaller-growing native American tree of the same genus.

Castanea mollissima (Chinese or hybrid chestnut) is usually offered as a substitute for the blight-stricken *C. dentata* (American chestnuts—still surprisingly plentiful in wild areas, but their bark is girdled by the fungus before they reach twenty feet). Unlike the American, Chinese chestnut adopts a spreading, leaning habit while still quite young. The first burrs appear after five years, opening to drop edible chestnuts. But even if high-pruned year after year, the tree continues to throw watersprouts from the trunk and doesn't develop a full, spreading crown until after ten years or more of cultivation. Dead leaves tend to remain on the branches during the winter.

Catalpa spp. is a genus of flowering trees whose native Southern species will survive in the North. Quick growth and enormous heart-shaped leaves of light green make the tree attractive when young, but cold weather and drought cause extensive die-back of older branches. Showy white flowers appear in June, but quickly ripen into seed pods nearly a foot long that fall and litter the surroundings. Older trees take on a ratty, half-dead appearance; and the huge leaves make the tree appear smaller than it actually is. If pollarded, however, catalpa can function rather effectively as a Second-Layer tree (see Chapter 6).

Ginkgo biloba is often touted as a "living fossil" that will survive city environments. But its form is unsatisfactory. The trunk goes straight up for several feet, with eccentrically placed straight branches. Except for the fastigiate variety, most mature ginkgos look mildly artificial. Trees bought as seedlings have a fifty-fifty chance of being female and bearing evil-smelling fruit. To eliminate this drawback, most nursery stock consists of male branches grafted to seedling trunks—which grow with annoying slowness.

Gleditsia triacanthos (honey or sweet locust) bears vicious thorns, long messy seed pods, and finely cut compound foliage whose leaflets usually begin falling long before autumn. A few new varieties —the 'Moraine', 'Sunburst', and 'Ruby Lace' locusts—have managed to eliminate the thorns and pods and offer attractive leaf color. But like their wild ancestor, they still have lousy form.

Any honey locust grows straight for the first six feet or so, whereupon its terminal bud loses its vigor and develops a welter of scraggy branches. Unless it's pruned early enough, the tree becomes open, sparse-looking, and wildly asymmetrical. The slow growth of the cultivars may be the result of the transplanting shock suffered by nursery-size trees—*Gleditsias* have notoriously far-reaching roots, and any balled-and-bagged specimen usually has had most of them chopped off. But seedlings grow slowly too.

Liquidambar styraciflua (sweet gum) looks great when it's small. The trunk is resolutely straight, and the regular side branches bear little "wings"—ridges of protruding cork. The young foliage resembles a Japanese maple leaf (in fact, this tree is frequently mistaken for a maple), but leaves from a mature tree are almost perfectly star-shaped. Fall color is either a creamy yellow or deep purple.

As the tree grows, however, it begins to bear seed capsules about an inch across—about the size and shape of a cherry bomb. Their color is dark gray, and the surface is embossed with short, blunt spines. These capsules fall copiously in late winter, covering the ground and bouncing into flowerbeds and corners so that you'll be coming across them all year.

Liriodendron tulipifera (tulip tree) is common in forests because it seeds itself so willingly. It's a quick grower, with handsome leaves and smooth bark when young. It's often sold for its "tulips"—large cup-shaped flowers produced in early summer—but they're not nearly as tuliplike as catalogs would have you believe. The petals' exterior is a reddish green that's almost perfectly camouflaged by the surrounding leaves. The only real flash of color is an orange throat—*inside* the flower, where you'll never see it unless it falls prematurely to the ground. To make itself even less decorative, a tree seldom flowers before it's thirty feet tall; and only then at the very top branches. So to enjoy the tulips at all, you'll need either binoculars or a hot-air balloon. Leaves break down very quickly, but falling branches and seed clusters are plentiful.

Platanus occidentalis (plane tree, sycamore) is widely planted in cities because it resists air pollution. Eventually the bark flakes off in large patches, revealing swatches of creamy white. (Somehow, this feature is not as attractive in a garden as it is on city streets.) Meanwhile, you have a real raking problem with stiff, outsize leaves in autumn, *Liquidambar*-like seed capsules, and possibly killing shade.

Ulmus (elm): Our native American and slippery elms are hard-pressed by the Dutch elm fungus, so increasingly, nurseries offer species or hybrids of disease-resistant Old World elms. Unfortunately, these trees never develop the classic weeping vase shape of the American species. But then, neither do the American elms until they've been grown for thirty years or so. When small, any elm is an open, sparse tree with rather dry-looking leaves, splintery bark, and a mongrel shape like outsized privet.

Despite their handsome compound leaves, I'd also omit the hickories (*Carya*) and the ashes (*Fraxinus*) because of their heavy drop of nuts and winged seeds. Hickories in particular take on a rather dull, dry look in midsummer. The shagbark hickory (*C. ovata*) has deep olive-green, almost blackish-green leaves and long narrow plates of bark that crack loose at top and bottom and hang on the trunk for years, giving it an unparalleled rustic look. But its main drawback is killing shade.

By forgoing the above species, you can concentrate on trees that are far more rewarding. Certainly you shouldn't plant any new trees until your Kill List species are gone, because the gaps they leave will suggest possibilities you wouldn't have perceived otherwise.

For example, what of the form of your surviving Canopy trees? Chances are that they aren't quite right either—because whoever planted them ignored the fact that a tree's shape and beauty (often its very survival) are determined by how it reacts to competition.

"Full-Sun" Versus "Forest Environment"

Any Canopy tree will do well in full sun, and a great many of them demand it. Choice species like Serbian spruce, tupelo, and the weeping and colored-leaf beeches show off only in sunny solitude. Planted in the shade of other trees or buildings, they'll become open and scraggly, never attaining the lush foliage and emphatic shapes for which you planted them. These are the *Full-Sun* species, which can't afford any competition for light. Since they'll need extra room on all sides, it's important that you either reserve their spaces, or plant them before anything else can get in their way.

In nature, the first tree of any specis to invade an open meadow adopts a classic spreading form to trap all possible light and also to forestall competition. But not all trees *require* such an advantage. Many species that normally grow under forest conditions not only tolerate shade and crowding, but actually look *better* when planted this way.

For example, inspect any property where a red maple was planted in full sun. The tree will be broad and bushy, but not as stately as you might expect. The handsome, furrowed bark is hidden by low

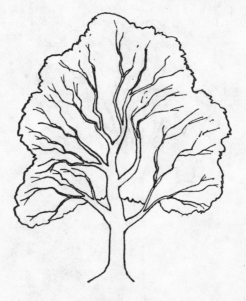

Figure 20

branches. Chances are the trunk divides only a few feet above the ground, as in Figure 20, with no single upward line for the eye to follow.

But compare this tree with one on a property where the developers left some red maples from the original forest. Their trunks soar up at least twenty feet without interruption, displaying the bark to great advantage. When the first branches appear, they jut sharply upward, carrying your gaze still higher. Then, finally, the crown bushes out in a broad arc as per Figure 21.

What you can't see is how the tree originally grew that way. For years, it was surrounded by others that shaded it from all sides, forcing all its new growth upward in a tight, narrow cylinder. When the competition was chopped down, its shape remained. The current spreading crown is simply the result of good health. I call trees that can be grown in this manner *Forest-Environment* species. Planted in full sun, they'll need extra pruning and training to make them tall and graceful. But planted with other specimens nearby, they will naturally attain this upward, reaching habit.

Of your present trees, chances are you'll find several Full-Sun trees languishing in the shadow of something else, and a few bushy Forest-

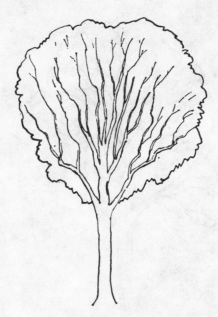

Figure 21

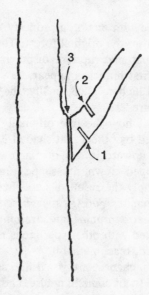

Figure 22

Environment trees out in the open by themselves. But to correct either problem, all you need do is begin high-pruning, which forces the tree to grow *up* rather than *out*. In Japanese parks, few Canopy trees have any branches within ten feet of the ground—the result of premeditated removal of lower limbs.

Since all Full-Sun specimens need light and as much space as possible on all sides, this means cutting back the lower encroaching limbs of *other* trees. But if their own present lower limbs are weak and sparse, these ought to come off as well. That goes double for any Full-Sun Canopy evergreens—hemlock, pine, or spruce—that may have been mistakenly used as foundation plantings under your house's walls. Eventually such a tree will get up above window level, ruining your view as its branches screen the light. Yet it's even more defeating to try and keep the tree to its present size by pruning it back down—or worse, arbitrarily cutting it off at the middle.

The solution is to get it up *over* your windows. Preserve the central trunk, but remove all the side branches up to the halfway point. (The larger the tree, the better this prescription will work.) It will then develop a straight, clean trunk that will carry it well up over your eaves. Further pruning will allow enough light below that you can begin *proper* foundation planting as outlined in Chapter 7.

All Forest-Environment trees need high-pruning even more. But since they haven't been trained until now, you may not be able to reduce them to a straight, single trunk. If their present spreading form is so attractive that you want to leave them as is, they should then be treated as Full-Sun trees, with no competing foliage within ten feet of their outermost branches. But do prune any branches that leave the trunk at a horizontal angle or below.

Getting all your trees' lowest limbs up at least fifteen feet gives you all the picturesque advantages of forest conditions: attractively exposed trunks with well-supported side branches, light dappled shade beneath, plus open headroom that makes raking and other chores vastly more convenient. Moreover, high-pruning allows you to grow a wide variety of other plants underneath—even shade-tolerant "Second-Layer" trees (see Chapter 6) with each retaining good appearance and vigor.

You may need the help of a local tree service, but on lower branches you can do a lot of the pruning work yourself. Larger limbs should be started with a preliminary "safety" cut on the bottom so that their fall doesn't tear bark loose from the trunk. (See Figure 22.) The second cut removes the limb. The third removes the stump,

Figure 23

leaving a wound that's conformed as closely as possible to the plane of the remaining trunk.

In general, the more susceptible a tree is to aphids or borers, the faster its exposed wood will decay. Even so, recent studies have proved that pruning injuries heal just as quickly—and with the same incidence of decay—whether they're sealed or not. Before bothering to seal a cut at all, ask yourself two questions: How vertical is the cut? Is it exposed to sun at least a part of the day?

A vertical wound in full sun will soon dry off, runs parallel to the grain of the trunk, and the tree's own bark will spread to cover it in two to three years. But a wide, horizontal cut (such as in the crotch of a tree, or across an upward-reaching limb) exposes the open grain of the wood to the elements. Especially if this wound is shaded, such a site can trap enough moisture to promote decay before the wound can be healed over. And when such "wet rot" gets into a branch or trunk, it follows the grain, turning the wood into a blackish, crumbling sponge that only absorbs more water. The healing cambium layer keeps turning inward, hoping to find solid wood on which it can build to close the gap. When cutting down hollowed maples, it's not unusual to find cross sections of cambrium that have described concentric spirals as the underlying heartwood rots away (Figure 23).

To forestall this, you still don't need a waterproof tar-base paint, just something to seal the grain. But before applying your paint, wait at least a week. An immediate application of sealer is often "bubbled" away by sap arising from the fresh cut.

Even if you have a tree service prune your trees, *never* allow the wood to be carted away. A tree surgeon will charge extra for transportation, and as I pointed out in the last chapter, pruned wood is too valuable to lose.

Chances are, the limbs will be in a high, chaotic pile. To dismember them, a machete (such as is used for cutting sugar cane) is more convenient than an axe. Standing on one side of the limb, for safety's sake, "throw" the blade at the base of branches on the other. A machete is a tool for one hand only, and branches as wide as two inches will slice through in a single blow. Finish detwigging the branches with a pruning shears, so that you're left with a series of straight, unbranched poles.

Smaller twigs are ideal for the mini-compost heap described earlier, but if your heftier branches are of willow, tulip tree, or mulberry, they'll make ideal stakes for later garden use. The fresh bark of these species is so saturated with sap that it will peel loose easily, exposing the clean white heartwood below. (Stripped-off bark is also good for the compost heap.) After the wood dries for a week or two, it stiffens and bleaches to an attractive driftwood sheen that makes it look better when supporting weeping trees (see Chapter 6) or tall perennials.

Branches thicker than three inches are best for firewood. Saw them into eighteen-inch sections, but don't stack them in the open unless you plan to burn them that following winter. Woodpiles that aren't used up in time attract termites and rodents, and enough dampness will creep in to make burning difficult. You can store a good amount of logs in the attic, close to the eaves where the house walls provide maximum support. Placing them on end speeds drying, and makes them easier to tip loose when called for. Firewood loses a great deal of its weight when thoroughly dry, so don't worry about it damaging the ceiling below.

Removing Kill List trees and high-pruning the rest should open room for at least as many new trees as you had originally. But no matter how much space you have, you'll enjoy any new tree far more if you plant it according to its most appropriate visual function. My rule of thumb is that any single Canopy tree serves *either* as a Silhouette Tree, as part of a Background Clump, or as a "true" Shade Tree.

I. SILHOUETTE TREES

The term "shade tree" becomes even more meaningless when you realize that very few trees are actually planted to provide shade. What the gardener is really after is something huge that he can look up at, that will lend his property greater scale. In California, significantly, most tourists do not visit the uncut redwood groves. The trees there may be massive and centuries old, but they're so crowded that the eye can't pick them out individually. Visitors prefer to photograph the few free-standing, solitary giants that can be viewed in the round. Similarly, most Canopy trees are planted for their silhouettes—as elements that break the horizon and show up against the sky. It's no coincidence that most of the best-loved Canopy trees —elms, hickories, oaks, maples, pines, and spruces—have trunks that are unusually upright and vertical, breaking free of the horizontal ground and lifting the viewer's eye in an exhilarating defiance of gravity.

To view a large tree properly, of course, you can't stand directly underneath it. But with today's smaller properties, too many gardeners plant a sapling Silhouette Tree right next to the house. When the tree grows, it can no longer be appreciated from inside, and its own form is partly obscured by the house itself. Therefore, all Silhouette Trees should be planted as far from your house as possible —ideally at the borders of your property where, eventually, they'll appear as tall verticals bisecting the horizon, their foliage made delicate by distance.

This arrangement also helps preserve your most vital garden resource—sun. A great many garden books have been written about how to solve the difficulties of gardening in shade—all because so many landscapers plug in trees just to fill empty ground, forgetting that almost all popular vegetables, flowers, and ornamental shrubs demand more than half a day of good sunlight. Situate large trees too close to the center of your yard, and you'll be permanently banishing a good third of the plants you could otherwise grow. Ideally, Silhouette Trees should frame—but not block—sunrises and sunsets. Nor, of course, should they be planted underneath telephone lines, or where they'll later threaten any pleasant vistas you presently enjoy.

Deciduous Silhouette Trees provide maximum seasonal variation —lush, leafy shapes in summer and attractively bare branches in winter. Especially desirable species are noted with an asterisk.

Acer saccharinum (silver maple) is so called because of its leaves' silvery light-green undersides. The leaves themselves are deeply scalloped. (A cut-leaf variety exists, but is too slow-growing for Silhouette purposes; use it as a Second-Layer tree.) Young trees grow quickly without compromising their basic delicacy, and slow down noticeably after they reach thirty feet. The wood saws more easily than Norway's and is said to be brittle, but few dead branches fall during windstorms. Larger limbs reinforce themselves with a girth of extra wood, and older trees take on a symmetrical shape midway between an oak and elm. (One private school took the stately silver maple on its playing field for an oak, blithely outfitting it with acorns on the school seal. The New York Thruway eventually was built over the site, erasing all evidence of the academic goof.) Autumn color is a pale yellow, and of all the larger maples, silver certainly appears freshest and most vigorous in late summer. Seedlings are moderately prolific, but easy to weed out.

* *Acer saccharum,* the native American sugar (or rock, or hard) maple, produces a craggy, textured bark that's far more picturesque than a Norway's gray elephant hide. Its fall colors are unsurpassed, ranging from a clear yellow through a breath-taking flame orange— with branches on the same tree often displaying different shades. Even in spring, sugars outdo the Norways: while the latter bloom with stiff nosegays of chartreuse flowers, the sugars are festooned with hanging catkinlike garlands of the palest yellow-green. In full spring sun, the trees suddenly seem hung with a gossamer Spanish moss.

Sugars sold by mail order are usually named cultivars, with more attractive upright form or more lavish fall color. You can also try to find seedling trees in your local area, but young sugars and Norways are extremely similar. To be sure, pick off a lower leaf. Norways are the only maples whose broken leafstems exude a droplet of a sticky milk-white sap.

Betula ermanii (Russian rock birch), difficult to locate in catalogs, has striking pinkish-orange bark and a thick, gnarled growth habit reminiscent of an old beech.

B. papyrifera (carol, canoe, or paper birch) is the large native American white-barked birch that should *not* be confused with the clump-forming "white birch" so often hawked in nurseries. Tolerating shade and loving dampness, it can get positively enormous. On the shores of Lake George, I've seen one growing at least sixty feet tall among hemlocks that cast a very deep shade. But its sun-loving crown was high above the conifers, and its dazzling-white trunk a good two feet thick. The mature bark peels only intermittently; after it has really aged, it forms a smooth horizontally ribbed girdle of white with no loose edges.

This vigorous species is not happy south of mountainous Pennsylvania, unfortunately, but it's ideal if you live in a northern climate. Look for small seedlings along roadsides and in open meadows: the leaves are distinctly oval-shaped when compared with the triangular ones of clump-forming gray birches. Give deep, rich woods soil for best results.

B. pendula (European birch) will grow wherever the above white-barked giants will not. Despite the Latin name, it's *not* a weeping tree (though some such varieties do exist). It's swift-growing, is widely available, has lovely form, and is thoroughly desirable.

Fagus (beech): All species have a gray elephant-skin bark, wrinkled around the knuckles and joints, that remains light and smooth until someone adds his initials with a penknife.

Beeches grow slowly at first, but look venerable at a fairly young age. Set flat rocks around the trunk so that the roots are cool and shaded. Once the tree has enough high branches to shade its own roots, high-prune drastically so that you don't get one of those ground-hugging specimens often seen on old estates. Though these low limbs offer ideal climbing for neighborhood children, they will arch down to form a skirt you can't walk underneath. Some limbs will actually sprawl along the ground, which is exotic but not too good for the lawn.

Fagus grandifolia (American beech) has green almond-shaped leaves with *exactly* parallel veining.

F. sylvatica (European beech) has fatter, more oval leaves and is more widely offered in nurseries. There are several varieties:

F. sylvatica heterophylla (cut-leaf or fern-leaf beech) has leaves so deeply cut that they resemble a red oak. Slower growing than most beeches, it produces thinner, more prolific branches that need high-pruning almost from the start.

F. sylvatica pendula (weeping beech) comes in both regular green and *purpurea* varieties. Young trees can be a bit sorry-looking, but patience brings a fountain of lush foliage and tormented, arching branches. Since new growth weeps down from the original branches, the bark *atop* each main limb is exposed, making a handsome contrast with the leaves. But unlike a weeping willow, weeping beech has hard, inflexible wood. Only very thin branches and new growth will sway in the wind.

This is definitely a tree for looking at, not sitting under, because the pendulous branches look best when allowed to graze the ground. But young trees should be high-pruned and staked to get their first branches up; *then* allow them to weep. Once twigs are actually touching the soil, clip them off.

F. sylvatica purpurea (copper beech): Several varieties of *F. sylvatica* are marketed as *purpurea,* period. All begin with pink leaves in spring, but some older cultivars turn dark green by July. However, the best trees keep a deep, rich mahogany red throughout the summer, a tint which is easily the match of 'Crimson King' maple.

F. sylvatica rohanii (Rohan's beech) is very widely offered. Its leaves are not as dark as *purpurea* and are ruffled along the edges; should be planted beside a tree with light green foliage for maximum contrast.

Juglans nigra (black walnut) is literally an investment. Should you tire of the mature tree, you can always sell it for several hundred dollars to a lumberyard. In fact, the wood is in such demand by cabinetmakers and veneer manufacturers that large trees are often pirated from parks and private woodlands.

Black walnut automatically grows a straight trunk that the sawmills require, but high-pruning will encourage it. The compound leaves are dark green and lusher-looking than those of hickory or ash. The "walnuts" are edible, but are encased in a green husk the size of a tennis ball that looks fairly exotic while it remains on the tree. The tree's only drawback is that its roots exude a poison fatal to tomatoes and other plants—another argument for placing this Silhouette tree at the border of your land where you're positive you won't want a vegetable garden someday.

Nyssa sylvatica (black gum, tupelo) is my favorite of all Silhouette trees. The rich glossy green foliage turns a clear, fiery red in autumn. The young bark is smooth and gray like a beech's, and the limbs—arranged in a perfect pyramid in young specimens—have an attractive wriggle to them that makes the tree look older than it is.

Older bark becomes dark and deeply furrowed. This tree almost never drops dead twigs or branches, yet never seems to get in its own way. The small blue berries are attractive, but unfortunately few ever germinate. This makes tupelo hard to find, but it's worth looking for.

Populus deltoides (cottonwood) is the species to pick if you hanker for a single, enormous, fast-growing tree that will reach seventy feet within your lifetime. A giant among poplars but used to growing in dry climates, cottonwood has roots that behave themselves while the trunk shots up to ten feet a year. Broad, triangular leaves are borne on a flattened, winged stem that twists gently in the lightest breeze. If the tree gets thirsty in midsummer, only the lower, older leaves will turn yellow and drop off. If so, pruning off the lower branches in July will maintain a neat, lush look.

Further high-pruning is required to keep the tree from developing a skirt of low, weak branches. But mature trees develop a beautifully furrowed bark and branches that arch gracefully downward. When the tree is quite large, the individual leaves themselves gradually become smaller, and the tips of old branches eventually begin reaching back down to the ground—all of which makes this species an ideal substitute for diseased American elms. The name "cottonwood" comes from the seeds, which are airborne in tufts of white even more gossamer than a thistle's. A large tree can carpet the ground beneath it with up to a half inch of "cotton" that is—unfortunately—flammable. Try to give your cottonwood room, so that the wind can catch it and disperse the fluff.

Quercus (oaks) come in two forms: the so-called *red oaks,* with sharp points to the lobes of the leaves; and *white oaks,* whose lobes are rounded. The following are of the red tribe:

Q. coccinea (scarlet oak) has dark green leaves, slightly plumper than pin oak's, that turn a screaming red in fall. But the mature tree takes on the sparse, angular look of a pin oak, and doesn't announce itself as dramatically as the other oaks below.

Q. rubra (northern red oak), the best of the reds, has wider leaves than scarlet oak and a deep mahogany fall color. Unlike most oaks, it doesn't resent transplanting and grows quite quickly, forming a craggy, dignified shape while still under ten years old. Lush and utterly dependable, it needs plenty of room.

Q. shumardii (red oak, Shumard's oak) is an uncommon species that ranges mainly in the South, but as far north as Ohio. It has good shape and fall color, but is worth substituting for a *rubra* only if your property falls within its natural range.

The following species are white oaks:

*Q. alba (white oak) is best-known for its distinctly cut leaves with wide, regular lobes. The color is a rich, deep green all summer. Old bark is rugged and furrowed, and limbs are handsomely arranged. Certain specimens take on the asymmetrical, gangling look associated with English oaks and the southern live oak, but only when they have plenty of room to do so.

*Q. muehlenbergii (chinquapin oak) has a long, thin leaf that closely mimicks the American chestnut, and so makes an ideal substitute. Growth is slow, and mature trees do not spread quite as widely as other oaks. It's particularly good, then, for a small property; or where you want a touch of glossy elegance.

*Q. prinus (basket, or chestnut oak) actually looks less like a chestnut than chinquapin, above. The leaf is fatter and broadens toward the top. Acorns are large and attractive. Although lacking good fall color, the leaves remain glossy green all summer and look more lush than the foliage of most other oaks.

Q. robur (English oak), only rarely available, exaggerates all the best qualities of our own *Q. alba.* But the tree grows slower than *alba* and the blue-green leaves are subject to the same leaf mildew that afflicts lilacs and roses. Because of *Q. robur*'s naturally tight growth, effective spraying is difficult, and the disease returns year after year. A fastigiate form exists and can be treated as a Second-Layer tree.

Unfortunately, our native oaks are seldom offered by nurseries or catalogs—chiefly since oaks of any size are notoriously difficult to transplant. Most throw only scanty side roots along a single deep taproot; if it's broken during digging, the tree is usually set back for several years.

Because oak pollen is borne plentifully on the wind, species in the wild tend to hybridize—hence the guidebooks' frequent confusion over nomenclature. In addition, the leaves of young oaks are often grossly broader and less deeply cut than on older plants. Rather than try to identify such perverse seedlings, prospect for adult trees in your vicinity, and then return in fall to gather acorns. Forgo any that bear small holes in the sides; this indicates that a weevil's larva has been eating within. Store the acorns over the winter in a plastic bag in an unheated attic or refrigerator. The following spring, plant them about an inch deep (as squirrels do) *at the sites where you want mature trees,* so that you won't have to transplant them later. By early June, the sprouts should appear.

Evergreen Silhouette Trees

There are many large-scale conifers on the market, but only a few form a good silhouette in winter.

*Abies balsamea (balsam fir) prefers cool summer nights and grows slowly in warmer climates. The fat needles are a lush, deep green, held horizontally on the twigs in a neat fashion not seen in any other conifer. Mature specimens have few bare lower branches, and their needles positively glisten in the sun.

Cedrus libani (cedar of Lebanon), originally brought to England by returning Crusaders, is good for any temperate climate but still little-grown in this country. Trees grow slowly, but with age produce a multibranched outline like that of a very neat white pine. The foliage develops in platforms, and early high-pruning assures a magnificent trunk. Definitely worth growing if you—and your descendants—have the patience.

Picea abies (Norway spruce) should be mistrusted. The needles are so thickly clustered on the twigs that the tree shades its own lower branches, which quickly become sparse and die back. The silhouette is almost always shaggy; on old specimens, the very top often dies back.

*P. brewerana (Brewer's spruce) is a still little-known Oregon species whose mature branches develop long pendulous twigs. Now available as seed from several firms, this is a gem worth germinating and waiting for.

P. omorika (Serbian spruce) has lovely sweeping branches, and twigs that hang—almost weeping at times—on either side of the branch like the hair on a collie's tail. The tree admits a great deal of light even when mature, so half-dead branches and thin spots next to the trunk are kept to a minimum. It seems to prefer a bit of shelter from winter wind, but will quickly repair any thin spots caused by winterkilling.

P. pungens (Colorado spruce) is best known in its many *glauca* varieties (collectively known as blue spruce). Old-fashioned blue spruces display a severely columnar growth, with neat, flat gently drooping branches. But many of the newer varieties sold by nurseries are disappointing. Bred for quick growth and color, their form has been wholly ignored: many get bushy as they grow older, and their branches do not droop at all. But the regular green Colorado spruce is neat and pyramidal, and its form better behaved than most modern *glaucas*.

Pinus nigra (Austrian pine) is perhaps the finest pine for Silhouette use. The needles are long and stiff, and trees are almost ideally symmetrical at any size. (They've been planted extensively along the Palisades Parkway just north of the George Washington Bridge, where virtually none of them looks the least lopsided or bedraggled.) The species' only disadvantage is that it's vulnerable to a pine blight, now affecting trees in the Northeast, that kills off lower needles and branches. If there are many other Austrian pines in your neighborhood that could serve to carry the disease, you may want to pass it by.

P. resinosa (red pine) has pairs of extraordinarily long needles and an unusually tall and straight trunk. The young bark is like any other pine's, but after the trunk widens to about a foot, the bark begins flaking off in flat reddish scales. Each looks like a piece of jigsaw puzzle that has been sand-polished to the satiny texture of driftwood, and the continual flaking of the bark maintains the trunk's ruddy brown color. To keep the coarse needles from spoiling your view of the trunk, high-prune the lower branches.

P. strobus and *P. sylvestris* (white and Scots pines) are probably the most widely sold species. But unfortunately, neither is ideal for Silhouette use. Each forms a bushy, fluffy tree that becomes erratic with time. White pines especially take on a wide, spreading habit that exerts a killing shade; often their trunks become streaked with drools of resinous sap that becomes chalk-white as it weathers. Prevention is best: be sure that any weakening lower branches are pruned off promptly while they're still narrow, so that the wounds can close promptly.

Better yet, pass up the ordinary white and Scots pines and look for the *fastigiata* varieties of these species, in which the growth is more upright and columnar than normal. Many species of Canopy trees (both evergreen and deciduous) are fairly unkempt, while their fastigiate forms are very neat indeed. A fastigiate pine's branches are angled up so tightly to the sides that the tree appears lush and cylindrical.

P. taeda (loblolly pine) is a particularly good Southeast substitute for *P. resinosa,* which doesn't like hot summers. Loblolly's top may become scraggly, but only in poor soil. With good moisture and nourishment, the mature pine assumes a terraced shape with gracefully curving branches.

Pseudotsuga menziesii (Douglas fir) forms a dense, craggy outline. Needles are unusually small, so that the tree seems more distant than it really is and better scaled to smaller properties.

Tsuga canadensis (hemlock) is too often used in places where a smaller tree is wanted. Without shearing, hemlock grows about two feet a year, adopting a shape more informal than spruce or fir, but still more delicate than a pine. But hemlock is so relentlessly common that I'd hold out for its distinctive full-sized variants such as 'Frosty' (with white-tipped new growth), *T. c. microphylla,* and *T. c. macrophylla* (with tinier and far larger needles than normal).

II. BACKDROP CLUMP TREES

In a crowded woodland, the eye easily picks out the trunks of individual trees, but their crowns intermingle into a single mass of leafy texture. The same effect can be created with only four or five trees planted closer than ten feet apart, in Forest-Environment fashion.

On your property, such a massed planting isn't likely to be all that deep, so you'll be able to see between the assembled trunks to the space beyond. Therefore, grouped trees do *not* take the place of a privacy hedge, as covered more fully in Chapter 7. Just the opposite: they let you see into your neighbors' yards while eclipsing the horizon. They also provide a shady environment as is required for a Wild Garden, and thus can substitute for a *single* "True Shade" Tree. (If your property is quite small, you can obtain the same effect with more appropriately sized Second-Layer Trees. See Chapter 6.)

Species listed without description below are Silhouette-Use species that can also serve in a clump-style planting without sacrificing their shape or fall color. (Note that a few "Second-Thought" trees are included here, because partial shade will curb their bad habits.) Again, the best for this usage are starred.

Deciduous Trees for Clump Use:

*Acer rubrum (red maple, swamp maple) is slower-growing than most of its genus. In the open, it eventually produces a rounded crown, but also does particularly well in competition with other trees about the same size. Planted three to four feet apart, red maples develop tall, straight trunks with attractive light-gray bark. (Locally, my red maples tend to preserve patches of smooth juvenile bark well into old age—a particularly attractive trait.) Branches are straight and open, so that a young grove of red maples will admit very light shade, if not dappled sun. (Deep shade is cast by mature trees.) In early spring, the tiny flowers are borne in bright red clusters. Mature leaves sometimes have a noticeably red stem; fall color is either red or yellow (though the color is strongest on trees grown in full sun). A number of cultivars promising better autumn color or a more symmetrical crown are now being marketed.

*Betula papyrifera (paper birch)

*B. pendula (European white birch)

*Fagus grandifolia (American beech: planted with other trees, it shows off its trunk and roots to best advantage)

Liquidambar styraciflua

*Liriodendron tulipifera

Quercus alba

Q. muehlenbergii

Q. prinus

Q. rubra

These shade-tolerant species usually look best if planted no more than ten feet apart. This way, each tree *begins* growing in full sun. High-pruning is necessary only until their branches touch and interpenetrate. Thereafter, the new growth will be competing against the adjacent tree and will be forced upward automatically.

The only caution is that all trees in any one group must be properly matched in size, health, and growth rate so that one doesn't outstrip any others. For example, a three-foot red maple will do well beside a four-footer of the same species. But plant a four-foot red oak beside a four-foot red maple, and the slower-growing maple will quickly be outdistanced. For ideal compatibility, obtain small trees and observe their individual growth rates while they're still small enough to transplant if adjustments are called for. Should one larger tree begin to overshadow another, its branches should be thinned out so that the smaller one's branches can interpenetrate it successfully.

Evergreens for Clump Use:

Most evergreens demand sun. If planted closely together, they shade one another and the lower branches die back, the fallen needles making the soil beneath too acid for most plants. To do at all well, however, the acid-loving Group D wildflowers mentioned in Chapter 12 need an annual mulch of evergreen needles. A clump of conifers not only provides this automatically, but creates a shady, protected spot where such plants can thrive.

All of the following conifers have relatively small needles that, rather than forming loose springy mats, tend to pack down neatly and tightly, conserving moisture even in midsummer. Remember, though, that you aren't growing these trees for themselves. Since the wildflowers are going to be the main attraction, avoid scarce or expensive trees that could be better displayed elsewhere. Use ordinary nursery stock, or seedlings from the wild.

Abies balsamea (balsam fir)

Picea abies (Norway spruce)

Avoid any other spruces, whose needles are too fat to break down quickly, and whose growth habit often produces killing shade.

Pinus strobus (white pine) is necessary if you want to cultivate pink ladyslippers. The needles are plentiful (five to the cluster) but thin enough so that they break down quickly and won't smother the low terrestrial orchids. But most white pines do not spread to throw enough shade until grown quite high. Trim back new growth to encourage greater bushiness—and thus, more shade and fallen needles.

*Pseudotsuga menziesii (Douglas fir)

*Tsuga canadensis (hemlock)

To encourage maximum growth, leave all branches on these clumped evergreens until they have grown to about fifteen feet (large enough to begin shading themselves). Thereafter, branches within four feet of the ground will make it difficult to spot your wildlings and cast too much shade; high-prune accordingly to encourage upward growth.

III. "TRUE" SHADE TREES

Planted deliberately to cast shade and cool things off, these can be either Full-Sun or Forest-Environment types, since either will get full and bushy in full sun. (They still need high-pruning, however, because presumably you're going to want to enjoy that shade by getting underneath the tree in question.) I personally find dappled or very light shade more comfortable than solid shadow, so I try to select trees whose branches can be opened up, leaving the crown as only a narrow veneer of leaves.

Remember that good sun is a must for the gardening environments discussed later, so ask yourself where you really *want* shade. Chances are you don't want permanent shade, but a broad transitory shadow that cools a given area during the heat of the day, moving to admit sunlight during morning and afternoon. This means that any "True" Shaders should go along the south and west of your lawn or outdoor area.

You'll also want one or more Shade Trees to the immediate south and southwest of your house to shade on the south face of your roof. This will drastically reduce the heat in your attic during the summer, helping to cool the whole house. *But use deciduous trees only* so that when the leaves fall, the house can be warmed by the winter sun.

Evergreens will cast unwelcome winter gloom. All of the following are also dependable fast-growers and will clear a roof within ten years.

Acer saccharinum (silver maple)

A. saccharum (sugar maple)

Betula pendula (European white birch)

Juglans nigra (black walnut)

Liquidambar (sweetgum) and

Liriodendron (tulip tree) are good for temporary shade while a better tree gets established.

Nyssa sylvatica (black gum)—good if you already have one as a Silhouette.

Populus deltoides (cottonwood)

Quercus alba

Q. rubra

No Canopy tree should ever be planted according to its *present* shape and size. This seems obvious until you hanker for two four-foot blue spruces on either side of your front walk. But Colorado spruces, of which the blue is a cultivar, reach ninety feet at maturity! If you admire them for their currently "cute" stature, you don't want a Canopy tree there at all, but one of the Second-Layer trees discussed in Chapter 6. Once your basic paths and walls are nearing completion, you'll begin to see automatically where Canopy trees would be inappropriate in the full sizes they'll eventually attain.

To help you plan ahead, a great many garden experts advise drawing up a map of your property. But even a perfectly accurate map traced with the aid of an aerial photograph is useless, because it exists in two dimensions only. It won't account for slopes, sight lines, or the actual *height* of plants. Compare any top-view garden plan—in which trees are represented as cloudlike circles—with an actual ground-level photograph or "artist's conception," and you'll see how hopeless it is for us laymen to picture the one from the other.

My method is cruder, but more practical. With a cheap box camera, shoot photos from several angles of the area you'd like to replant. Have some fairly large prints made. Then with a needle or corner of a razor blade, you can doodle directly on the film emulsion, scratching in new trees, enlarging bushes to the outline they'll cast next year, sketching brick paths on one print and flagstone on another for comparison. Which species of Silhouette tree would look best against the sky? Cut out photos of mature specimens from catalogs (great rainy-day project for the kids) and move them about like paper dolls on the photos. The effect will be approximate, but far more understandable than anything you could map out.

Obtaining and Planting Canopy Trees

If trees that seed themselves onto your property are often more vigorous than ones transplanted from a nursery, it's because of the poor condition of most nursery stock.

These trees, grown from seed or cuttings, are ready for market when they have reached about three feet. Each is dug up with a flattened ball of soil around its roots. (But since few trees produce roots in a strictly symmetrical ball, most of the feeder roots are chopped off during the process.) To help avoid dehydration, extra clay is often packed around the ball, which is then wrapped in burlap or plastic prior to shipment. But the tree's remaining roots are pretty well fixed in the directions they originally took to account for their nursery's original subsurface rocks and patterns of drainage. By the time the tree has recovered an efficient root system, a seedling of the same species—whose roots have suffered no setbacks—will often have overtaken it.

The smaller the tree you plant, the better its chances for fast growth and a satisfactory mature appearance. But nurseries don't offer smaller stock because customers want "instant" results in their gardens and will pay over one hundred dollars to have a ten-foot specimen installed. I'm trying to wean you away from the balled-and-bagged route because many of the best trees I've described are rarely available from nurseries. You must obtain seed or seedlings from mail-order firms, or prospect in the wild for young, transplantable specimens.

An ethical Bermuda Triangle surrounds the issue of digging plants from public or private lands. Obviously no honest person would sneak home desirable plants from a neighbor's garden. But when you are tempted by a seedling Christmas fern on the eroding bank of a state road, or a colony of spring beauty in a lot that's awaiting the bulldozer, or a single field hawkweed in a park where literally thousands run wild, is this "stealing," or conservation? In many cases, seedling trees I've collected would not have survived in the shady environments where they'd originally germinated, and their land's owners—had I managed to identify them—could hardly have cared less. Yet when an article taking this point of view appeared on the New York Sunday *Times*' gardening page, it drew a volley of fierce letters from moralists.

This is a debate that each gardener must resolve for himself, but do try to obtain digging privileges beforehand. Most landowners will understand that the seedlings you want are so small and insignificant that they can be dug loose without notice. Secondly, *never take any trees taller than a foot*. Their root systems are too large to move without some loss, and the holes they'll leave will be conspicuous.

If you dig the first desirable tree you see, chances are you'll come upon an even better specimen later on, just as you're hurrying back to your car. Therefore, always make two trips—the first for prospecting and identification. Leave the actual collection for your second visit—preferably in early spring or late fall, when transplanting shock is minimal. But how can you locate your trees again later? Here's where your old plastic garment bags come in handy. When you see a choice seedling, tie a plastic "scarf" about eight inches long around the base of the trunk. Later, you'll have no trouble picking it out of a lineup. Also save plastic shopping bags, especially those with a flat rectangular bottom and molded plastic snaps that hold the top closed. The flat bottom will hold a seedling upright so that the soil around its roots doesn't fall apart. And the snaps can close around the seedling's trunk, keeping the roots from drying out before you get it home.

If seedlings measure under six inches tall, without a deep root system to tie them down, they can be heaved and uprooted by winter's end. Be sure to plant them a bit deeper than they were originally growing. The tinier the tree, the deeper it can go, up to an inch below its original starting point. No later correction is necessary; the tree will automatically adjust.

Not all desirable trees occur in the wild, however, and sooner or later you'll have to depend on nursery stock. Once you get a nursery-grown tree home, while it's still in its bag, move it about. Take sample glances from different locations—both inside and outside your home—to see how it looks. A tree should be precisely positioned and angled so that its full spread is visible from the most common angle of viewing—from your picture window, a specific point along a garden path, or the center of a patio. Sometimes I spend up to ten minutes of adjusting and "posing" a tree before actual digging begins. To carve the hole, a long-handled spade with a narrow blade results in far greater precision than a larger shovel. With it, you can shape a hole to match the spread of the tree's roots, or lift earth from the bottom of a steep pit where a wider blade would cause cave-ins.

Many nurserymen advise you to plant a tree "as is"—ball, bag, and all. To put it bluntly, they don't know what they're talking about. *Always* remove the bag from any tree you buy, especially if the roots are wrapped in plastic cloth. If the root ball was ever mulched for any length of time, the tree may have grown new roots that penetrate the bag. No matter: the plastic or burlap must go; feeder roots still inside the soil ball will not be seriously affected.

Most larger trees and shrubs are field-grown in a poor clay soil that, when dry, hardens into a primitive form of cement. You won't see any appreciable new growth until the newly formed roots break through that clayish enclosure—which may be never. And since extra soil is often packed around the trunk during the balling and bagging, the tree is usually planted too deeply in its "new" soil ball. If left this way, the bark will remain damp and vulnerable to fungus. The *entire* ball of clay should come off, so that the tree is bare-rooted in its new hole.

Another advantage to removing the clay ball is that you can tell how the roots are positioned—and if there are enough for the tree to survive. I once bought an expensive Japanese *palmatum* maple, and removed the burlap but not all the clay. The new growth promptly withered and crisped, and the bark turned a sickly purple. When I uprooted the dead tree for an autopsy, I found that its large single taproot had been carefully sawed off so that the tree would fit the burlap bag! This mutilation proved that the tree would not have lived even with the best of care, and I obtained a free replacement.

To wash the clay loose, use a hose with a strong spray—if the clay is brick-hard, a hammer helps. Such clay is usually *far* worse than your existing subsoil, so let it collect on a plastic shower curtain. You can cart it off later and use it as fill in a brick walk or cobblestone path.

Now bare-rooted, the tree should be planted in a custom-dug hole that holds the roots securely. (When digging a hole on a slope, always place the dirt uphill, where it'll slide down easily when needed.) The base of the first *strong* side root should go just beneath the new soil surface. Pack the soil in around the roots with your bare hands. Gardener's gloves are an asset if you're pruning prickly shrubs like roses or barberry, but even the thinnest glove reduces one's sense of touch. And when digging or transplanting, you have to be able to feel your way along—where the main roots are, where the soil is hard and resistant, where a small rock has fallen in the way. Simply pare your fingernails to the quick and admit that your hands, like any other essential gardening tool, are going to get dirty.

You'd think that the soil you've dug out of a hole would be enough to fill it up again. But with grass sods and rocks removed, somehow it never works out that way! Whenever you transplant anything, keep handy a bucket of fresh humus. This not only adds the extra volume you'll need, but improves the soil around the newly forming roots.

Once the hole is packed as tightly as you can force it, flood it with water and pack it down again. An amazing amount of extra soil will bubble down between the roots, but that's the whole idea. Add still more soil, packing it down until the mud simply gushes up again whenever you press down. (Now all the air pockets that caused the bubbles will be filled with good soil) If you place heavy rocks on the mud surface, the roots will usually be held so securely that no staking is necessary.

Since any balled-and-bagged tree has lost some of its roots, you should reduce its foliage to bring the root/leaf ratio back into a healthy balance. As soon as it's transplanted, begin your high-pruning by clipping off one or two bottom branches, as well as any twigs that conflict with the main flow of the trunk or that duplicate the lines of existing higher branches. (This also helps reduce the "top rigging" that makes a newly planted tree vulnerable to wind.)

If the tree has no branches that need pruning, then some of the foliage should go. Don't cut leaves in half as some books advise—this results in a lot of ragged brown edges. Instead, remove *all* leaves on the lower third of each branch. (The upper leaves are usually younger, and therefore healthier and best left alone.) Don't pull a leaf loose, or you'll risk tearing off a strip of bark too. Snip the stem with a pair of clippers. The remaining stub will soon fall off by itself.

Never remove *more* than a third of the leaves, however. When a friend of mine took delivery of some of my spare dogwoods, she misunderstood me and removed *all* the foliage. Unable to photosynthesize enough energy to weather their transplanting shock, the trees never recovered. Better to let a tree wilt slightly, and let *it* decide which leaves to drop.

Young trees often get their "shins" scraped, especially if you have a self-propelled lawnmower. If so, a light injury quickly announces itself by a flash of chartreuse green cambium—the living layer just beneath the bark surface. As long as they're *uniformly* green, such wounds don't need attention: the cambium will soon generate new bark. But a glint of ivory means that the injury has penetrated to the sapwood. Last July, a sapling wild cherry in my front yard suddenly turned yellow and wilted. When I dug the tree up, I found that a low (but apparently superficial) crack in the bark had split downward and festered, girdling the tree below ground level. So unless the trunk is wide enough to heal itself quickly, the injury should be sealed.

"Temporary" Trees:

I have to admit that the lovely black gum doesn't grow as fast as the horrid Norway. If you're going to axe your Kill List species and start anew with seedlings, must you put up with an open, sun-scalded, barren yard until you can coax your new arrivals to an enjoyable height?

Not necessarily. I still suggest that you reserve space for those superior, slow-growing trees I recommend. But in the meantime, plant any of the fast-growing species listed below.

Acer negundo (box elder) grows up to ten feet a year under average conditions. It's not usually found in nurseries, but vigorous seedlings are always available in the neighborhood of mature trees, now growing far outside their original Midwestern range. Severe pruning can restrict them to a strictly upright habit.

A. platanoides (Norway maple) is your best bet for sunny, dry locales. Since the tree is only temporary, forego expensive cultivars like 'Crimson King' and 'Schwedler'—as well as nursery stock. In April and May, you can find vast drifts of seedlings in the vicinity of any mature tree, and these smaller specimens will grow quickly if you preserve their roots.

A. pseudoplatanus (sycamore maple)

Liquidambar (sweet gum)

Liriodendron (tulip tree)

Populus deltoides (cottonwood)

Yes, there are a few Kill List trees in the above list. But all of them look fine when small; not until they mature do they start to develop their bad habits. *Never* use ailanthus, sumac, or Lombardy poplars as temporary trees, since their roots sprout when the main trunk is cut down.

Most really desirable Canopy trees require full sun, but that means full sun *eventually*. For now, you can plant a choice seedling between two Norways. And as long as the Kill List trees are severely high-pruned for a good five years or so, your choice species won't be noticeably affected by the competition. However, high-pruning tulip trees, sweet gums, and most young maples will activate dormant buds just under the bark, so that sometimes the entire length of the trunk will sprout with clusters of leaves. The effect can be rather lush and neat at first, but such trunk-sprouts should be rubbed off before they become long and unsightly.

The only problem with Temporary trees is that they won't die of their own accord. In fact, they'll continue to grow lustily, casting your better trees into a deep coma of shade. So any Temporary tree should be removed when it reaches a height of around twenty feet— in fact it *must,* because high-pruning will no longer restrain it from becoming obnoxious.

Usually, the Temporary can be removed without leaving too much of a visual gap. Probably you'll notice the loss—in fact, your landscape may look a bit empty for the first summer. But when a small tree is suddenly relieved of shade and root competition, it increases its growth rate. Within a year or two, the Permanent tree will have come into its own, and you'll no longer have any reason to mourn its former surrogate. The Temporary's stump will often raise a few new sprouts, but stubborn debudding will discourage them. Until the stump rots, it can be concealed with the same groundcover that should surround any Canopy tree's roots (see Chapter 10). Because you want your Permanents in just the right places, however, the Temporaries must always be planted a few feet *to one side* of where you actually want a tree to be. Otherwise, when the Temporaries are gone, your Permanents will look as if *they* were out of place.

❧ PART TWO ❧

SPECIES
THAT CARE FOR THEMSELVES

6

SECOND-LAYER TREES

Who would imagine,
alas! that in the garden my
dear wife and I
planted together
the trees could have grown
so dense, so high? . . .

—ADAPTED FROM A MEDIEVAL JAPANESE POEM

If your place measures less than an acre, too many enormous Canopy trees will dwarf everything else, making your tract look even smaller by comparison.

My own property measures less than a third of an acre. Three huge existing oaks, plus the tupelos I've introduced, are really all I can afford without sacrificing most of the sunlight my smaller perennials demand. So I've been forced to specialize in smaller trees that adorn the space they occupy without overflowing it.

It's relevant to remember that a tropical rainforest is composed of two main layers: first the forest giants, and under them, a second layer of smaller-growing species that soak up any sun the taller trees admit. Our North American forests are no different. Except where Canopy trees have wholly taken over, most woodlands support naturally smaller-growing species that mature at under 40 feet and are far more in scale with a one-story bungalow and a 50-foot frontage. If these smaller trees are used in place of larger ones, a property looks far larger—more colorful, too, since these sizes include all of the best-loved flowering trees, such as the dogwoods, crabapples, flowering cherries, and other so-called "ornamentals."

The basic arrangement of trees for any property is shown in Figure 24. While the biggies look best at a distance, you'll want smaller trees closer to the house where you can appreciate 'them. These Second-Layer types will still leave you plenty of room to glimpse the larger Canopy trees beyond them. (The dotted mounds represent the shrubs you'll be planting as per instructions in the next chapter.) Most flowering trees perform best in full sun, but as long as no Canopy tree directly overshadows them, they can be planted fairly close together without any compromise of bloom. (Any established apple orchard is a good example.) Many others tolerate forest conditions, and will do satisfactorily even under high-pruned Canopy species.

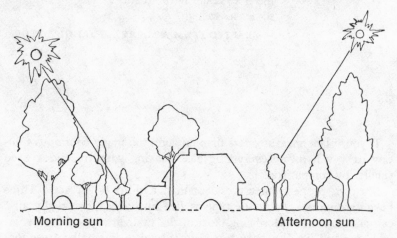

Morning sun   Afternoon sun

Figure 24

My front yard is dominated by a mammoth pin oak but nevertheless, it also boasts a dozen Japanese maples, a weeping beech and weeping hemlock, dogwood and striped maple, three shadblows, four birches, and assorted crabapples and conifers. Not all of these Second-Layer trees have reached maturity, but when they do, they'll be wholly compatible.

I. SHOWY FLOWERING TREES

All should be planted in full sun, or at least where no other tree overshades them.

Amelanchier spp. (sarvice tree, serviceberry, shadblow) is a must for any property. In mid-April (supposedly just at the time shad enter coastal rivers to spawn), these trees erupt in long racemes of small white apple-like flowers. The earlier magnolias and the later crabapples will make splashes of stronger color, but the effect of a shadblow is far more gossamer and ethereal. Within a week, the flowers fade just as the neat oval leaves emerge, at first colored a ruddy olive.

There are two main species, and I cultivate both—*A. laevis* from a nursery, and *A. arborea* (or *canadensis*) from seedlings gathered near Long Island Sound. *A. laevis,* more frequently offered in catalogs, has deep reddish bark and fatter, rounder buds. Its roots usually sprout several trunks of equal size. (This means you must prune most of them to avoid a spreading, multitrunked shrub that casts excessive shade.) But *A. arborea* usually forms a single trunk. With increasing age, its smooth, very light gray bark becomes lightly furrowed by darker lines (sometimes tracing faint zigzags or triangles). The trunk contours with extreme grace from the roots to the highest branch. It responds eagerly to high-pruning, becoming tree-like far earlier in its career. Winter buds are long and pointed, like a beech's, and flowers open a few days earlier than those of *A. laevis*.

But all shadblows are literally self-pruning. Few older branches ever *die;* instead, the tree aborts younger twigs that are getting in each other's shade. When dry, they become brittle and usually fall within the year. The trunk quickly expands to cover their sockets.

Cornus florida (flowering dogwood) is widely planted for its showy white or pink bracts. (Like poinsettia, its "flowers" are actually modified leaves surrounding the small, greenish true flowers.) In their naturally shady woods habitat, dogwoods grow into eccentrically shaped trees with only a few greenish-white blossoms. But grown in full sun, they become straight and symmetrical. The bracts bleach to a dazzling white and are borne in great profusion, literally covering the tree, rivalling the azaleas in the late-spring finale.

Like other widely planted trees, dogwood does have its disadvantages. Grown in even part shade, a dogwood comes into bloom later and more sparsely. Yet in full sun, it will branch thickly enough to cast a killing shade. (High-pruning is necessary every other year.) Meanwhile, the fairly large "petals" litter the ground in mid-May. In autumn, the tree ripens small football-shaped red berries that drop and readily germinate into quantities of new seedlings. Each year, I give away at least two dozen sapling dogwoods, and am forced to uproot many more as weeds. Because dogwood seedlings are so plentiful and grow so quickly (about two feet a year once established), it's foolish to buy nursery stock—unless you want the new fragrant white or weeping varieties. Otherwise, if your neighbors already have *one* dogwood, you can easily have many more for nothing.

Pink varieties make a marvelous contrast to the white, but avoid the variegated-leaf varieties. The lack of pigment in their leaves makes them vulnerable to sunscald, and they seldom attain more than the stature of a small bush.

*Cornus kousa (Japanese dogwood) has larger, more distinctly X-shaped white bracts that appear in very late May after the American dogwoods have quit. Better yet, they stay in bloom for a solid three weeks, offering a wonderful reprise to the faded *floridas*. The branches form distinct layers of foliage that are even more closely packed than *florida*'s, but high-pruning exposes more sinuous, eccentric branches.

Crataegus (hawthorn), a wide genus of native American and European species and hybrids, are seldom offered by nurseries—probably because they are so slow-growing and often sprout wicked thorns. But their leisurely growth makes them ideal for Second-Layer plantings. Moreover, hawthorns can tolerate extreme drought and cold, which is why mature specimens survive to shade the arid picnic grounds of Fort Ticonderoga on the shore of Lake Champlain, where winter temperatures plunge far below zero. The leaves are small and deeply cut, never more than 2½" long. A six-foot trunk is already gnarled and stately. Mature trees produce a dense, rounded crown and, in late May, thick clusters of flowers that ripen into red berries in late summer and autumn.

I obtained all my hawthorns as seedlings that resist precise identification because they haven't yet bloomed. However, I would try to locate the cultivar 'Paul's Scarlet' that bears bright red double flowers in masses that resemble nosegays of old-fashioned roses.

Magnolia is the showiest of the early spring-flowering trees. If shadblow is subtle, magnolia is joyously blatant, with huge flowers on bare branches. The leaves, which follow later, roughly resemble a healthy avocado's. All magnolias have smooth light-gray bark, slow growth, a "mature" look at about ten to fifteen feet.

A number of species and hybrids abound. Though my climate forbids me the lush evergreen species of the South, those that are winter-hardy in the North also happen to be among the most attractive. *M. soulangeana,* or "saucer" hybrids boast a distinctive purple-pink, lotus-like flower whose petals open flat at maturity. Avoid *M. stellata* (star magnolia) that bears sparse-looking white flowers with thin, drooping petals. These flowers always look as if they'd been through a short war; the tree itself remains huddled and shrublike— and its slow-growing multiple trunks resist effective pruning. Most *soulangeana* flowers range from red to pink. For a full, succulent white, try *M. denudata,* one of the Oriental species from which the *soulangeana* hybrids were developed. For a smaller, pink-flowering tree, use *M. liliflora* variety *nigra* (often sold as *Magnolia nigra*). Both of the above are dependably hardy Chinese species.

All magnolias' flowers are rather short-lived. Even barring a late spring frost (such as the ones in spring 1976 and '77 that blasted magnolia petals to a rusty brown), a week of extravagant show is the most you can hope for. Thereafter, the enormous petals begin sifting loose. Still gorged with the water that supplies their fleshy translucence, they don't dry up readily like the petals of apple or cherry and make a royal mess on any lawn; so underplant the trees with a deep groundcover.

All magnolias are basically spreading, shrubby trees, and "clump"-style mags become ratty-looking as they mature. High-pruning them isn't enough; you must also clear the trunk and lower limbs of the suckers that arise hopefully year after year. Once the tree develops a good crown, it will stop suckering and concentrate on stately branches.

Malus is a huge genus comprising the domestic apples and flowering crabapples, which make among the most splendid spring displays. As with hawthorns, there are so many native species and natural and artificial hybrids that specific recommendations are difficult. I can say, however, that crabs with flowers of deep purple or red do not carry visually; to my taste they present a needlessly sullen shade beside their white and pink counterparts. If you like that raspberry sherbet tint, you can find it among the flowering cherries and plums (see below), so restrict your crabs to the lighter shades. More than one variety has double white flowers, and many others begin with coral-red buds that open slowly to perfect white, giving you two colors within the space of a week.

Most wild apple trees are equally attractive, though their flowers are less spectacular. One shrubby species I've seen in the Jersey woods bears tiny clusters of white flowers in late April. Despite its dark brown bark and glistening, perfectly oval light green leaves, it's too modest for any but a Wild Garden. The coast of Long Island Sound abounds with (apparently) hybrid seedlings whose single white flowers carpet the tree in profusion and last for an unusually long time—up to three weeks.

All *Malus* trees have fairly identical foliage, however, so that an unknown tree that's not in bloom is almost impossible to identify, let alone evaluate as to color. Catalog descriptions are seldom adequate, so make it a rule to choose your selections when they are actually in bloom, whether at the nursery, along roadsides and backsides, or in orchards gone wild.

No matter how lovely the flowers, always consider the shape and habit of the tree—which determine what you'll be looking at for the other eleven months of the year. All too many hybrids tend to get squat and shrubby. Even mature trees send up persistent water-sprouts from the base of the trunk and from exposed roots. The darker-flowering varieties seem to be the worst offenders: look for wine-dark flowers, and you'll usually see a multiple trunk and a welter of self-conflicting branches. A lean, upright, open growth habit is a model of what a proper crab apple should be.

These reservations apply only to ornamental trees, of course. If you grow ones for edible fruit, invest in the dwarf or medium-size trees—larger trees are increasingly hard to spray, prune, and harvest. Much fruit-tree wood is highly vulnerable to decay, and any crop-bearing tree should be low enough so that you can reach it for convenient surgery.

Since a crab grows so vigorously, you may be tempted to clean out its silhouette in a single orgy of pruning. But restrict yourself to removing only a few branches at a time. Most trees of the apple family have an unusually efficient root system, and wholesale pruning tips the foliage/root ratio in favor of the roots. This stimulates an explosion of vertical watersprouts that will ruin the tree's shape. With crabs, pruning should be an ongoing weekly chore, concentrating chiefly on smaller branches headed in the wrong directions.

Oxydendrum arboreum (sorrel tree, sourwood) has oblong, glossy leaves resembling those of a richly endowed wild cherry. Sprays of tiny white flowers are borne in July and August, when no other tree is in bloom. The invariably upright habit saves you a great deal of pruning, and the tree's entire appearance is clean and trim.

Prunus is a huge genus, comprising native American species of wild cherry and wild plum as well as the ornamental and fruit-bearing hybrids of cherry, plum, almond, and so on.

Avoid peaches and apricots unless you're willing to cultivate them for the fruit alone. Most strains are not as vigorous as a crabapple or cherry, and only rarely assume good shape: branches tend to jut straight out from the trunk. They are vulnerable to borers that announce themselves with sudden outpourings of amber-colored resin along the trunk. The fruits are regularly afflicted with a fungus that turns them brown and withered before they ripen; the resulting drop of mummified pits is unsightly and hard to clean.

Ornamental flowering cherries have rather brief flowers, and their shape is often awkward and ungainly—the very worst of the cherries form an inverted cone of branches with a flattened top. As far as shape is concerned, however, the weeping cherries of Japan are outstanding. I recall one ancient Japanese weeper in Wallingford, Connecticut, whose black-barked, sinuous, craggy trunk jerked itself up into high, gnarled limbs and finally tapered down into pendant twigs of amazing delicacy.

But this specimen was planted in the nineteenth century. To get market-size trees in less time, today's nurseries graft weeping twigs onto the 4- or 5-foot trunk or "standard" of an ordinary cherry—usually one with rather humdrum bark. This technique deprives you of ever seeing the weeping cherry's own free-form trunk. Sooner or later the site of the graft swells into a large cankerlike ball of "proud wood" from which the weeping branches protrude. The tree eventually takes on the appearance of a sea anemone—a straight, fat trunk with disproportionately slender "tentacles." Meanwhile, the non-weeping base of the trunk below the graft begins sending up watersprouts that need cutting back, and later leave unsightly scars.

Insist on trees that have been rooted from cuttings. If there are none available, take winter cuttings yourself from a weeping cherry you admire and try to root them yourself in moist sand. The resulting tree—if it survives—will cost you no little time and effort. But it will be a weeping cherry to the tips of its roots, rewarding you when its trunk begins to fissure into recurved plates of bark and the branches actually *develop*—rather than simply emerge—from the trunk.

Flowering plum hybrids are showy, well-formed, and frequently available with purple foliage—a trait hard to find outside of the peaches. Plum foliage greatly resembles that of apple, but the bark is distinctly smooth and shiny—as is the bark of all *Prunus* trees. Trees seldom bear fruit, but are unusually slow-growing and upright when compared to the rest of the genus.

There are also gracefully shaped native plums and cherries. Though their flowers are nowhere near as spectacular as the hybridized ornamentals, they are vigorous, hardy, and especially apt wherever a subtle bloomer is called for. Probably the most widespread species is *P. serotina* (wild cherry). Birds carry it so widely that most vacant lots have at least a half dozen seedlings, if not a good-sized tree or two. Wild cherries are so plentiful locally that I no longer bother to transplant seedlings; I just let them arise wherever I want them. Leaves on younger (up to 10 feet) trees are often small and undistinguished. But above this height, the tree produces larger leaves that are glossier and darker green. Four-inch panicles of small white flowers are borne in May.

Wild cherry can get up to be 60 feet and more, but this is rare—fortunately, because an older tree drops a truly boggling quantity of fruit, turning any well-trodden path beneath it into a thick layer of jam. But any sizable wild cherry serves as fodder for caterpillars of the tiger swallowtail, probably the most spectacular American butterfly after the monarch. Large and swift-flying, this swallowtail's wings combine sulfur yellow with velvet black. The bottom of each hind wing bears a short "tail" that gives the butterfly its name.

Other native species of *Prunus* have larger, showier flowers than wild cherry, but are not as prolific. All are roughly similar; many interbreed and hybridize; few if any are offered commercially. This means you'll have to locate trees in the wild, collect the fruits before the birds do, and mash them to extract the pits. Planted in a flat, some *may* germinate before the summer is out, but the rest will prefer to wait out the winter.

PLATE 1   Black gum
(*Nyssa sylvatica*) is the best
large-sized tree for shade
or silhouette, quickly forming
a dense glossy pyramid.
The heavy leaves are
seldom troubled by pests
and turn fiery red in autumn.
(*Dennis Yeandle*)

PLATE 2.   Japanese maples seldom grow above 25 feet and are ideal for
smaller properties. *Acer japonicum* var. *felicifolium*, shown here, is a
"true" Japanese maple; most sold in nurseries are hybrids of *A. palmatum*.
(*Dennis Yeandle*)

PLATE 3.   A series of large-leafed *Rhododendron roseum* will form an evergreen hedge for year-round privacy. Avoid hybrids with pale lavender flowers (shown here) in favor of the showier reds and pinks. (*Tom Andron*)

PLATE 4. Until it blooms, the European sundrop (*Oenothera pilosella*) is only a few inches tall. After the flowers fade, the stalks remain neatly upright, the leaves turning deep red in fall. (*Dennis Yeandle*)

PLATE 5. Rose of Sharon (*Althea*) has many hybrids; choose only those with large flowers and bright color. Plant between azaleas or other low shrubs and prune to a single trunk so that the plant branches well above the ground. (*Dennis Yeandle*)

PLATE 6. Though biennial, foxglove (*Digitalis*) hybrids seed themselves readily under Low Garden conditions. First-year seedlings form attractive leafy mounds. (*Tom Andron*)

PLATE 7. Jack-in-the-pulpit (*Arisaema triphyllum*) multiplies quickly in a Wild Garden. Taller plants can be moved to a pachysandra bed, as shown here, where they will thrive for years. (*Dennis Yeandle*)

Sorbus (mountain ash) is a fast-growing but neat tree for sunny locations. Naturally fastigiate, it bears hairy compound leaves and stiff, straight trunk and branches. Older trees (over 15 feet) bloom in May with tight clusters of white flowers that ripen into bright red-orange berries. There are a number of native species, but most commonly seen and offered by nurseries is the European import, *S. aucuparia.* Since the berries germinate readily, it's easy to find seedlings near any mature specimen. Given good light, these small trees will grow up to two feet a year.

Syringa amurensis var. *japonica* (Japanese tree lilac) has a spreading habit but, unlike most shrub lilacs, offers shiny bark and a single trunk that can be high-pruned to form a thick, rounded crown. Flowers are borne in plumes that are larger and later than ordinary lilac's.

Aphids will often throng a flowering tree's new growth as soon as it emerges, stunting and curling the leaves. With most species this is only a temporary problem, since the twigs soon thicken and harden enough that the aphids' tiny beaks cannot penetrate. But trees of the rose family (the crabapples, plums, and mountain ashes) keep producing soft new growth throughout the season, maintaining a permanent aphid population. A hard, tight spray from the garden hose helps knock them loose. Since aphids usually cluster on the underside of foliage to escape sun and rain, try to aim from underneath the tree.

II.   SECOND-LAYER EVERGREENS FOR FULL SUN

Ilex (holly) is instantly recognizable: stiff, extremely glossy evergreen leaves whose lobes terminate in sharp points. Trees sold in nurseries are almost always hybrids of the English *I. aquifolium* and/or the American *I. opaca.* (Do not confuse these tree-forming hybrids with the shrub and bush hollies used for foundation planting.) Recent hybridization has so increased the winter hardiness of holly that specimens can now be grown in the Far North; your main problem will be selecting from among the hundreds of varieties available. Avoid variegated hollies: yellow or white veining looks good on small twigs, but an entire tree with this color scheme is garish, and not as winter-handy as plants with pure green leaves.

Larger specimens are very expensive, but the rotted cuttings usually offered by mail are unsatisfactory. Poorly rooted, they usually grow very slowly and thus take quite a while to develop. So one good solution is to grow your own holly from seed. After Christmas, collect as many berries as you can from discarded wreaths and decorations. Seal them in a plastic bag and leave them until spring in the vegetable bin of your refrigerator. Then in May plant the berries in rich loam in part shade. A few will sprout to give you holly hybrids of your own. Not all will be equally vigorous or winter hardy, so transplant only the best: though they prefer full sun, hollies need protection from strong winter gales, so should be planted downwind of other evergreens.

Remember that only the *female* tree bears berries. For wind pollination to occur, a male has to be nearby. Therefore, in any stand of berry-bearing hollies, at least one—preferably upwind—has to be a visually barren male. (If you've germinated your own berries, the law of averages will assure you about an equal number of males and females.) For better display, plant your female hollies in *front* of the males, so that their berries are more visible. And when a male holly becomes mature, solid, and lush, there's no reason you can't high-prune it to show off the gray bark and craggy branches.

Chamaecyparis obtusa (hinoki cypress) grows large enough in its native Japan to be used for temple beams. But most garden-shop hinokis are more or less dwarf varieties. For Second-Layer purposes, look for specimens in gallon pots, already two to three feet tall and displaying a good *single* trunk (dwarf hinokis seldom produce a recognizable single top leader). These faster-growing trees are far more open than their congested dwarf counterparts and can tolerate part shade.

Even in sun, the threadlike top leader usually meanders off at a crazed angle, as if the tree were about to become a weeper. But don't stake it—as the stem thickens, the new growth somehow manages to straighten itself up. Like arborvitae, old foliage turns brown, gets brittle, and falls of its own accord: a gentle manual "frisking" in spring will usually neaten the tree considerably.

Picea pungens glauca (Colorado blue spruce): For Second-Layer purposes, use the 'Koster' cultivar, an asymmetrical dwarf.

Pinus (pine): Most gardeners covet the look of a small pine. But the Silhouette pines discussed earlier will shoot up like telephone poles. Happily, a number of other species are fairly slow-growing and stay under 30 feet even at maturity.

**P. albicaulis* (white-bark pine) develops smooth bark of a very light gray. Naturally you'll want to high-prune it to expose the bark. But the bluish needles are bushy and attractive, and the branches naturally twisted.

P. aristata (bristlecone or foxtail pine) has attained fame since some California specimens were discovered to be the oldest living things on earth, antedating even the redwoods. But during its first thousand years of life, *aristata* leaves something to be desired. Growth is wildly erratic; even with patient pruning, trees quickly grow into incoherent Rorschach blobs. And since the thick needles are retained along the older branches, larger specimens have the furry look of an artificial Christmas tree. I would recommend bristlecone pine for the collector only.

**P. banksiana* (Jack or scrub pine) is a modest-sized, naturally craggy species. Careful pruning of central "candles" will produce a bushier, healthier-looking tree than specimens usually seen in the wild.

**P. cembra* (Swiss stone pine), the most formal of this group, maintains a tight pyramid shape, with branches closely packed together at a sharp upward angle. Surprisingly, it's quite happy in part shade. Needles are a lush bluish green shot through with silver, and no pruning is ever necessary except for removal of the very bottom branches to expose the base of the trunk. Eventually *cembra* gets up to twenty feet, but remains lush, in proportion, and kind to more delicate neighbors.

**P. flexilis* (limber pine) is a Western native only beginning to be appreciated in cultivation. Its branches are graceful and upright; its bark remains gray and smooth like a beech. It's slow-growing, and if given full sun, it remains neat and pristine well into old age. It naturally grows in semi-arid, rocky soils and thus is perfect for any high, well-drained slope where other trees have suffered from drought. But this pine is perfectly winter-hardy, too—my father and I collected seedlings from a Wyoming mountainside where winter temperatures plunge to 30° below zero.

P. parviflora (Japanese five-needle pine) is most often sold as a bonsai subject. But left to grow normally, it produces pleasant, thick tufts of bright silvery needles aboard long, meandering branches. The trunk leans and twists gently, and the bark eventually turns a scaly brown. A bit of early candle-pruning makes a bushier, more compact tree. After it reaches about six feet, the tree begins taking care of itself, requiring no further pruning and bearing cones at a very early age.

P. pumila is similar to *P. cembra,* above, but slower growing.

*P. rigida (pitch pine) is a low-growing, shrubby species that takes on a leaning, gnarled look while still under ten feet tall. This is one of the few pines that commonly sprouts new growth from old wood, giving you a second chance to coax out branches where needed. But otherwise, bursts of new needles should be discouraged along the trunk and main branches, lest they make the tree look ragged and unshaven.

*Sciadopitys verticillata is one of the very best Second-Layer evergreens. A few sources call it "Japanese umbrella pine," but that's the common nursery moniker for *Pinus tanyosho*—this close relative of the pines simply has no common name. Its broad, deep-green needles are arranged in plump rosettes that resemble an Egyptian papyrus in tree form. Old needles fall promptly, so there's never any unsightly scruff along the reddish-tinted branches. Growth is slow, never much more than six inches a year, and so rigorously symmetrical that even an aged tree maintains a strict conical shape.

This is the species that my father "mistakenly" grew in full sun. It positively adores growing in part shade, with good morning sun on its needles and a groundcover keeping its roots cool and moist. The very lowest branches—as with all Second-Layer evergreens—should be pruned, especially if they have to penetrate groundcover to reach the light of day. Otherwise, the only time a *Sciadopitys* needs a saw is when it develops two parallel leaders which then compete for supremacy. (This usually occurs when the tree is still under three feet and so loosely branched that it forgets itself.) Remove one of the two leaders as soon as possible because it takes longer for a larger specimen to regain its trim, full-form appearance.

Many fastigiate evergreens also lend themselves beautifully to Second-Layer plantings. These are naturally upright trees with narrow lateral branches like the "Skyrocket" juniper. *Juniperus chinensis torulosa* (sometimes called California or Hollywood juniper) forms a lush-green free-form pyramid like a hinoki that's really enjoying itself. Also notable are *Taxus baccata,* the so-called Greek, Irish, and Chinese junipers; Italian cypress, especially *Cupressus sempervirens* 'gracilis' and 'stricta'.

III. WEEPING VARIETIES TRAINED AS FASTIGIATES

Most common deciduous and evergreen Canopy trees have weeping or *pendula* varieties. Left to their own devices, some tend to grow out of bounds: weeping hemlocks form enormous mounds much wider than high. Very old weeping Atlas cedars tend to sprawl horizontally, forming a wavy trunk from which decumbent branches hang. The result is an enormous shower curtain of foliage that's a real barrier to access and visibility and acutely vulnerable to snow damage.

Oddly, no one thinks of overcoming these drawbacks by growing weeping varieties as *upright* trees. Once the trunk is firmed up with a few seasons' new wood, it becomes a fountain of lush foliage that seldom gets any taller. The new pendulous growth cascades straight back down to the ground, and the tree's circumference can easily be kept narrow by a minor pruning every two years or so. After all, what other evergreen drops its major branches *down* to where your clippers can get at them?

The trick, of course, is getting the tree up there in the first place. Some canny nurseries graft weeping stock to the tops of normally straight trunks, producing "standards" that resemble a rose tree. But these constructions omit the sinuous trunk of a true weeper, which to me is one of the plant's main charms.

It's easy (and far cheaper) to make the tree ascend yourself. Simply get a stiff bamboo pole a good deal higher than the already planted weeping tree. Sink it at least a foot deep, as close to the trunk as possible without compromising the main roots. Since the new growth of most weeping trees is extremely floppy and flexible, you should have no trouble straightening it up. Tie the trunk to the pole, gently but firmly, with separate lengths of rope spaced six inches apart, until the tree's at the ultimate height you want. Since most weepers do not get up but a few feet under their own power, a tree trained to a certain height will stay there—more or less—for years on end.

Leave it attached to its "mast" for at least three growing seasons. (Loosen the rope each summer to avoid creasing the tree's bark.) When you think that the tree's been locked into place by the growth of new wood, check by loosening the *middle* ropes only. Both trunk and pole should stay more or less as they were. The places where the trunk *most* diverges from the pole are those which should be recinched as tightly as possible. Try again next year. But when you finally release it, watch it for a week or two to be sure the tree doesn't go into a slow, imperceptible slouch under the weight of its new growth. You really don't need to prune a weeping tree at all, except to remove shoots that are getting in each other's way, to trim branches that are trailing down onto the ground, or to maintain a clear view of the trunk, whose curves and twist will become even more lovely with age.

The following is a list of weeping trees that I've seen offered by various firms. (Unless identified by specific cultivar names, all are usually designated by the variety adjective *pendula*.)

Cedrus atlantica pendula (green Atlas cedar)

C. a. glauca pendula (blue Atlas cedar)

C. libani pendula (cedar of Lebanon)

Cercidiphyllum japonicum pendula (Katsura tree)

Chamaecyparis nootkatensis pendula (blue-foliaged false cypress)

C. pisifera pendula (thread-needled cypress)

Cornus florida pendula (flowering dogwood)

Fagus sylvatica pendula (beech)

F. s. purpurea pendula (copper beech)

Ginkgo biloba pendula (ginkgo)

Juniperus rigida pendula (needle juniper)

J. scopulorum 'Tolleson's Weeping'

J. s. 'Tolleson's Weeping' *viridis* (green form of above)

J. virginiana pendula (Virginia juniper)

Picea omorika pendula (Serbian spruce)

P. pungens glauca pendula (blue Colorado spruce)

Pinus densiflora pendula (Japanese red pine)

P. flexilis pendula (limber pine)

P. strobus pendula (white pine)

P. sylvestris pendula (Scots pine)

Pseudotsuga menziesii pendula (Douglas fir)

Sequoia gigantea pendula (giant redwood)

Thuja occidentalis pendula (arborvitae)

Tsuga canadensis 'David Verkade' (Canadian hemlock): a good substitute or companion for 'Sargenti' (below).

T. c. 'Kelsey's weeping': normally lower and more spreading than other *canadensis* weepers.

T. c. 'Sargenti', sometimes just plain *T. c. pendula* (Sargent's weeping hemlock) is the oldest, most widely propagated of the *T. canadensis* weepers and quickly adopts a form far wider than high. Be sure to clip adventurous horizontal branches.

T. caroliniana 'LeBar's Weeping': More dramatic falls and twists of branch than 'Sargenti', but does get big. Best left untrained in an open environment; consider instead of clump-style evergreens as a cover for Group D wildflowers.

IV. INCONSPICUOUSLY FLOWERING DECIDUOUS TREES

Except as noted, all can afford part shade, or at least very close group planting.

*Acer buergeranum (trident maple) eventually gets to forty feet or so, as has the splendid specimen by the entrance of Yale's Peabody Museum. But it grows slowly enough and with such a sinuous, twisted trunk that it's a fine companion for more common Japanese maples. The neat leaf resembles a highly elongated red maple—one sharp triangular point at the bottom, flanked by two triangular side lobes.

A. campestre (hedge maple) is so called because when young, its lush, thick growth allows it to be sheared to a coherent form. Unpruned, it forms a stout, symmetrical tree that needs high pruning and a bit of competition for best results. Leaves are dark green, as broad as long, and shaped like fat Maltese crosses.

A. ginnala, sometimes called *amurensis* (amur maple) should be avoided. The leaves are attractive, more narrow than trident maple (see above). But after a few years, the tree sprouts multiple trunks, resists pruning, and starts looking like an untamed forsythia minus the flowers.

A. griseum (paperback maple) has a deep red-brown bark that eventually starts peeling—which is unusual for a maple, and the tree's only claim to fame. The sullen deep-green leaves are compound, resembling a cross between box elder and hedge maple and are hardly distinctive—in fact, all photos of *A. griseum* I've seen have been carefully cropped to show the bark only.

*A. japonicum translates as "Japanese maple," a term mainly used to describe the more common trees whose Latin name is *A. palmatum.* True *japonicums* are known as full-moon maples because the leaves are broad and full, like a horse chestnut's. Pick of the litter is the variety *filicifolium* with huge ferny leaves and a severe need for high-pruning. My mouth waters for some of the native Japanese species of maples not yet widely available in this country, many of which are incredibly accurate mimics of well-known Canopy trees. *A. nikoense* (Nikko maple) has leaves divided into three segments, like box elder's—except that each is equal-sized and borne on such widely splayed stems that the leaflets precisely resemble the foliage of a copper beech! The Japanese hornbeam maple has a long, oval leaf that looks exactly like an American hornbeam. Closer examination reveals parallel veining, so that it could also be mistaken for a beech or chestnut.)

*A. palmatum (Japanese maple) has literally countless varieties, thanks to the hybridizing efforts of Japanese and American connoisseurs. Nurseries usually stock the purple, red, and green-leafed varieties, and the cut-leaf *dissectum* varieties thereof (see next Chapter). If you have outdoor floodlights, try to obtain a deep red *A. palmatum* to plant in the spotlight for night viewing. Especially in spring the illumined foliage glows a piercing red almost as strong as that of

a flowering crabapple. But these common types represent only a few drops in a horticultural Inland Sea. Once you've succeeded with a single *palmatum,* why settle for a common duplicate when more than one mail order catalog offers over three hundred different varieties and cultivars?

Listing them here would be pointless because few are available from more than one source and because—as is true with so many hybridized plants—names often disguise the extreme similarity between varieties. One stunning exception deserves mention, however —the variety *sangokaku.* Its bark is a rich coral red, winter and summer, and the leaves a deep chartreuse. Abetted by high-pruning, the tree soon assumes a classic upright vase shape.

A. palmatum maples have been so thoroughly hybridized that any one specimen is a seething caldron of recessive genes. The next generation of seedlings often displays characteristics of long-forgotten— and often more desirable—trees. For example, when my father grew seemingly ordinary green *palmatums,* many of their seedlings displayed red leaves. Across the street from me is a light-purple *palmatum;* its various seedlings are green, dark purple, fully leafed, extremely cut-leaf, upright, and arching in habit. I can't wait for these offspring to have seeds of their own, to see what they'll do next.

Japanese maples are often considered dwarfs, but given enough nourishment, they will grow up to three feet a year, topping out at about thirty feet with a flat, spreading crown. The trick is to keep them high-pruned for the first ten feet so that they don't develop into broad, multi-trunked shrubs. Planted in part shade, *palmatums* usually grow in the direction of available light, so that they often begin leaning away from larger trees nearby and may need staking.

Characteristically, a healthy *palmatum* often keeps sprouting new growth until late September. However, these tardy sprigs seldom harden off before winter and will be dead long before March. You can tell a dead maple twig by its color: a dull grayish-brown or sallow purple. (Live twigs are glossy and a deep olive green.) By about April, dead twigs are dry and so brittle that they can be snapped off by hand as easily as the stalks of last year's goldenrod.

A. pensylvanicum (moosewood, striped maple) is an utterly splendid tree for even a tiny property. The light green leaves are as wide as a wild grape's, with three pointed lobes. (The leaf actually has five lobes, but the upper pair are usually vestigial; on certain leaves even the bottom pair are scanty, represented only by "tails" twisting out from the side margin.) But the tree's real glory is in its bark, which remains smooth with age. The glossy green "background" is shot through with eccentric vertical stripes of chestnut brown and chalk white. (One cultivar, 'Erythrocaldium', is said to have pink branches that turn red in winter!)

What makes moosewood maple even more desirable is its preference for part shade. In fact, its leaves will distort and brown at the edges if given full sun. So it makes an ideal planting beneath a Canopy tree or between other taller Second-Layer trees.

Only recently has moosewood begun appearing in catalogs, and then at regrettably high prices. But it grows abundantly in the woods of the Catskills and other hilly country, where its unique leaves make even tiny seedlings easy to spot. Forest-grown seedlings often lean horizontally to escape the total shade of larger trees. If you carefully plant such a seedling so that its slanting trunk is partly buried in the soil, chances are that it will sprout extra trunks from the horizontal wood. The result is a specimen I have growing in my Wild Garden— originally a single-leadered seedling, the tree now boasts four magnificent trunks instead of one.

One word of caution, though: the tree's cambium layer is so close to the surface that it's vulnerable to disease, which can cause unsightly cracks and sudden black patches of discoloration. Because a moosewood's bark is so neat and smooth, even careful surgery will leave an unsightly scar. So be sure you high-prune your moosewood so that *some* light strikes the trunk for at least an hour a day. Sun helps dry and cauterize any breaks in the bark and also assures that the white streaks will gleam out to best advantage.

Acer rubrum (red maple) will attain 120 feet, but it's so slow-growing that it can be interplanted with Second-Layer trees. Deprived of sun, it generates a straight, gray-barked trunk as described in Chapter 5, and when it finally achieves Canopy status, high-pruning will keep it from competing with its counterparts. The red spring flowers are produced when the tree reaches 15 feet or so—far earlier than most maples—and until a tree is really established, the branches remain slim and open, admitting plenty of light to other trees nearby.

Acer spicatum (mountain maple) has fat, quilted, sharply toothed leaves that look like a cross between moosewood and red. It seldom exceeds 15 feet, enjoys the same shade as moosewood, and makes a delightful companion tree. It's almost never offered commercially, so you'll have to prospect for it in the Appalachian Mountain Range. If given enough moisture in summer and fall, smaller specimens readily adapt to lower elevations.

All Second-Layer maples tend toward flat-topped, wider-than-high silhouettes, but fall into two major growth habits. Left to their own devices, hedge, moosewood, mountain, paperbark, and red maples will grow a single trunk with multiple opposite side branches. However, the *japonicums, palmatums,* and amur maples adopt a shrubby appearance, with erratic trunks and low-seated, conflicting branches. High-pruning during the early years is crucial, or the final result won't look much like a tree.

Betula lenta (black, cherry, or sweet birch) lacks white bark, but more than makes up for it in symmetry, hardiness, and vigor. I once came upon some *lenta* seedlings, and because of their neat, elongated leaves and smooth glossy bark, decided to try them as bonsai. Despite root-pruning, they prospered in their pots and grew so rapidly that each week, I had to pinch back their new growth. Finally I decided they'd never become good artificial dwarfs and released them to open soil—partly to see what they'd do. One of these former bonsai is now a double-trunked twenty-five-foot tree outside my bathroom window. Though tall, it's loosely branched enough that I can see through it even in summer: in shade—as this one now is—*B. lenta*'s leaves are far more widely spaced and the tree grows more slowly.

B. populifolia (gray birch, paper birch, white birch) has only two virtues: it has white bark, and it forms clumps. Otherwise, it's by far the worst birch you could choose. The tree grows quickly when young but when it reaches about 25 feet, it produces wild tangles of black branches and twigs. Many of the latter die during the winter, so a tree needs constant pruning to avoid a seedy appearance.

The species' main drawback, though, is that it's short-lived: a tree genetically programed to colonize open ground, seed itself, and then pass away. If you've ever spotted a wild stand of small-to-medium-size birches broken off halfway, with many white trunks littering the ground, that's *B. populifolia*.

Should you already have one of these clump-forming birches on your property, never cut off the vertical suckers that arise from the base. This is the clump's own way of increasing itself with new trunks. Left alone, these sprouts will grow as tall as their parents within a few years; and when they're about three inches thick, their amber-colored bark will begin peeling to a chalky white.

If there are too many suckers, or if the old trunks are clearly exhausted or decay-ridden, you can cut them off about six inches *above* the ground. But be sure to seal the wounds lavishly, because no other species' wood rots so quickly—should decay of any sort enter the base of your clump, you can expect the trees to rot away completely within five years.

There's one more drawback in store for you. The leaves of *populifolia,* more triangular in shape than any other birch, are highly susceptible to leaf miners—small flying insects that lay their eggs on new foliage. Larvae hatch and burrow into the middle of the leaf. On the leaves of perennials like columbine and snakeroot, they leave attractive pale squiggles that widen as the growing grub increases its girth. But when attacking clump birches, these insects hollow out all the cells between the upper and lower surfaces of the leaf until the entire structure resembles a small brown teabag swinging from a stem. You can easily split the leaf in half, horizontally. At the bottom of the "bag," now translucent, will be a few black dots—the larva's droppings. Look closely and you can see the plump green bulges of the larvae themselves, about the size of a grain of rice.

For some reason, leaf miners vastly prefer birches growing in full sun, while a more shady birch is seldom affected at all. Since birches put out new foliage all summer, any chemical spray used to control miners must be repeated every ten days. Meanwhile, I water plentifully (to encourage new growth) and visit infested trees every other day with a pruning shears. For some reason, leaves do not die until completely excavated—and so, each infested leaf you clip off means fewer adults to carry on the species. Collect the leaves as you remove them and burn or drown them afterward.

An even better solution is to axe your *populifolias* entirely and get three or four seedling *Betula pendulas.* If you plant them in a tight clump, they'll lean out from one another just like a natural clump of *populifolias,* and no one will know the difference. (*You* will, because they'll be a lot healthier!) Clumps of *pendula* also make a winding driveway easier to follow in the dark, because their broad, glossy white trunks do a great job of reflecting headlights. (To emphasize the outsides of unexpected curves, variegated hosta adds an accent of warning white.)

Carpinus caroliniana (blue beech, hornbeam, musclewood) is practically never offered by mail—a definite oversight when you consider this tree's enormous appeal to bark freaks. The leaves closely resemble those of *Betula lenta,* but with slightly more irregular and fine serrations. (When young, the two species are barely distinguishable, though *B. lenta* shows more vigor.) But when hornbeam gets up about ten feet, its branches become a bit less symmetrical and its wood thickens into incredibly attractive vertical ridges. It's as if there were indeed, sinuous muscles beneath the smooth gray bark, whose color is similar to that of cast iron. These facts—along with the wood's surprising hardness—leads to its common name of ironwood. Mature trees display a most lovely silhouette, winter and summer, but never grow too rapidly. The rigid roots make this tree very difficult to transplant, however, so obtain the smallest seedlings you can.

Cercis canadensis (redbud) is an extremely delicate-looking tree with rose-purple flowers in spring. Its neat heart-shaped leaves are borne with precise alternation along straight, often nodding branches. Like some other "forest" trees, redbud prefers almost full sun, losing a great deal of its vigor in part shade. But in windy sites, it takes a while to become robust.

Pruning the long branches' tips back after flowering will encourage a bushier, more compact plant. If your soil is not rich in humus, fertilize regularly. European and Japanese species and cultivars are frequently offered, and make good substitutes or companions for *C. canadensis.*

Hamamelis virginiana (witch hazel) is a small shrub that usually grows upright for three feet or so, before it levels off and begins leaning—probably a natural genetic trait that helps it glean additional sunlight. Preventive pruning is necessary if you want to train it as an upright, single-trunked tree. Still, the root system is weak and the wood flexible: my trees often lean precariously after a shower or hard wind, so some staking may be necessary.

There's a reward, however: witch hazel bears fat, asymmetrical leaves of a lush olive green that turn bright yellow in fall. Then in November, the tree blooms—tiny bursts of contorted yellow streamers that arise directly from the wood of the larger twigs. Pruned leaves and branches exude the familiar witch hazel aroma, and the flowering twigs make arresting Thanksgiving centerpieces.

Rhus spp. (sumac) is only occasionally offered by mail, and it's probably just as well. Their autumn color is an unparalleled acid red (old leaves will take on the same hue throughout the summer as they fade) and some species bear colorful cones of berries in late summer; but those assets more or less exhaust their charm. The roots are extremely invasive, and drought causes premature leaf drop. In winter, the branches are bereft of their compound leaves and look bare and forlorn. Sumac is best on a *single* level of a sharply terraced hillside, where its roots will creep to form a fairly level "forest" about 15 feet tall at maturity. Sumac needs full sun; otherwise the trunks become long and spindly and the roots will spread erratically in search of better conditions.

When two or three high-pruned trees are gathered in the corner of a lawn, they eventually widen at the base, heaving the lawn enough to make the soil dry out quicker. Together with the overhead shade, you get a high, hard, difficult lawn. It's easier to turn the entire grove into an "island" by filling in the soil between the trunks with a shade-loving groundcover (see Chapter 9), tying the trees together at their base as well as at their intermingled crowns.

To make such an island even more attractive, plant flowering ever-greens between the trunks and lay a path right through it so that visitors can appreciate it from the inside. The arrangement of Second-Layer tree trunks will probably forbid a strictly straight path in any case, but try to avoid its being so. An elbow or dogleg makes the most intriguing route for any narrow expanse.

Because Second-Layer trees are naturally small to begin with, high-pruning is even more important than with Canopy species. All too many gardeners let their dogwood, crabapple, or Japanese maple sprout low branches that make mowing difficult—and underplanting impossible. Prune these trees so that their lowest branch is well above the head of your tallest guest—I'd suggest ten feet.

I suggest a Darwinian method of pruning. First, remove branches that the tree *itself* will eventually allow to die back. A good wet snowfall—temperature just above freezing, so that each twig gets flocked with an overhang of snow—bends down into your gaze the same branches that, next summer, will again sag just this way under the weight of their new growth. Therefore, these branches should be pruned before the spring expands them. Against a white backdrop, naturally, you can also pick out any twigs that are diverting the growth of the tree.

Another good time to check young trees is just after a rain in early summer. Too-lavish new growth often looks acceptable until a downpour wets the foliage. Then, with the extra weight, the new growth—and often the entire tree—begins to droop. Inspect your younger trees while it's still humid and their leaves haven't dried. Any branches you find nodding across your path should come off immediately so that the tree's encouraged to balance its growth.

Some extremely top-heavy trees will continue to lean. If so, start just below the main leader and prune off *every* branch that points in the unwanted direction. The tree will not straighten up immediately, because its wood still "remembers" the original tilt. But the remaining branches will tend to pull it back the other way. As new wood forms and hardens, it will become upright again—and you'll have accomplished a good deal of your high-pruning when the task is easiest.

The easiest way to avoid the decay, splitting, and other problems of tree crotches is to keep them from developing in the first place. If a tree forms a fork, you'll see that one leader is *always* slightly thicker and more upright than the other. Given another few years, this leader will outstrip the other—and the eventual loser might as well come off now.

Pruning is best done when twigs are small. At that stage, your effort is minimal and the tree is not yet so "committed" to that branch that it loses a significant amount of foliage. But oddly, no garden book follows this principle to its logical conclusion. Last winter, I was inspecting a young birch that had, as most young trees do, a number of buds down the length of its trunk. I sighed to think of the pruning job I'd have next spring, when it hit me that I wouldn't *have* twigs to prune if I removed those buds now!

Buds on deciduous trees are attached by highly brittle "joints." I rubbed loose a dozen or so, and visited the scars again in late spring to see if they were bleeding sap. They weren't—the cold, dry winter air had apparently cauterized off these pinprick injuries. Encouraged, I rubbed loose a few more unwanted buds. *Twig*-pruning at this late season would have left bleeding stumps, but, again, the bud sockets cauterized themselves. I now debud all my trees wherever and whenever they threaten to produce an unwanted branch.

Once in a while—as with a heavily pruned crabapple—the new growth may be *too* vertical. To make it more horizontal and in keeping with the tree's other branches, you'll have to stake it down. The average hemp rope is too heavy; unravel it into its three component strands. You have over three times the length you had originally. And because of their built-in corkscrew torque, each strand has more tension than either twine or rope. For tying two lengths of short strands together, the old-fashioned square knot assures no slippage (Figure 25). For tying the rope to a tree, use a bowline, whose fixed loop prevents binding and is far easier to adjust or remove as needed (Figure 26).

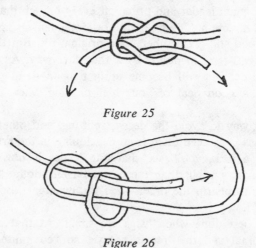

Figure 25

Figure 26

An orchard may look lovely in spring, but for the rest of the year, sameness of size and shape lends a certain monotony. Why not use young Canopy species as "temporary" Second-Layer trees? Again, once your "permanent" Second-Layer species are in their final positions, plant the faster-growing temporaries. Where I live, ashes, tulip trees, hickories, mountain ashes, dogwoods, and wild cherries regularly seed their progeny onto my land. While I don't want any more of these trees in full size, I don't mind them as fast-growing juveniles. When they get to about 15 feet or begin forming overshadowing branches, out they go.

Pollarding

Every so often, you may want to preserve a Canopy tree for its foliage, but not let it grow tall enough to overshadow other plants. For example, I have a sport of Norway maple whose leaves' lobes are so severely blunted as to resemble the foliage of English ivy. But left to its own devices, this tree would develop into a full-scale Norway with all its attendant problems. Across my yard is a natural hybrid of sugar and red maple, with extremely lengthy coral-red stems and outsize palmate leaves. But probably because of some genetic defect, it produces long, weak new growth that fails to harden off in time for winter. Twigs are often so succulent that they break under their own weight.

What's interesting in both these trees is their foliage, so I want to keep them low enough for easy inspection. The answer is *pollarding*, a technique that dates back to Roman times. In fall, *all* new growth produced since spring is pruned back to the main branches. The stubs callus over during the winter and in spring, erupt with a vast number of new twigs, creating a neat, spherical crown. The effect is wonderfully formal, and while the trunk and branches continue to expand, the tree never gets any higher. Pollarding works best on fast-growing trees like willow, poplar, apples, and the larger maples (though the same technique is used on grapevines and roses). The trees do look a bit empty over the winter, but after a few years, the ends of the remaining branches swell into dumbbell-shaped knobs of "proud wood"—a rather exotic and not unattractive deformation.

Bird Feeders

Any feeder should be low enough to replenish easily. A Second-Layer tree usually provides a conveniently low branch, but choose one that's close to a window where you can watch the traffic. If you admire neatness, never hang any feeder over a flat surface or lawn. Instead, position it over a thick groundcover into which the spilled seed and dropped chaff automatically disappears.

Of all feeders on the market, I prefer one sold by Droll Yankee, Inc.: Basically a plastic cylinder pierced by metal perches, it's designed mainly for smaller birds like sparrows or chickadees. The metal lid swivels to the side, so that you can pour in seed right to the top of the cylinder. (Baffles prevent the feed from running out of the side holes.) A metal bottom pan that can be ordered separately catches seed that would otherwise be lost, and gives a comfortable perch to larger birds like jays, waxwings, and cardinals.

The Droll Yankee feeder is claimed to be squirrel-proof—but isn't necessarily. When I hung mine directly from a limb, a squirrel soon learned to climb out, hook his hind feet into the corners of the feeder's handle, and hang upside down like an acrobat on a trapeze, nibbling seed from the holes and gnawing the plastic to sharpen his teeth. In any case, the feeder's wire loop is far too narrow to pass over most branches. So get some fairly heavy wire and bend it into the shape shown in Figure 27. The longer the wire, the higher the limbs you can reach. The double arc at the top fits over a limb without binding. The hook at the bottom holds the feeder, which is easily disengaged at refill time.

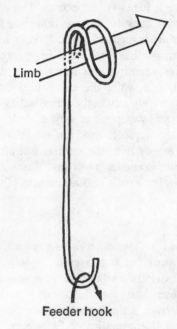

Limb

Feeder hook

Figure 27

The squirrel who used to raid the feeder is now utterly baffled by this wire extension. He has tried to reach his goal by a flying leap from the tree's trunk, but the feeder, now free-swinging, dumped him to the ground each time. With this wire extension, the feeder swings so easily that any bird large as a cardinal must use it alone. (A bluejay objects furiously when smaller birds light on the silo's opposite side and upset his balance.) But a Second-Layer dogwood, cherry birch, or ironwood has plenty of twigs on which birds can wait their turn.

7

SHRUBS, HEDGES, AND FOUNDATION PLANTING

Too many shrubs and bushes are used just because they're the right size, because they flower, or because they grow quickly enough to withstand clipping. Just like a Canopy tree, a given shrub must be matched to its proper function or you'll find it a permanent source of disappointment.

I. LOW HEDGES

Hedges are of two types: ones you can see over, and ones you can't. Obviously, your goal for any hedge is something that (1) keeps its leaves all year, and (2) needs as little pruning as possible. But most low-hedge plants in use today are naturally shapeless in growth habit and drop their leaves in fall, leaving your property open to view a good half of the year.

Kill List for Low Hedges

Berberis (barberry), a staple hedge item in old-fashioned gardens, bears tiny oval leaves and thorns on thickly branching stems, and oval red berries in autumn. The original green Japanese *thunbergii* species has been bred into hybrids with yellow and dark-purple foliage. All barberries need full sun and frequent shearing if they're to look at all decent, but even when carefully pruned, barberry's stems are too soft and pliable to hold themselves rigid. Old branches sag out of line, or cause gaps when an interior stem dies or shifts position. The thorns make pruning and nearby weeding needlessly painful.

Ligustrum (privet) is widely used for hedges because of its compact twigs and glossy leaves. But most strains are only semi-evergreen and take on a sorry look in winter. Privet demands sun too, and even the part shade of overhanging trees reduces its vigor and the density of its branches. The bottom half of an old hedge usually becomes sparse and awkward. This syndrome is obvious on old privet hedges, which are often a three-inch veneer of foliage sprouting from an open core of loose, bare branches.

Taxus (yew) is a short-needled evergreen that produces bright-red berries recessed at the tip to show the dark seed within. Though it takes well to pruning, it's a sun-lover—so much so that the lower and interior branches usually lose their needles. After a moderate pruning, a new growth begins promptly, even from old wood. But repeated clipping produces wide calluses at the tips of the branches and leaves ugly brown scars on needles that got in the way of the blades.

Before getting rid of a hedge of these Kill List species, remember their sole advantage: they will sprout new growth if pruned back severely. Since they're spoiling for a confrontation anyway, there's no point in being gentle. Cut them back to the shape you want, all in one swoop. Then—if they still haven't given a satisfactory effect by the end of the summer—squat down and get a firm grip on each plant's lower stems. (Barberry will require thick garden gloves for this move.) Then straighten your legs *only*. Your leg muscles are so much stronger than your arms or back that you can uproot even good-sized shrubs without feeling it the next day. Pulling shrubs up by the roots leaves a shallow trench. Replace the missing soil with good humus, and begin planting a new hedge comprised of any of the following replacements:

Buxus sempervirens is the long-leafed English boxwood featured in English topiary gardens and Colonial Williamsburg. It is not hardy in the North, however, where the Japanese species *microphylla* is a good substitute. The variety *koreana* (Korean boxwood) forms a naturally flat top at a height of eighteen inches. But its stems are weak: under the weight of rain or snow, it splits like a cracked muffin and the sides need continual shearing. Therefore, opt for the higher-growing varieties that keep relatively straight sides with little clipping.

Pinus strobus nana (dwarf white pine): the terms "miniature" and "dwarf" are practically synonymous in many garden guides and catalogs. Strictly speaking, *dwarf* refers to any variety or cultivar that's smaller than normal—which is *not* to say it doesn't get large with time. (The giant sequoia has a "dwarf" variety that results in a fifty-foot tree.) Dwarf white pine ultimately grows to twenty feet, but does so with exquisite slowness. A thick contorted trunk bears a tight bun of feathery blue-green needles.

All pines like full sun, but will survive if shaded for no more than half the day. Dwarf white pines are expensive, so plant them at least two feet apart so as to cover as much distance as possible. Allowing them to mulch themselves with their own fallen needles will help speed growth. To control their shape, simply twist off the candles of new growth. This takes a bit longer than trimming with shears, but spares the existing needles so that the final effect is far more elegant and attractive.

Pinus sylvestris nana (dwarf Scots pine) is ideal if you want a thicker, more prickly, but still upright hedge. The needles are more squat and of deeper blue than *strobus nana,* but branches arise so thickly from the trunk that there's no natural crown to speak of. Plant at least two and a half feet apart. Thorough candle-pinching in May will keep the plants immaculately formed.

Either pine can also be kept to its desired height by preventive debudding. In March, when the new buds begin to swell, pry off the ones that threaten to grow out of bounds. Lower buds will then take over, and after a few years, these pines can be trained to geometric shapes without the cut-off twigs and hacked needles that shears would leave behind.

If you don't want to uproot an existing hedge all at once, you can also make a gradual transition. Simply remove Kill List plants at intervals—every three feet or so. Plug the gaps with desirable plants, and prune the edges of the original hedge so that the new additions have enough room. Thereafter, your only task is to prune back the old ones so that the new can expand. When any one Kill List specimen is more than half pruned away, you can yank it completely.

Except for boxwood, no hedge plant grows solidly down to the ground without drastic pruning. It makes better sense to anticipate this dieback: eliminate weak lower branches from the start and give the hedge a "foundation" of groundcover.

II. HEDGES
YOU CAN'T SEE OVER

. . . are usually grown in place of a wall or fence, or as windbreaks. Many gardeners let their privet grow to ten feet and more, or for year-round privacy, plant a row of hemlock, spruce, or pine. Because these species get up quickly, they give gratifying results at first. The problem is that they keep *on* trying to get up, and long hours on a stepladder are needed for proper results.

My property's original owner planted a row of hemlocks that provided excellent privacy between him and the neighbors. But any dense evergreen allowed to reach six feet or more begins shading itself drastically. So as the hemlock hedge grew, branches at the center soon dropped their needles.

Unlike privet or taxus, hemlock, spruce, and other needled evergreens do *not* sprout abundant new growth from old wood. And so the zone between the trimmed new growth and the bare interior wood becomes increasingly narrow. To keep gaps from appearing, you must allow the conifer to slowly enlarge outward by about a half inch a year. Thus while my side of the hedge is still "solid" in most places, it now extends at least three feet out from the hemlocks' original trunks! And since hemlock produces new growth all summer long, constant shearing is needed to keep the twigs in line.

To make things even worse, any trimmed conifer of any size sprouts fast-growing top branches in an effort to escape the frustrating shears. If pruned in time, these vertical shoots can be controlled so that the hedge remains relatively flat and even. But if it runs up sloping ground, as mine does, mounting a ladder is hazardous work. I haven't been able to get all the sprouts I should have, and as a result, my hedge's top growth has escaped beyond easy reach, sapping energy from the side branches, which are now starting to thin beyond repair. Soon this hedge will be little more than a filigree of new growth that gives a clear view of the bare branches within.

Therefore, hemlock, spruce, and pine are all on the Kill List for high trimmed hedges. The best all-around substitute is *Thuja* (arborvitae) of which several fastigiate varieties are now on the market. Planted in full sun about three feet apart, their edges will eventually meld to form a solid wall of foliage. And since arborvitae is naturally straight-sided, shearing is necessary only once a year, if that. *Thujas* insist on maintaining lush foliage clear to the ground, so that the gaps of even a radical pruning are quickly filled. And the upright top leaders are more succulent than hemlock and quite easy to keep in trim.

Of course, you can't uproot a tall hedge of Kill List evergreens without sacrificing your privacy until their replacements grow tall. However, you can use the technique of gradual succession, as I did. First I hired a tree service to cut off the trunks of my hemlocks at a uniform eight-foot level. Removing those overgrown, sprawling tops was exactly like lifting the roof from a dollhouse: noon sunlight now filters through the bare interior branches to the ground. Then I purchased a lot of young arborvitaes. By planting one between each pair of hemlock trunks, I am positive that they're evenly spaced. In that fairly dim light, they are now growing leggy—but tall, which is what I'm after. When they reach the four-foot level, I can begin pruning back the hemlocks' side branches. Eventually the *Thujas* will fade in as the hemlocks fade out, preserving my privacy all the while.

Trimming Tall Hedges

Even with arborvitae, I believe in pruning the bottom growth up at least six inches. With these lower branches gone, a groundcover can spread back under the fringe of the hedge, increasing the tidiness of the whole.

For keeping the sides vertical, the old-style hedge clippers are quite heavy to operate and don't give very neat results once your arm muscles begin to tire. A hand-held laser beam would be the ideal clipper, but for now, I prefer cordless electric clippers that can be recharged by plugging into a household outlet when not in use. They run for a good twenty minutes and can be angled back and forth easily to sculpt perfectly flat surfaces.

The best time to shear *Thuja* is about the beginning of July, when the weight of new growth has pulled a number of branches out of plumb. Yet the new growth is still fairly succulent and easy to cut. To insure accuracy, after dusk I usually place a high-powered flashlight at a raking angle to the plane of the hedge. Any unwanted bulges, even on hedges with rounded corners or along sloping ground, are immediately "spotlighted," while the shadows indicate where I've already clipped enough. (Best of all, the work is far cooler after dark.) If the hedge's base is edged with groundcover, leave the clippings where they are. The next morning's sun will dry them and they crumble into the leaves.

In general, however, I'd advise you not to trim any new hedge until it gives you an idea of what it will do on its own. Many tourists who marvel at the topiary boxwood of England and France aren't aware that *Buxus,* left to its own devices, forms a perfectly acceptable free-form hedge with lush mounds and bumps, but fairly straight sides. Even if you allow arborvitae's top leaders to go unchecked, they'll form neat spires without compromising the vigor of the lower branches. The formality you lose by not clipping is often more than compensated for by the attractive texture of the foliage.

III. FLOWERING SHRUBS FOR HEDGES OR SINGLE PLANTINGS

When the neighboring view isn't too obnoxious, many gardeners edge their property with shrubs—almost all of which make the Kill List:

Cornus alba sibirica and *C. sericea* (Tartarian and red-osier dogwood) have multiple trunks and are rather shapeless; despite their brilliant red bark, they make a rather forlorn winter display.

Cydonia japonica (flowering quince) blooms in the spring with stiff-petaled apple-like flowers that attract hummingbirds. To my mind, that's its only asset, since the plant's shape is wildly erratic and impossible to prune neatly.

Forsythia is widely planted for its masses of yellow flowers in early spring, but looks like hell the other fifty weeks of the year. Wishful thinkers sometimes plant it as a hedge, but forsythia positively chuckles at pruning, let alone shearing. (To install some semblance of order, recent hybridizers have introduced fastigiate and semi-weeping strains.) But give forsythia even a touch of shade and it thins drastically, becoming even more erratic and unkempt.

The chore of keeping forsythia in line is only compounded by the plant's uncanny willingness to root. When I hauled out a towering bush one November, a few small branches broke loose and fell among dry leaves. The next spring, I wasn't too surprised to see them burst into flower—large apple branches pruned in fall often bloom the next spring, relying on sap retained in the heartwood. But these forsythia twigs began putting out new *leaves*. Despite the freezing temperatures of winter, they had put down healthy six-inch roots.

Hydrangea is just as shapeless as forsythia, and its huge quilted leaves and outsize pompons of blue or white flowers never seem to blend in with surrounding plantings. Before they fall, the petals often begin to rot, turning the flowerheads a filthy brown.

Philadelphus coronarius (mock orange) has creamy white flowers —once, in June. Flowers tend to appear more plentifully on younger plants; older ones become sparse and unsightly especially if grown in part shade or dry ground.

Spiraea (bridal-wreath), smaller than mock orange, has a similar vase shape. Perfectly lovely clusters of white flowers are borne in drifts along the branches in May. But they last only a week. Then the thousands of tiny white petals begin falling, drifting like confetti with the wind and making a royal mess. They're too small to rake or sweep up, so you have to wait until they dry up or decay. New growth often leans drastically, and winter reveals the plants as untidy clumps of undistinguished stems.

Syringa (lilac) has flowers that last only a week or so before wilting. But my main quarrel with lilacs is that they never seem to neaten up. Once a shrub is of blooming size, its trunk erupts with suckers. Other shoots arise from the lazily creeping roots, and many branches die back, leaving gaps and clusters of bare wood.

Viburnums have maple-like foliage and clusters of white flowers in spring. However, the new growth is usually weak and unbranched, so that even plants grown in full sun begin leaning every which way and spread to form forsythia-like mounds.

Weigela species and hybrids bear appealing white to rose trumpets in May. But the flowers are too small to show up at a distance. Mature shrubs are extremely gangly, resembling a healthy forsythia.

On my place, I have decided to forgo deciduous shrubs entirely. Not only do they make life difficult for nearby perennials, but many are subject to more than their share of diseases. When I bought my property, it was bordered on the west with lilacs, then at least fifteen feet tall. Originally they had been planted in full sun, but neighbors' trees were now large enough to cast over them the moist shade in which disease prospers. What leaves were not already blanched with mildew were withered and blackened with fungus. Many central stems had died and, as a side course, the live bark was infested with scale insects.

It's best to uproot sickly flowering shrubs like this and start from scratch. After heavy spring rains had softened the ground, I grabbed hold of my lilacs' long trunks and used their own leverage to crack loose their shallow roots. It's harder to root out large forsythia, mock orange, and other strongly rooted shrubs. The best method, I've found, is to cut them down to the ground in late winter. The next spring, vast amounts of sap will gush from the stumps, exhausting the roots. Every week, visit the site and break off any succulent new growth arising from the old wood. By July, most of the roots will be so weakened that they can be pried loose far more easily.

I had eliminated my sickly eyesores, but I still needed privacy. Ideally, I wanted a flowering evergreen shrub that was disease-free and needed minimal pruning. But it had to provide dependably thick growth under a variety of light conditions ranging from full sun to part shade. Fortunately, rhododendrons fill that bill exactly. But I also wanted to duplicate the tall, upright, leafy look of the original lilacs. My solution was a free-form hedge composed of *both* rhododendrons and Second-Layer trees.

A superb example of such a hedge is just up the street from me. One house has a rather narrow street frontage, and a regularly clipped hedge would only emphasize the small dimensions. But instead, a myriad of details slow the eye: azaleas and rhododendrons have been interplanted with birch, dogwood, and other Second-Layer trees; and the entire planting row is underlaid with a strip of pachysandra groundcover that swallows leaves and integrates the separate shrubs into a single visual unit. Both the pachysandra and shrubs are evergreen, offsetting the trees' bare branches in winter.

Such a planting can be kept low as a roadside border, or grown higher for utter privacy, all depending on the varieties you originally select. And in addition, a free-form hedge can help you "pirate" your neighbor's landscaping.

It's usually impossible to *wholly* screen out glimpses of adjoining properties. Yet the average American gardener more or less ignores what's growing next door, hoping that his own private selection of plants will eventually grow higher than his neighbor's. Such rugged individualism doesn't always look too good at maturity; if two radically different plantings are intermingled and competing, both properties are spoiled.

Long before us Americans, the overpopulated Japanese were faced with the problem of landscaping tiny suburban lots. The Japanese gardener realizes that plants on another's property are part of his own visual landscape. Therefore, he often plants visual compatible species on his *own* property. After a few years, the casual eye reads both sides of the fence as members of a single grouping, and each gardener's eye can stray a good distance into the other's yard without meeting an arbitrary line of demarcation.

This technique works best, naturally, if your neighbor has good plants to begin with. My property abuts one lot that's edged in mountain laurel. Anything I'd plant would take years to equal their size, so I've chopped down some of my own shrubs that were blocking the view. Now those shrubs seem to be *my* hedge, and so I give them the same water and fertilizer I lavish on my own plants.

The ultimate in such "pirating" is actual cooperative landscaping. When another of my neighbors bought the property I described in the Introduction, the privacy strip bordering our properties was taken up with monstrously overgrown spruces, pines, and sun-bereft deciduous shrubs. And even though my neighbor actually owns those plants, we agreed that I'd start cultivating them as if they were my own, high-pruning the trees and eventually planting a free-form hedge underneath. Already I've removed two enormous forsythias that were invisible to him, and the empty space vastly widens the apparent extent of my own land. I'm also introducing pachysandra along the dry strip of his property that borders the street. From my point of view, it makes my driveway that much more elegant. From his viewpoint, it's grass he no longer has to mow.

The main components of a *low* untrimmed hedge, of course, are flowering evergreens. Only one is on the Kill List:

Pieris japonica (andromeda, lily-of-the-valley bush) is evergreen, but its leaves have an unhealthy bronzy tint, borne on eccentric branches that become gangly and sparse with age. The pendant white flowers are borne in very early spring from buds visible throughout the winter. But somehow the shrub always seems to be in a more or less undecided state of becoming. Any of the following evergreen shrubs have far lusher foliage and more spectacular bloom:

Azalea is actually a member of the Rhododendron genus (see below), but those you'll want for your garden are invariably listed as azaleas. You already have enough bare twigs to look at during the winter months, so avoid deciduous and semideciduous azaleas like the hybrid Exburys. They bloom in wild colors, but their foliage is a nondescript green and not very glossy; their growth sparse and willowy, not nearly as compact as the evergreen strains.

Garden-shop azaleas are often so low-growing and spreading that many gardeners are tempted to go nature one better and shear them into smooth upright mounds. The result *is* attractive, but when a clipped azalea comes into bloom, the flowers often do not cover the plant evenly: the blossoms are usually sparsest toward the top. This is because an azalea becomes most unruly toward the top—therefore, that's where clippers remove most of the flowering buds that form atop new growth during the summer.

To shear an azalea properly, you must steer a narrow course between form and flowers. Clip *immediately* after the flowers begin to fade, and the plant should have time to set enough new-growth buds for a blaze of color next spring. But most small-leafed azaleas naturally keep themselves in trim, so my main pruning targets are the lower, horizontal branches and the occasional high vertical shoots.

If your property features old azaleas, you may have an expected bonus when you go to prune them. My shrubs had long, ground-hugging branches that had to come off to encourage the plants upward. But to bare the spot where these removable branches left the main trunk, I often had to dig into an inch or more of oak-leaf mulch. Many cut branches came loose with tufts of what looked like long white mold—actually roots that the branches had sprouted through natural layering. In other words, each branch was a rooted cutting two feet tall (formerly long) that in a nursery would cost at least $5.95.

We were then in the midst of an August drought, and I doubted these juvenile roots could survive in the full sun where I wanted to plant them. But a half hour's pruning had given me over a dozen hefty rooted cuttings! I felt reckless, and went ahead. I forgot to water them several times, but surprisingly, I lost only two—and those were ones with sparse foliage! Other fully leafed branches that had far fewer roots survived with no setback, and bloomed the next spring. (Younger azaleas come into full bloom about a week sooner than their parents.) The odd vertical angle of the original leaves (which had been hoisted from their original horizontal plane) is now wholly corrected by the new growth.

Mature azaleas have another characteristic that makes hedge-growing easier—you can get them to straighten up by cutting them down! One plant's spreading branches were sweeping a brick path I wanted to widen, so I cut at least half of the azalea back to the ground. By September, the pruned stubs had grown new shoots a foot tall, and straight as arrows.

I've since discovered you can cut any well-rooted azalea flush to the ground and have it respond with a bundle of upright new growth. Thereafter, selective twig pruning will maintain a shape that's higher than wide. Remember, though, that this trick works only with *old* plants whose roots are very well established. A younger azalea puts more of its energy into new branches than into roots; and when it loses its leaves, it hasn't the energy to recover quickly.

Though brittle, azalea wood is extremely hard and rot-resistant. On the other hand, an azalea takes many years to work new bark up around a ground-level cut, so any branch stubs should be sealed off.

Camellias are largely Southern plants, but some hardy hybrids have recently been developed for Northern growing. (Naturally, they're always advertised as such.) If you find a particularly desirable flower whose underpinnings may not be perfectly hardy, buy two specimens. Plant one outdoors, and treat the other as an indoor houseplant. Even if the outdoor specimen succumbs, your indoor one will definitely thrive.

Kalmia (mountain laurel) has leaves of deep waxy green that glisten in the sun. Then in late May come the lovely hobnail buds opening into wide clusters of cup-like flowers, each up to an inch across, that resemble an old-fashioned glass paperweight.

In the wild, most *Kalmia* flowers run a short gamut from pink to white, but recent hybridization (working from atypical wild variants) has developed flowers of deep pink, and others decorated with bands, dots, and stripes; and when these new varieties reach the market, mountain laurel will hold its own with the most lavish and exotic of American wildflowers.

After years in full sun, *Kalmia* reaches about twenty feet with a richly contorted trunk and rounded crown that would make it ideal as a Second-Layer tree. But when planted in a low hedge, simple pruning after the flowers fade will keep it low and bushy. *Kalmia*'s new flowerbuds are produced atop the new growth in fall, and pruning after midsummer will seriously compromise the spring display.

Rhododendron ("rosy root") is a huge genus. In general, the leaves and flowers of *so-called* rhododendrons are larger than those of azalea. But most *species* rhododendrons are too small for hedge use. For *low* hedges, your best selection is among the hybrids classed in catalogs as "small-leafed." Their plump foliage is never more than four inches long and usually far glossier than taller-growing hybrids. These plants grow to around four feet and then level off without any pruning required.

Most dependable is the widely sold hybrid 'P.J.M.'. Its neat oval leaves turn a deep purple in winter, warming up to a lush dark green. Small pinkish-lavender flowers are borne in April. Older plants sometimes become a bit leggy, but this is easily forestalled by twisting loose the light green sprigs of new growth that arise in May at the tip of each branch.

Installing your untrimmed hedge

When introducing these plants, leave plenty of room for them to spread. Mature azaleas are about four to five feet across; camellias, kalmias, and dwarf rhododendrons three to four feet. Most experts advise you to plant lines of shrubs with an identical distance between trunks. But if specimens have branches of unequal length, the line may *be* evenly spaced but not *look* it. Therefore, measure the distance between existing *branches*. If those gaps are equal, all your plants should join together at about the same time.

Few shrubs are perfectly round; most are oval or even downright elongated. For hedge purposes, you want each plant to fill as much space as possible from the beginning, so make sure the plant's longer axis is parallel to the line of the hedge.

You can use a Kill List species to fill in the temporary gaps. But for increased visual interest, a free-form hedge can even take a break or two. My own azalea hedge has a natural gap, in which I planted a few ferns. Then I let a rivulet of pachysandra trickle down from the top of the slope—a path not for the feet, but for the eyes.

Because all your low-hedge evergreens are shallow-rooted, any Second-Layer trees you plant among them will delve deeper and offer no competition. All of the above evergreens can also stand part shade, so as long as intermediary trees are high-pruned from the start, the shrubs should enjoy uninterrupted vigor.

For a *low* hedge, the best Second-Layer trees are:

> *Amelanchier* (shadblow)
> *Betula pendula* (European white birch)
> *Malus* (crabapple hybrids)
> *pendula* varieties of any deciduous or evergreen tree
> *Prunus* (especially dwarf and weeping cherries)
> Any of the Second-Layer conifers mentioned in Chapter 6

Eventually, the foliage of the shrubs will grow to camouflage the lower trunks of the trees. Result: twice the amount of plants in the same growing area, and a taller border to your property that you can still see through. Now you can also interplant the evergreens with a few highly desirable deciduous shrubs that would make a barren winter display if planted by themselves:

Althaea (rose of Sharon) would ordinarily make the Kill List because of its bare, leggy growth. But usually it can be high-pruned to only a single trunk, so that it spreads out above a low evergreen hedge. In August, when little else is in flower, it bears series of hibiscus-like blossoms ranging from white to deep purple (see Color Section). The deep-red and purple varieties don't always show up well, so restrict yourself to the pink and white shades.

Also avoid cultivars with variegated leaves and specimens with branches of different-colored flowers grafted to a single trunk. Both look busy and arbitrary among the more sedate azaleas and rhododendrons. Vigorous pruning right after flowering will keep rose of Sharon from getting the unbranched, "stalky" look that overtakes most older specimens.

Clethra alnifolia (pepperbush) is a native American species that's deciduous, slow-growing, and has no coherent shape until late in life. Still, I do feel it's worth the trouble. The quilted leaves are small and dainty, and the shrub as a whole stays within bounds, seldom sprouting extra trunks or throwing dense shade. In July it erupts with six-inch white sprays of a shape midway between lilac and wild cherry. The individual flowers later ripen into peppercorn-like seedpods, hence the name.

Pepperbush casts long, searching, woody roots and thus is extremely difficult to transplant unless you come upon a small seedling. Better yet, gather the "corns" for germination. Because of its modest growth under even ideal conditions, pepperbush takes a few years to show up properly, so locate it where it can remain unmolested. Full sun to light shade are acceptable, though flowers increase with available light. A cool, moist soil is a must for vigorous growth, and I give my young pepperbushes a deep mulch of raw compost for good measure.

Rhododendron nudiflorum (pinxter) makes me waive my reservations about deciduous azaleas. This native American azalea is sometimes mistermed "shrub honeysuckle" because of the extravagant form of its flowers (see Figure 28). The shaft of the trumpet is a rich coral pink, as are the upturned anthers. The petals in between are a light pastel pink, lending marvelous contrast. These flowers appear in sizable globe-shaped clusters around the first or second week of May. Leaves begin expanding fully just as the flowers begin to fade, remaining a light green (that lends a rather fresh look) throughout the summer. The bush itself is upright and fairly compact.

You can often find small pinxters in oak woods, usually sprawling over the dead leaves in search of better light. The delicate foliage would seem to suggest that the plant prefers part shade, but my finest pinxter flourishes in full sun in a poor clayish soil. When transplanting, get an *enormous* ball of soil that contains as many of the weak rambling roots as possible (Warning: pinxters stem can amble horizontally for a foot or more; don't insert your shovel until you uncover obvious *roots*. This means a slow downward baring of the

Figure 28

trunk by hand.) But few wild plants respond so positively to better conditions, and the first flowerhead will more than reward your patience. The flowers need to be seen close-up to be appreciated, so place your specimen to the near side of the hedge for easier viewing.

IV. HIGHER FREE-FORM HEDGES

If you can wait ten years or so, the plants mentioned above will slowly approach privacy height. If you're in more of a rush, though, it's easier to choose a set of faster-growing plants. By far the best are the large-leafed rhododendrons that quickly get up around ten feet.

Try to avoid the long-leafed native species *longifolium*, however. Many landscapers are wooed by their rapid growth and pinkish white flowers borne on the last days of June, when most other rhododendrons have quit. But these old-fashioned foundation plantings develop extremely straight trunks with a minimum of side branches.

(Many nurseries disguise this drawback by selling specimens with six or more trunks, but they remain spindly as they grow.) On the other hand, the best of the hybrid rhododendrons start out with more branches at ground level, more delicate foliage, and more colorful, earlier bloom.

Don't order tall-growing rhododendrons by mail. These are usually rooted cuttings under a foot tall that will take several years to reach three-foot size. (One "white" I ordered eventually bore pastel pink flowers.) The ones balled and bagged at the nursery are more expensive, but a better size to start with, promising faster results.

By visiting the local garden shops in mid-May, you can be *sure* of flower color. Most offered by nurseries are tagged as *roseum*—actually a generic name for a wide variety of hybrids, not all of them pink. But most bloom with the pale lavender shade typical of many species rhododendrons (see Color Section). For contrast, therefore, search for at least a few reds and whites. The *deep* acid-reds don't show up too well, so go for the bright, clear shades.

However, since your first priority is a hedge plant that looks good all year, the question of flower color is almost secondary. The following rhododendron characteristics are not necessarily a specialist's criteria, but ones that I find make for a tighter and more attractive hedge.

Desirable "privacy" hybrids have rather small oval leaves whose length is not more than three and a half times the width—and seem to bear these leaves in greater profusion. For maximum privacy, the leaves should have a very slight droop and not stand out at right angles to the stem.

Try to select specimens with two or more trunks, since they will soon become denser and wider than single-trunk specimens. Trunks should lean outward from each other at a low angle, not slanting up again for at least six inches—an assurance they they won't grow together at a later date. Check for stumps or gaps in the bark where lower limbs have been torn off in transit.

Lastly, don't forget to remove the bag and clay "overshoes," as described in Chapter 5. For years I've noticed that even shrubs grown in plastic containers of good soil seem to do best when transplanted bare-rooted. Finally I think I've found out why—houseplant experts now recognize a problem called "soil interface" that interferes with a plant's success after transplanting.

The roots of certain species, it seems, accustom themselves to the soil in which they're growing. If the rootball is removed intact from its pot and placed in a wider container, chances are the new surrounding soil is different in density and chemical composition. Quite often, the plant considers it as "alien turf," and its roots refuse to expand beyond their present limits. As a result, plants moved to the most spacious containers can remain effectively "potbound" below the soil surface. I wonder if this isn't true of outdoor plants as well. Of course, invasive-rooted trees like mulberry, pine, spruce, and poplar will penetrate even plastic bags in their lust for *Lebensraum.* But I've often moved fibrous-rooted shrubs like rhododendron and boxwood that have spent several years in the ground. Again and again, the roots break loose in a neat bun that suspiciously resembles the outline of the original soil ball.

For indoor plants, the only remedy for soil interface is to force the plant to adjust by removing *all* soil from the roots and replanting them in a homogenous mix. Though any outdoor plant should certainly go into a pocket of *improved* soil, let it be bare-rooted within that pocket, just like a tree.

While your rhododendrons are getting up, keep them shapely by debudding the tops of outsize branches. (Be sure not to remove the distinctly larger, fatter buds that will form flower heads the next spring. Foliage buds are slim and sharply pointed at the end.) Also snap off exhausted flowerheads so that no extra energy is siphoned off into seed production. In any case, hybrid rhododendrons do not self-seed dependably, and it's easier to propagate them by layering— cut partway through lower, trailing branches and bury the broken sites under piles of leafmold. Three years later, the branches should have roots and be ready for transplanting.

If you plant Second-Layer trees among these larger rhododendrons, they must be straight-trunked species that can be high-pruned to at least ten feet. Good choices include:

> *Betula pendula* (European white birch)
> *Cornus florida* (dogwood)
> *Fagus grandifolia* (American beech)
> *Prunus* (especially the cherries)
> *Sorbus* (mountain ash)

V. FOUNDATION PLANTINGS

These are usually selected to "tie a house down to the ground." But a few comely Second-Layer trees can do that better than any shrub. Again, no evergreen Canopy trees should be there in the first place. High-prune any Canopy or Second-Layer trees. Eliminate the Kill List shrubs discussed earlier, as well as the following:

Juniperus (junipers) are widely sold as foundation evergreens, but inevitably grow out of shape. Not that most junipers have much shape to begin with—and even if carefully pruned back, the Hemlock Hedge Syndrome eventually catches hold. Older junipers usually display a broad underside of dead, dry foliage, and these sharp needles make close pruning a painful chore.

Mahonia aquifolium: the species name of "water-leafed" describes the shiny, waxed surface of the compound leaves. Individual leaflets resemble those of holly. If only the plant could learn to stand upright! Instead it throws weak, rambling branches that are only semihardy. Careful (usually drastic) pruning is required. The yellow flowers and later blue berries are exotic, but not terribly attractive.

Taxus (yew) takes pruning well. But all except the fastigiate *hicksii* variety grow into multiple-trunked trees or irregular spreading mounds with lanky horizontal branches. Even with pruning, age does little for a taxus; it simply gets bigger without developing any form or grace.

Foundation planting's only real function is to hide the bald expanse of concrete, stone, or brick between the ground and the beginning of the clapboards. In a sense, a brick house's "foundation" goes all the way to the roof, so a high free-form hedge is acceptable there. But clapboards or siding should show as much as possible. Therefore, why not think of your foundation planting as a low free-form hedge! But no trunk should be within three feet of the wall; leave a broad avenue for access and later growth. Next to a house, plants should be as neat as possible. Forgo azaleas and other rough-outline plants in favor of small-leafed rhododendrons. The following plants also keep a flat, compact habit well into old age:

Acer palmatum variety *dissectum* (cut-leaf weeping Japanese maple) is often sold as a lawn accent. But while an ordinary Japanese maple grows to become a Second-Layer tree in full sun, *dissectum* stays put.

The reason is partly the shape of the leaf. The more deeply cut a plant's foliage, the less surface it has for photosynthesis. Therefore, any cut-leaf plant will be less vigorous and slower growing than its full-foliaged counterparts. A most extreme example is the so-called "Thread-Leaf" Japanese maple, whose leaf surface has been narrowed so drastically that the veins alone remain, jutting from the stem like the fingers of a skeleton. Each rib bears a tiny, narrow flange of leaf surface. This tree is exceedingly hard to raise to marketable size, simply because it needs three or four years to accumulate the energy a normal *palmatum* could obtain in a few months.

Dissectums, on the other hand, are rather widely available. Their seedlings take so excruciatingly long to mature that virtually all nursery stock has been grafted to ordinary *palmatum* trunks—but this doesn't matter for foundation purposes. If grown on the sunny south side of a house, a *dissectum* overlaps its old branches with new semi-weeping ones, eventually disguising the straight trunk under a neat, rounded bun of foliage.

Buxus (boxwood) is ideal for foundations, especially when left to form its own lush, billowy mounds. In fact, I'd use boxwood almost exclusively around smaller houses. For a very low foundation border, use the flat-topped *koreana.*

Chamaecyparis pisifera filifera aurea nana (plain old golden thread-needle cypress) forms a buoyant mound of weeping foliage whose new growth is an attractive yellow against the older chartreuse scales. Because new growth sprouts readily from old wood, the tree can always be pruned down again if it becomes too sizable.

Ilex crenata is a small-leafed Japanese holly that spreads into a wide, low mat and takes very well to shearing. Unlike the tree forms, it never bears berries, but its foliage is dependably shiny and evergreen.

Picea abies variety *nidiformis* (bird's-nest spruce) never gets above three feet, growing into a perfect round mound of neat, short needles.

Picea glauca conica (Alberta spruce) forms an upright, deep-green cone that looks as if it had just been carefully pruned. For foundation use, it's much better than any fastigiate evergreen because it never grows above six feet tall. Because of the slow growth rate, large specimens are quite expensive. But smaller plants can be fertilized and high-pruned to get up quickly.

Also suitable for sunny foundation use are the host of other low-growing "dwarf" evergreens, too numerous to mention here. Check catalog descriptions to make sure each grows wider than high. Avoid dwarf hinoki cypresses, which form bare trunks in their old age, as well as:

Pinus mughus (Mugho or mughus pine), widely offered as a rock garden accent. *Mughus mughus* is an even more low-growing variety, but neither plant attains a really respectable shape. With age, mughus pines become lanky, with a series of loose, meandering branches that ultimately resist pruning. Substitute:

Pinus strobus nana (dwarf white pine) usually arises from a single trunk, but forms low, quickly dividing branches and a dependably even crown. Unlike *mughus,* it's upright enough that you never have to worry about branches crawling along the ground and getting choked with dead leaves.

All of the above species need at least half a day of good sun. For the shady north side of your foundation, use *Prunus laurocerasus* (cherry laurel). It has larger, darker, glossier leaves than mountain laurel, spreads thickly and widely, and tolerates pruning. (In fact, it should be pruned early in its career to forestall semi-upright trunks.) Plants grown in shade usually withhold their flowers, but do spread their branches more evenly.

Foundations usually contain lime that leaches into the nearby soil, making it alkaline. When you first plant acid-loving evergreens, make heavy use of an acid fertilizer. When the plants get large enough to begin dropping needles, their own mulch will keep the soil acid—as long as you don't rake the needles loose.

Some gardeners let all their foundation shrubs grow to a given height and then shear off the entire intermingled line. This looks a bit odd in the final analysis, and as with Second-Layer trees, a planting

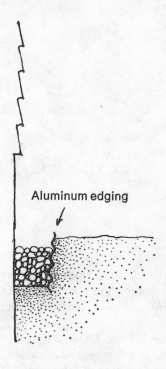

Aluminum edging

Figure 29

of different-size shrubs is more attractive. I prefer a series of discrete mounds, like a plate of closely packed gumdrops. If one plant *really* starts spreading, however, you might as well give it extra room by moving its smaller competition. They'll appreciate the move, but if a plant is doing very well where it is, why mess with success?

To neaten the foundation "row" even more, underplant with a groundcover. (For very low shrubs, pachysandra may be too tall—try vinca minor or foamflower.) But always leave a six-inch space between your foundation and the groundcover. Dig to a depth of six inches or more, edge on the outside with aluminum edging, and replace the gap with pebbles (see Figure 29). This makes it more difficult for termites to invade your house, and a regular dusting of insecticide among the pebbles will also reduce the number of ants, beetles, and spiders that find their way indoors.

8

VINES FOR CLIMBING

When used properly, no other kind of plant can lend so satisfying a look of finished elegance. Yet take the rattiest spot in a garden: chances are it contains vines—or, more accurately, the vines contain it.

Unfortunately, many of the fastest-climbing species are also the worst to have around at all, whose appearance really detracts from your local landscape. And so, the following Kill List for vines is a fairly long one:

Kill List Vines

Celastus scandens (native American bittersweet, waxwork) is on many states' preservation lists. If you have one, you'll know it by its truly enormous quantity of brightly colored fall berries. Given a strong Open Trellis (see Figures 31 and 32, below), *C. scandens* should be sure to please you. But you're more likely to find *C. flagellaris* (Korean bittersweet) or *C. orbiculatus,* the similar—and infamous—oriental bittersweet.

Originally from Asia, the latter is frequently sold at nurseries and by mail, which is truly irresponsible. Oriental bittersweet is attractive and robust, but the plant is a shameless spreader. New growth winds itself around any available branches. If no support is available, the shoots arise more or less straight up for about three feet, then bend under their own weight—and come to rest. Once the stem has a chance to harden off, it branches off again.

Given enough light, *C. orbiculatus* crawls up to twenty feet a year, racing out of bounds, strangling any smaller plant that gives it the least purchase, smothering everything beneath it with deep shade. Flowers are negligible. In autumn, the leaves give only a brief hint of yellow before falling to reveal beige coils of stem and a few soggy orange-yellow berries. These fruits are eaten by birds, and because the seeds are highly fertile, new vines will quickly arise in flowerbeds, under trees, and in other neglected areas, quickly getting out of hand.

Even if bittersweet has woven its way into the branches of something else, getting rid of it is fairly easy. First, trace its stems back to the main root system where all the branches (some a good three inches thick) congregate at ground level and abruptly disappear. Cut off all branches or trunks at soil level and, with a pipe or crowbar, pry loose as much of the root system as you can. Repeat if new sprouts appear.

Convolvulus spp. (bindweed, field bindweed) are wild relatives of morning glory, annuals with white or pink flowers that self-seed and returns year after year, twining up the trunks of young trees and over shrubs. Old stems become quite stiff, and if you try to pull them loose, they can strip the foliage off their hosts.

First uproot the plant at its base. Then loosen the coiled stems from their support and cut them every six inches or so with pruning shears. The next day, the sections will have wilted enough so that they can easily be pulled loose.

Hedera helix (English ivy) is often used as a groundcover—a most common garden mistake, as I'll explain in the next chapter. A vine should never be allowed to trail on the ground. If it *can* climb, plant it where it can do so.

Lonicera (honeysuckle) is an immense genus whose species range from paltry groundcovers to overweening shrubs. Even though the hybrid honeysuckles offered for sale have lovely, fragrant flowers, their rank, utterly formless growth makes them unsuitable for a small, neat property unless you cultivate them on an Open Trellis (see below).

You'll note that such really unkempt vines don't have the self-attaching mechanisms of the more dependable species discussed later. Honeysuckle, in fact, has no way to attach itself directly to its support. Rather than trying to climb, it simply overruns its own stiff dead stalks until it builds up a high perch from which it can ooze onto nearby plants. The very worst examples are the semi-evergreen honeysuckles of the Northeast, which flower inconspicuously and form immense tangles, layer on layer: entire acres of low woodland have been ruined by these plants that hitch themselves over Second-Layer trees and shroud them in a net of dense gloom.

You *may* want to give any small seedling vine a trial probation to see if full sun will coax it into attractive bloom. But like any other vine, a large honeysuckle is fairly easy to kill once you trace the stems back to their roots. Pulling out the main clump usually isn't sufficient, however, because broken roots and underground stems will sprout to form a second generation. Applying a layer of plastic, covered with a functional or cosmetic mulch, will solve the problem once and for all.

Polygonum aubertii (silver lace vine) is too wild and frizzy for my taste. The unassuming flowers appear in August and September when little else blooms. But the nondescript foliage is deciduous, and the growth so rank that heavy pruning is needed.

Rhus radicans is deceptively good-looking. Three blocks from my house is a very old elm, swaddled in the abundant green foliage of a gnarled and stately vine that seems to have been planted there deliberately. If so, I pity the gardener—*R. radicans* is poison ivy!

Poison ivy is of the sumac genus, and thus able to spread below ground as well as above. It can form a full, dense groundcover in fairly dense shade and is one of the few plants that will survive in the dry acid thatch under mature pine trees. It can grow into a contorted small bush or become a thick climbing vine—all depending on light and available support. (As a vine, its ascending stems sprout thick tufts of modified rootlets that wedge themselves into the cracks and irregularities of textured surfaces. Consequently, poison ivy can climb straight up the bark of a tree, up a brick or cement wall, even over painted wooden clapboards.) Its leaves vary widely, often embossed with bumps like the ones their oil raises on human skin—but not always. The leaves range from rich dark green to light chartreuse, and can be narrow or extravagantly wide. But the leaflets always come in threes. The berries (usually borne only on plants growing in strong light) are a bluish white.

Around the turn of the century, poison ivy used to be sold (in relatively safe seed form) for training along fences and stone walls as a deterrent to any trespasser who could recognize its rash-producing leaves. But unfortunately, poison ivy's irritating toxin exists throughout the plant. One midwinter, while excavating antique bottles from an old dump, I took care to avoid a leafless shrub of poison ivy growing nearby, or so I thought. A few days later, my hands erupted in a rash after all. I then realized that I had been digging among the plant's *roots,* which had penetrated the loamy soil surrounding the old bottles. Even worse, poison ivy toxin can be removed from the plant and still retain its virulence. The smoke from burning plants is said to cause severe distress if inhaled, and a woman I knew was once hospitalized with a severe rash after plucking a pheasant her husband shot. Evidently the bird had nested in poison ivy, and picked up the toxin in the oil of his feathers.

Oddly, man is the only animal who seems susceptible to it. Birds not only nest in poison ivy but eat the berries and are largely responsible for the plant's spread. Horses find poison ivy a particular delicacy and will browse on it with gusto, often infecting anyone who handles their bridles afterward. And even some humans do seem immune: my father once transplanted a sizable vine, thinking it would look nice against the kitchen wall. It did, and though it later turned out to be poison ivy, he suffered no reaction.

The clue may lie in the fact that the poison ivy rash is basically an allergy. The "desensitizing" medicine now available for sufferers works by dampening the skin's reaction; and as an allergist will tell you, it usually takes repeated exposures before the body's reaction to an irritant erupts in full cry. (Although I suffer a reaction nowadays, my parents swear that as a baby I once *ate* some leaves without suffering ill effects.) On the other hand, my father continues to uproot *R. radicans* without gloves and still claims to be immune. But the skin of his hands is thick and callused from long years of mechanical work, and at the end of the day, he usually has to wash his hands thoroughly of oil and grease—thus perhaps removing any toxin before it can penetrate. In other words, those who are "immune" may just not have been exposed sufficiently—which is all the better reason to stay clear of poison ivy in the first place.

If you *are* exposed, quick washing with soap and water should dissolve the oil before it can penetrate the epidermis. And a friend who lived in West Virginia insists that household ammonia neutralizes the toxin, even when the prospective victim has made love in a thicket of *R. radicans,* as one of his pals once did.

In most cultivated gardens, you're likely to come across small seedlings whose roots have not yet dug deep. The leaves of young poison ivy are easy to spot—distinctly shiny and often reddish along the margins. Never touch their stems directly. Instead, pick a number of wide, thick leaves from the handiest tree or shrub. Fold these "safe" leaves into a shield between your thumb and forefinger (see Figure 30). Then grip the ivy's stem at ground level. If you pull *gently,* you won't tear your leafy shield, and the seedling will usually come up with all of its roots in one piece.

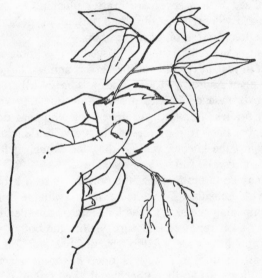

Figure 30

To get rid of larger plants, you don't want to contaminate your tools by cutting it or digging it up. Get a defoliate spray from your hardware or garden shop. Mix a highly concentrated solution inside a wide-mouthed jar, and set the jar firmly in the soil beside the poison ivy. With a stick, push one of the branches, leaves and all down into the liquid. The vine's own sap will absorb the chemical and carry it back to the roots, killing the entire plant.

Smilax (greenbrier) is a genus of largely native American varmints. The heart-shaped glossy leaves resemble those of clematis (see below), but there are no noticeable flowers, and slender stems are lined with thorns that tell you you're in for trouble. This is one pest that never seems to grow thicker with age: the stems remain well under an eighth of an inch thick, rambling over anything nearby. Dry soil doesn't bother them, and so they often turn poor, sunny ground into an unsightly tangle of barbed wire.

In the open, greenbrier will trap leaves, slowing their decomposition. When its own deciduous leaves fall, the stems themselves often die back too. But dry or fresh, they contain a highly inflammable oil. A thicket of greenbrier will burn hot and high, but not even fire will kill the well-protected underground roots. So the plant has an even better chance of reclaiming the burned-over land when it sprouts in spring.

Perhaps the best time to get rid of them is in early summer. Follow the new stems as deeply into their tangle as you can and clip them off. New growth that emerges in late spring or even the same fall will help you zero in on the roots.

Wisteria chinensis (Chinese wisteria) is the hardiest species and the one most frequently offered by nurseries and by mail. The lavender flowers are lovely in spring but they drop all at once, making a really dismal mess. In fall the vine produces a host of pods like lima beans that also dry and drop, again littering the ground. But wisteria has other, more serious drawbacks.

My father once planted a *chinensis* wisteria tree in his back yard. He soon discovered that such "trees" are nothing more than high-pruned *vines* that constantly try to revert their twining habit. From its base, this one throws sudden three-foot suckers of new growth that go snaking across the patio until they are stepped on or cut back.

To distract the plant in the hopes that it would climb instead, my father planted an iron stake beside it and ran a few guywires up to bolts anchored in the concrete brick wall of his house. The idea was that the wisteria's tendrils would twist around these wires, forming a nice shady "roof" over the entire patio.

Obligingly enough, the wisteria shoots coiled around the wires and took off skyward. But wisteria doesn't simply *follow* a support. It literally pulls itself along by tightening its coils. As this vine's shoots thickened, they exerted such pressure that soon the guywires themselves were as twisted as the shoots coiling around them. The resulting tension grew until two of the toggle bolts broke loose from the concrete! When my father introduced some slack, the shoots—nothing daunted—made direct for his color TV antenna. Now they have to be restrained from clinching their way along the telephone cables.

A determined *Wisteria chinensis* can throw up to fifteen feet of new growth a year, often traveling confidently in the shade beneath clapboards, shutters, or wood paneling. Then it finds the light of day and enough new vigor to pry loose whatever it's tunneled through. According to reports, the "famed untamed wisteria" of Sierra Madre, California, was innocently planted next to a house in 1892. In ten years, it had smothered the house, and the residents had to move, claiming that they could hear the vine prying shingles loose as it grew up to ten inches a day. That single vine has now swallowed the house and spread over several acres, its weight estimated at better than 150 *tons*. Bearing over half a million blossoms each spring, it is a major tourist attraction. I thought this account was an exaggeration until I found a wisteria growing into a hayloft closed by two tight-fitting shutters of solid wood. At least two feet of vine protruded through the locked jamb and into the totally darkened room. Most plants automatically turn their new growth toward the source of greatest illumination. Wisteria, obviously, does not.

To grow vines properly, simply observing the forgoing Kill List still isn't enough. The problem is that while *all* vines are usually described as "climbing," they have quite distinctive methods of doing so. Some species like Boston ivy actually support themselves, while others like honeysuckle simply *hang*. Wisteria can easily twine up a slender pole, but is utterly unequipped to scale a brick wall. English ivy can climb bricks, but can't extend itself on the kind of trellis on which a grapevine thrives.

You have to select vines according to *where* you want them to grow; if you don't, the result is a disastrous tangle. And except for a few exceptions mentioned later, you can forget about a trellis. Once most vines get going, they will smother a trellis so completely that maintenance—painting, replacing rotten wood or rusting metal—is exceedingly difficult and awkward. I much prefer vines that don't demand special favors, selecting them so that they can take best advantage of supports I want to camouflage.

I. NONFLOWERING VINES FOR TEXTURED SURFACES

Vines in this group will do well against brick, concrete, stone, even the bark of a tree, but *not* on a clapboard house. Wood shaded with vines is extremely susceptible to decay. (Show me the original wooden trellis for any vine planted twenty years ago, and I'll show you a pile of rotten lumber.) Even if you plant a vine against the dry south side of a house, it will make future painting practically impossible.

These vines do best on many old trees—especially oaks, hickories, and Norway maple—whose bark can be downright dull. These vines give lackluster trunks an elegant camouflage, while the tree itself gives the vine an ideal trellis—and with no trimming usually necessary. (One note of caution, however: carefully inspect the bark and larger limbs of any tree on which you plan to train a vine. Any wounds you find should be dry and well on their way to healing. If there's any decay beginning within twenty feet of the ground, a clinging vine will only camouflage and exacerbate the problem.)

Hedera helix (English ivy) is what most people mean by "ivy," period. The leaves are usually evergreen, and cut stems root easily in water—two reasons why the plant is so widely grown. It will also climb any flat surface. Like poison ivy, its stems sprout modified roots on either side, like the legs of a millipede. Pulling a healthy plant away from its supporting surface is like removing adhesive tape —the vine comes away in short stretches, making a noticeable tearing noise as its rootlets break loose. Even if your outside walls are of unpainted brick, you should keep any *Hedera* well away from the windows. Once English ivy's stem rootlets get clotted in the wire mesh of your screens, they are practically impossible to remove. Smothered in shade, the window jamb and casement will soon begin to rot, and as the vine gets thick, birds will nest in it. An exposed chimney is the only part of your house where English ivy won't cause trouble. But if you like to build roaring log fires, you should omit a clinging vine entirely, attach an aluminum trellis, and get a Deciduous Vine that can climb it (see below).

There's one decided plus to growing English ivy on a tree, however—it discourages squirrels. Eventually its foliage juts out about six inches, making an effective barrier to any small mammal trying to navigate the trunk. Since *Hedera helix* tends to grow straight up a tree, intervening avenues of bare bark will remain for a few years. But once they close in, the average squirrel will stay out of the tree unless he can reach it from the branches of ones nearby. So if you want *H. helix* to grow up only one tree, choose a hickory or an oak.

This species has been very extensively hybridized. Because individual plants produce sports—sudden genetic mutations—at a very high rate, hundreds of slightly different cultivars are available. I'd avoid the variegated ones from the start; an engulfing mass of variegated foliage gives an unsettled, noisy look. My preference leans to the so-called "primitive" ivies, whose leaves are generally slimmer than usual for the species: *caenwoodiana, helvetica, pedata* (bird's-foot), *sagittifolia* (arrowhead-leafed), *triloba* (three-lobed). Even on a single plant, the width and shape of individual leaves will vary significantly, but this is true of all *Hederas:* the first leaves on a vine are often narrower and smaller than those produced later. On the other hand, if a stem starts growing quickly, it will often sprout widely spaced leaves noticeably narrower than those below.

Before sending them up a high trunk, however, you should understand the reason why most English ivies don't bloom.

For years, the front entrance of my father's house was swathed with a woody, slow-growing, most attractive evergreen vine. Its wide pointed oval leaves were so dark they appeared black, borne on stubby contorted twigs that branched out into the air. If my father hadn't secured its main branches to the wall with toggle bolts, the whole plant would have toppled under its own weight.

It remained pretty much at ten feet tall; moreover, it bloomed. For most of June, it bore green flowerheads about the size of a halved golfball. Their slightly bitter, syrupy scent attracted hundreds of flies, honeybees, yellowjackets, and paper wasps. Truly enormous cicada killers, their striped abdomens an inch long, hovered about and preyed on bumblebees. During those few weeks of bloom, using the front door meant running the gauntlet of a motley hive. Later in autumn, plump black berries ripened and persisted through the winter.

I had always hoped that this vine would seed itself. But in the fertile soil beneath it, all I could ever find were ordinary English ivy seedlings. For years I simply just assumed that these young *H. helixes* had been dropped by the birds roosting in the larger vine. But these seedlings *were* the larger vine's offspring! Like a butterfly, *H. helix* exists in both adult and juvenile form. The slow-growing oval-leafed vines are the sexually mature adults, of which the familiar English ivy is the prepubescent stage. But why does this dramatic transformation usually go unnoticed? Why do we cultivate the caterpillar and ignore the butterfly? For one thing, a great many juvenile *Hederas* are made to creep on the ground, where they have no opportunity to climb. Unless the juvenile vine has gotten up and feels confident of getting unobstructed sun, it does not pass go and collect its adult growth habit.

On the tree I advise you to plant it on, English ivy will take at least ten years before the big switch. Meanwhile, it's absurdly easy to keep it from getting tall enough. Just cut the stems off at eye level every two years or so. (Do this in very early spring so that you can enjoy your ivy's lushness throughout the late winter months.) My eye-level suggestion is for maximum convenience. Naturally you can climb a ladder and prune higher. But don't go any lower: cutting English ivy back too drastically will weaken it, and it'll take longer to get back up. But be sure to clip *all* stems, as if you'd drawn a knife blade straight around the trunk. If you prune only a few, you'll find that invariably they cross under stems that you *haven't* pruned— pull loose dead stems, and you'll pry loose the live ones.

Then grab hold of the lower edge of the cut stems, and start peeling up. Since you are pulling the ivy from its thickest, stickiest side, it should strip off easily, baring the bark surface. But since the ivy's lower portions remain undisturbed, they will sprout new leaders, and in not much more than a year, the upper stretch of the trunk will be green again. This technique also keeps English ivy from shinnying out along a tree's lower branches—never a pleasant sight.

On the other hand, you may *want* mature English ivy. It does attract stinging insects, but it never suffers winter damage and it limits its yearly growth to a few inches of stiff horizontal stems that are easily pruned from below. Happily, you don't have to plant juvenile ivy and wait for it to grow up. Mature *H. helix* cuttings will root without reverting to juvenile form. (They should be rooted in sand like any hardwood cutting, not put in water like "young" ivy.) Such cuttings can be trained into what's called "tree ivy"—a more or less freestanding shrub.

English ivy is the only dependably *evergreen* vine for general use.

However, you can also dress up an uninteresting surface with vines that drops their leaves during the winter, providing some seasonal variety.

Parthenocissus is a splendid genus with two common and versatile species. *P. quinquefolia* ("five-leafed") is the widespread Virginia creeper or woodbine; *P. tricuspidata* ("three-cusped") is the venerable Boston ivy.

Each has the same distinctive way of climbing: it sends out tiny branched tendrils that, when they contact a solid surface, widen to form small structures much like the footpads of a tree toad—and serving the same purpose. Interestingly, the very new growth of both plants always hangs *down* from the tip of the vine and only later curves back up to meet its supporting surface, exactly like a roll of wallpaper being applied from the bottom up.

Since the tendrils stick to what they touch, these vines can climb anything that English ivy can. But because the tendrils appear only at intervals, these vines are more loosely attached to their surface. The tendrils eventually become stiff and dry, so that should the need arise, pulling a *Parthenocissus* off its surface is very quick work. The old, dry tendrils break off easily, leaving their "pads" still attached to the original support.

Virginia creeper is the perfect vine for heavy duty and quick covering. The compound leaf is usually divided into five lobes. Large vines' leaves often approach dinner-plate size, and are showy and conspicuous even at a distance. With nothing to grab hold of, the plant will run pleasantly amuck, eventually forming a high, loose groundcover. If given anything at all to climb on, it will do so swiftly —up to several yards each year. This is the vine you often see in rural areas, running up tree trunks, out along one of the lower limbs, and hanging down again in long garlands.

Boston ivy is far more genteel. While V.C. goes straight up, B.I. will climb for two or three feet and then level off, creeping horizontally *across* its supporting surface. (This makes it ideal for low stone walls you may want to camouflage.) B.I.'s leaves are *usually* three-lobed, but highly variable. Leaves at the bottom of a vine are often wholly compound, like those of a box elder. But toward the top, the three lobes often coalesce to form an undivided single leaf strongly resembling a red maple's. B.I. leaves tend to dovetail under one another like the scales of a fish.

In general, V.C. turns a bright yellow in fall, while B.I. ranges through reds and pinks. But individual plants sometimes display no fall color at all, or different colors from year to year. B.I. regularly retains its leaves for several weeks after V.C. has already gone bald. But neither is exactly invisible during the winter. Boston ivy displays blue berries when its leaves fall. On a snowy morning, the leafless stems form an intricate network that catches and holds remarkably fragile ridges of snow. The sight is fleeting, but hard to forget.

One thing a young Boston ivy cannot tolerate is full shade. Unless a young vine gets a few hours of direct sunlight, it wanders about in a forlorn daze, bypassing obvious upward pathways that a V.C. could detect from three feet away. Eventually, a V.C. will always outrun and smother Boston ivy. But by putting both vines to work on the same tree, you can judge their respective merits for several years before deciding in favor of one or the other.

B.I. and V.C. are both sold in many garden outlets, but their seedlings often abound along roadsides and vacant lots. If you're looking for V.C., make sure there are *five* leaflets, however! Poison ivy leaflets somewhat resemble Virginia creeper's, except that invariably the poisonous leaflets look oily (not dry, like Virginia creeper's) and its leaflets come in threes.

But so do Boston ivy's! The only *sure* way to tell B.I. apart from poison ivy is to examine all the leaflets. *All* of poison ivy's leaves will be fully compound. A young B.I. will have at least a few resembling the undivided leaf of a maple or grapevine. (If you're still in any doubt, however, it's far safer to purchase your plants from a nursery.)

Both *Parthenocissi* are easy to transplant when young. Scratch away at the spot where the vine enters the soil and you'll find that the trunk begins to widen just under the surface. This swollen root-stock goes down about three inches, then tapers again into a fairly short taproot. Get as much of the root system as you can. As long as the main rootstock is intact, the vine will survive.

Before growing any vine up a tree trunk, determine the quality of the soil at the tree's base. A tree may seem to enter the ground like a telephone pole, but if its roots splay out just below ground level, the surrounding soil may be actually quite shallow and dry. It's best to plant the vine's roots a foot or more away, where they'll have enough room to spread. Obviously a vine planted at any distance from the trunk will have to be guided toward the bark, but once it makes contact, it will reward you with untroubled growth.

Boston ivy's only drawback is that the long, thin stems often die back in winter. As a result, entire sections of the vine will unexpectedly fail to bud the following spring. You should remove them promptly. Left alone, a dead stalk eventually comes loose—but usually detaches the living stems that have grappled themselves to it in the meantime Because both B I and V C. sprout adhesive tendrils on *new* growth only, a stem that pulls loose will never reattach itself. Better to chop it off right above the spot where it has lost its support and let new growth start over.

Flowering Vines for Poles or Dead Trees

I know an actor whose heart-rotten apple tree failed him during a hurricane. He sawed off the smaller branches for firewood, leaving the tree's torso where it fell, and then let an adjacent honeysuckle overrun it. On Fire Island, summer residents whose Japanese black pines die often send a Virginia creeper aloft to crawl around in the bare branches. The result in either case is an untamed snarl. But if you use a neat, trim dead *sapling* instead, you'll get a neat, trim vine. This is the secret of a truly stunning flowering "tree."

My own choice for the all-round best flowering vine would be *Campsis radicans* (trumpet creeper, trumpet vine) Extremely hardy, it survives frigid winters and has attractive compound-leafed foliage that's darker and glossier than wisteria's. *Campsis* grows slowly, but its lovely trumpetlike flowers of warm orange-red appear continuously throughout the summer

C. radicans likes full sun, as do all vines and climbs like English ivy, so you must secure it to its supporting surface for a year or two so as to give the stem rootlets a chance to develop. If you can't give it a slim dead tree trunk, the best alternative is a twelve-foot pole of metal or cedar, planted in a sunny corner of the lawn. (Edge its base with brick, of course, to avoid mowing trouble.)

Still, I must admit that wisteria gives faster results—and certainly its seedlings are more widely available.

In my yard, I have a young fifteen-foot tulip tree I don't want to grow any larger. Pollarding a tulip tree is not practical, of course, because of its vigorous growth and huge leaves. But considering this tree against its backdrop of dark arborvitae, I realized that something delicate and light green would look good in its stead. Then I saw a positively ancient wisteria in White Plains, New York (now chopped down) that had enormous baroque coils like that of a python and towered a good thirty feet in the air. Whatever tree once supported it had decayed years before. So as an experiment I dug up a seedling wisteria and planted it at the foot of the tulip tree. I then rewound its tendrils up the trunk. (Older tendrils of wisteria become woody and set in their ways, but while still flexible, they'll readapt to the pressure of a new support.)

This wisteria is now well on its way to becoming spectacular. I figure the tulip tree has only a few more years to go before the vine overgrows it completely, whereupon I can simply girdle the tree's bark at ground level and let the wisteria inherit its dead branches. Result—an automatic "trellis" that will eventually decay, but not before the wisteria has grown a strong and tightly coiled trunk that will be self-supporting.

If you have pachysandra underneath to catch its litter *and* enough room so that the tendrils don't latch on to other shrubs, a "treed" wisteria (as opposed to a wisteria tree) can be fairly attractive. Try to obtain the *floribunda* (Japanese) species. It grows more slowly and to a lower height than the more common *chinensis*. Each *floribunda* leaf has more and smaller leaflets as well, giving the vine a more refined and delicate appearance. But the more unruly *Wisteria chinensis* will do, as long as you have seedlings on hand.

Flowering "Deciduous Vines" for an Open Trellis

These vines' entire stems usually die back in winter, often right to the ground. The result is a brittle, ropy tangle that has to be cleared out every spring. But on the other hand, all species in this group bear spectacular flowers. They're worth growing if you can provide a special trellis all their own to keep them looking neat.

Because these vines die back, any trellis they grow on should be easy to clean up and refurbish—annually, if need be. But since their stems will never grow thick enough to be self-supporting, the trellis will have to support them *permanently*. The trick, then, is to make a trellis sturdy without resorting to those closed spaces that make painting and disentangling that much harder.

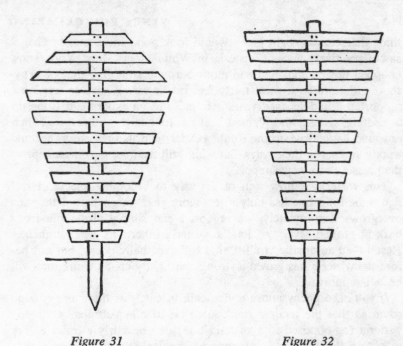

Figure 31   Figure 32

Figures 31 and 32 are variations on my basic kite design that you can adapt to your own preferences. This trellis can be built in any proportion or size, limited only by how far the vine it supports can grow by midsummer. The central feature is a stout $2'' \times 4''$ cedar or redwood beam, sharpened at the bottom so that it can be sunk in the ground. The matched rows of holes are drilled through it (see Figure 33), admitting screws which will hold the slats. Note that slats toward the bottom should be shorter, so that they adapt to the vine's eventual shape. (Since the trellis is tapered, individual slats will look more elegant if their cut ends are angled accordingly.) Individual slats that peel or decay can be removed easily. But the heftiness of the central beam means that those slats can be relatively flimsy, while still providing enough support for the vine.

This entire assembly can be cut and finished during the winter. Then in spring, the beam is set in a sunny, protected location with good drainage. Beside it, dig out a cylindrical pit of soil about eighteen inches deep by eighteen inches wide. Fill with good raw leafmold

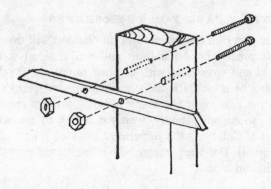

Figure 33

and grass clippings, heavily mixed with sand. (For clematis, add a good amount of crushed limestone.) Then plant any of the following vines so that its crown and the soil surface inside the pit both remain at *least* three inches below the surrounding ground level. This depression makes it much easier to water in summer, when these vines need good moisture. In winter, filling the depression with a mulch of heavy bark chips or straw will protect the roots from frost, assuring the vine a much healthier start the next spring. (As soon as the danger of frost is gone, strip the mulch away or you'll risk rotting the new growth.)

Slats can be added one at a time as the vine climbs them, or all at once. The height of the beam and total number of slats is up to you, but don't expect any seedling vine to scale a twelve-foot trellis in one season.

Aristolochia durior (Dutchman's-pipe) has exotic speckled flowers shaped like a squashed-down pitcher plant. They are not terribly conspicuous, however. The real show comes from the enormous heart-shaped leaves of medium dark green that cover their support with a neat and even upholstery of foliage. Often grown on front porches during the nineteenth century, Dutchman's-pipe is also a good selection for wire-fence use (see below), if the location isn't excessively exposed.

Clematis is a large genus whose species have been hybridized into hundreds of different strains. Most flowers have enormous brightly colored sepals, usually in groups of four or eight, and are produced for the better part of the summer. But no clematis will do well unless you meet its precise needs: a deep and well-drained soil enriched with leafmold and sweetened with crushed limestone, good sun, and roots kept cool by mulch. Clematis is rewarding but takes some years before it shows real vigor. In many hybrids, flowers appear on old growth only, so before pruning, wait for spring to see what's alive and what's not. Enlarging the uppermost slats of your trellis so that they form broad T-shaped wings will allow extra growth and, of course, additional bloom.

Convolvulus (morning glory) is an annual, but no perennial vine can match it for sheer majesty of bloom. Start seeds indoors in pots about April, so that they can be moved outdoors in May. Provide a high trellis. "Heavenly Blue" is the usual all-blue hybrid, which I prefer over the all-white "Pearly Gates" and other red strains.

Passiflora (passionflower) is sold mainly on the strength of its large and complex flowers, which allegedly recall the Crucifixion but in fact look simply rather decadent. Each combines a strange horn-shaped anther, tendrils, multiple thin petals, and a suitable purple cast. The genus comprises twenty-odd species, most of which are tropical and thus not hardy for most climates. (Avoid any passionflowers advertised for indoor growing. A vine is messy in a pot and downright awkward once you add the necessary trellis.) However, new *Passiflora incarnata* hybrids are being developed for nothern gardens, and some specimens are now reported to survive the winter in sheltered locations as far north as Missouri and mid-Ohio.

If you don't want to take chances, grow *Passiflora* in a large plastic pot sunk in the earth beneath your trellis. When the first frost hits, cut back all stems. Lift the pot, and so you don't have to water it too often while dormant, encase in a plastic bag. Then store in a very cool garage or attic. Add water once or twice a month if the soil seems dry. Once the frost danger is past, bring the pot out again and sink it in its former locale.

Passiflora is a rampant grower, and new growth will keep coming if you fertilize heavily. (For a really bizarre touch, hang the open trellis with some Spanish moss.) The short-stemmed flowers are quite interesting if floated in snifters or fingerbowls, and make a corsage that definitely gets comment.

Vines to Cover Fences

Vines with modified roots or adhesive tendrils find it hard to spread across gaps, so unless your pickets or slats are very close together, the result can be disappointing. Training vine along *metal* fences is even trickier. Uninsulated metal heats up in summer sun, and new growth is often withered before it can grab hold. Try to train the vine straight for the top so that it begins shading itself as soon as possible. You can also plant a fast-growing tulip tree or Norway to provide noon shade until the vine reaches the top of the fence; then the tree can be cut down.

I'd prefer small-stemmed vines to types like wisteria that grow so thickly that they strangle themselves in the metal. (Wisteria won't mind its bondage, but a Laocoön group of trunks trying to swallow metal alive is not a neat or pleasant sight.) Silver lace vine and clematis, often touted for metal fences, are such sun-lovers that they soon shade their own lower branches, causing large gaps of open view at the fence's base. Methodical Boston and English ivy are most likely to cover evenly from top to bottom. But if you have a really *high* chain fence, you can have some fun with the wild grapes, perhaps America's most neglected native plants.

Vitis riparia and *V. vulpina* are still widespread throughout the East. Usually they overgrow brush and small trees along meadows and roadsides, but I once came upon a most amazing specimen in an Adirondack hemlock forest. Its trunk—thich as my arm, shaggy with tufts of reddish bark—was apparently hanging in midair. Its foliage was lost in the crown of a hemlock whose trunk rose for twenty feet before the first side branch. The forest was now far too dark to support any but shade-loving plants, and *Vitis* is a sun-lover. Therefore, while these hemlocks were still saplings, this one must have germinated, clambered aboard its present host, and grown up with it. Despite its girth, this grapevine was still flexible, so that after a hard shove, it swayed back and forth for a minute or so.

All grapevines grow basically like Virginia creeper, climbing with the aid of auxiliary tendrils. But unlike *Parthenocissus,* grape tendrils do not end in holdfasts. They simply twine around anything they touch—twigs, the vine's own stem, each other. (Eventually these tendrils dry out, becoming hard and stiff and able to support the vine for a good many years.) Since these tendrils must *encircle* in order to cling, a grapevine cannot tackle the bark of trees. Instead, it casts around for a low-hanging branch, gets a grip, and then climbs up the host's smallest outer twigs. But because a grapevine grows only one layer thick, the tree is usually not smothered as it would be if penetrated by honeysuckle. A wild grape bears neat, dwarfish clusters of steely blue fruit, and its massive maple-like foliage turns gold in autumn.

It's easy to find seedlings twining through thickets and along roadsides. Even if it isn't a species grape, it may be an escaped hybrid or the even more desirable Manchurian *V amurensis, V. coignetiae* (Japanese glory vine), or, in the South, the delicious scuppernong. And a chain-link fence's wire is just the right size for tendrils to latch on to. Once the roots are established, stems will cover a fence with rewarding speed. Tendrils that die in hot summer sun will often continue to support the vine nonetheless. Best of all, any eventual grapes are low enough for easy picking. But prune back any nearby trees and shrubs so that they're safely out of reach of inquisitive tendrils.

9

PACHYSANDRA,
THE ULTIMATE GROUNDCOVER

In the broadest and most practical sense, a *groundcover* is something that covers the ground, allowing no other species breathing room. Nurseries offer a wide range of "groundcovers," from vigorous alpines to low-growing trees and shrubs. But most groundcovers don't, for various reasons.

You can divide all groundcovers (and their shortcomings) into four basic groups, according to their manner of spreading. Species not dependably evergreen are noted with a "D" for deciduous:

1. Woody, or branched groundcovers (dwarf barberries, D; cotoneaster, D; all prostrate junipers): These are basically bushes, flat shrubs or trees. Low-growing or prostrate branches arise from a single rootsystem, rarely if ever forming new plants. Their twigs spread out in a wide fan—not only to capture sun, but to discourage competition. But such infighting exists even among the branches of a single plant: when they overshadow one another, the lower ones begin to drop their foliage and die out. I have nothing against junipers or cotoneasters planted as individuals, but they don't look their best when miscast as part of a mob.

Of course, yearly pruning will keep these plants democratic and at a smooth, even contour. But there are worse problems ahead. For one thing, dead leaves falling on such thick foliage have trouble drifting down through to the soil, where they could break down and do some good. Instead, they are held aloft and have to be removed by hand. As a result, the soil suffers: I once dug into a bed of juniper twenty years old, and the shovel came up with a lump of unregenerate clay. Most rainfall is broken by the bushy foliage, but there are always a couple of gaps where a heavy downpour can make its way to unprotected soil. On a fairly steep bank, erosion needs only a small foothold. Soon roots wash loose, branches die back, and the entire "groundcover" starts going downhill—literally.

And any groundcover that leaves the ground surface bare, with tempting sunlight only inches above, can't restrain a fast-growing weed that doesn't mind sinking its taproot in poor soil. Until your bed attains a truly *solid* six inches of foliage, with no gaps, you'll have weeds. Not just dandelions, either, but hefty mullein, burdock, ragweed, and vigorous seedling trees.

2. Vines or vine-like groundcovers (bearberry, euonymous, English ivy): These plants arise from a central root system, but trailing shoots remain relatively thin in diameter, branching every few inches. Shoots will often climb if given the chance; if left to trail, they will often develop new roots intermittently, sometimes producing new trunks.

Ivy—and any other trailing vine, for that matter—will crowd out weeds with a thick carpet of shoots. But once it establishes itself, up to four feet of new growth a year will cascade over other plantings, sidewalks, and driveways. Your only alternative to horticultural havoc is constant pruning to encourage lateral growth. But even if you have achieved a neat bed of these plants, their ambitious shoots often die back in drought or cold, leaving unsightly snarls. Secondary plants such as azalea are quickly climbed and smothered, and as with Group 1, raking is a yearly task. You simply can't depend on them for all-purpose, carefree, year-round service.

3. Truly creeping groundcovers (ajuga, D; arenaria, ground myrtle, D; hay-scented fern, D; certain violets, wild mint, D; lily of the valley, D; perwinkle [*Vinca minor*]; *Veronica repens*): This group sends out modified stems, either on or just below the soil surface, for the specific purpose of starting new plants. Unlike "beds" of

Groups 1 and 2 groundcovers (formed when a *single* plant extends itself), these species reproduce to form a colony. But most Group 3 groundcovers are deciduous. Worse, they often grow loosely, covering the ground more like a fishnet than a blanket and doing little to halt weeds or grass. Very low growers (like arenaria) actually encourage the germination of foreign seeds, and during the winter, are often smothered in wind-blown leaves.

Massed violets provide a dense weed-killing shade, but since violets grow taller as they age, it takes a single bed several years to attain a uniform, finished look—by which time the elder plants have literally shot their seed into nearby lawn and flowerbeds. Since the rhizomes grow right under the surface, violets are easily susceptible to rake damage—except when escaped to the lawn, where they assume the status of weeds.

I'm not saying that each of the above species doesn't have its rightful place. Even ivy as I explained in the last chapter, can be delightful in the proper spot. But *all* of Group 4 should be on your Kill List:

4. "Tidal Wave" Groundcovers usually spread as in Group 3, but much taller and more quickly. Crown vetch, a rampant relative of clover, grows in billowy mounds of deciduous stems that look good only in summer—and at a distance. *Cytisus* (Scots broom) has deep olive-green stems lined with acid-smelling yellow flowers, and spreads into shapeless, untamable masses. The worst of this group, *Aegopodium* (goutsweed), throws tall-stalked compound leaves from invasive underground rhizomes. It's almost impossible to eradicate, since the tiniest rhizome fragment soon leafs out and starts a new colony of its own

Any garden groundcover you ultimately select should free you of weeding, pruning, *and* raking. It should be at least six inches tall, enough to discourage germinating weeds, but short enough (under eight inches) to allow a wide selection of shrubs, bulbs, and perennials to grow up *through* it.

Ideally, it would reach its ultimate height in one season, presenting a trim and level appearance. It should be evergreen, of course, masking the earth both winter and summer. It should also flourish in sun *or* shade and grow thickly, with the leaves of one plant overlapping —but not competing—with the next. Lastly (and most importantly), its shoots should be springy and flexible enough so that they "swallow" dead leaves, even small twigs and branches, packing them down under its own foliage where they can decompose to form effortless compost, thus eliminating both raking and mulching.

Happily, such a plant already exists.

Pachysandra, a genus of the boxwood family, is better known by its Latin name than by its common name of spurge. *P. procumbens* (Appalachian spurge), a native American species found in the Southeastern states, is rather sparse—its sprigs appear here and there, several inches apart. Purple bursts of small flowers rise from the ground on independent stems. Preferring shade for the most part, it's a classy addition to any Wild Garden, but not thickly growing or hearty enough to serve as a groundcover.

The ideal species, hands down, is the better-known Japanese spurge, or *P. terminalis.* The species name refers to the way both new growth and flowers arise from the end (or terminal) of last year's growth. The glossy, toothed, dark green leaves are staggered in a loose rosette around a single stem never more than seven to eight inches tall.

Pulling on a terminal, you will find that the stem makes a right angle at ground level, and you are now drawing up a fairly stiff, greenish stalk that was lying flat on the ground. Other upright terminals have usually branched from this horizontal stem, and they will lift up too. Each green stem in turn arises from a whitish runner that travels just under the soil surface (often for a foot or more). Often the rear ends of these runners simply rot away into nothingness—a condition that doesn't seem to bother the new terminals growing lustily from the other end. In a pachysandra bed, these runners branch and interweave to such a degree that they form a tight mat just below the soil surface, two to three inches deep.

Despite their rootlike appearance, however, these runners are merely stems that haven't bothered to develop chlorophyll. Pachysandra's true roots emerge from the white runners and (less plentifully) from the aboveground stems. They are fairly thick, blunt, and quite similar to the roots that a cutting of ivy or pussy willow develops when placed in water. Any one runner's roots seem fairly spindly and ineffectual for a plant that can win out against grass and weeds, but a *single* pachysandra terminal has no intentions of going it alone. Each root system is adapted precisely to *avoid* competition, since the moisture and protection it needs will all be provided by nearby members of the same colony. Most garden books repeat the misconception that pachysandra does best in shade. Actually, its leaves prefer full sun. Only its *roots* need shade, but once a colony is established, shade is automatically provided by the thickly growing terminals.

P. terminalis reproduces by three separate means. In the spring, about when the early daffodils are in bloom, an occasional bud (formed above the leaves the previous autumn) opens into a turret of tiny white flowers. Each resembles the stylized squash blossoms on Navajo jewelry, but they are inconspicuous at best—especially since only one of a dozen or so terminals sets a flower bud in any given season. On the other hand, the seeds—if any—drop directly under the foliage of the parent terminal, so you won't find pachysandra seeding itself into unforeseen spots.

Apparently pachysandra practices sexual reproduction only to keep its hand in, since it relies mainly on asexual methods. Each spring, a horizontal pachysandra stem usually produces new buds, each of which will produce a new terminal that same season. Each "old" terminal keeps putting out new growth, of course. But unlike a branched groundcover or a vine, the pachysandra stem does not widen or strengthen to support the weight of this new foliage. So the whole terminal simply flops over to one side. The newly formed terminals bend upward, seeking the light, and wind up at more or less the exact height of those produced the year before. As a result, pachysandra forms one of the most dependably flat beds in existence. There's *never* any need to prune.

After the old stems slump from vertical to horizontal, the old leaves drop off, quietly and invisibly. What was once a terminal becomes a horizontal stem, ready to root and bud to form new terminals.

But its most rapid spreading action takes place just under the soil —from those long white runners whose tips resemble asparagus in miniature. Each is the bud of a new terminal, carried along as the runner glides along at a depth more or less determined by the degree of moisture at the surface. If conditions are hot and dry, individual runners dive to a depth of four inches or more. In a humid, heavily established bed, they may even skim along the soil surface, branching and dividing as they go.

Depending on obstacles in their path, available light above, or sheer whim, they suddenly arch upward. As each one breaks the surface, its sharp bud enlarges, and the growing stem begins to develop the scale-like vestigial leaves that remain on adult terminals. The larger leaves turn from a pale matte green to a waxy chartreuse. In about a month, they enlarge further; their color deepens. The new growth of established terminals settles down beside them, and by early summer the entire surface of the pachysandra bed is wholly renewed.

Although terminals are crowded together, pachysandra still has plenty of empty space underneath its leaves and stems into which dead autumn leaves can collapse. And to help dead leaves disappear even quicker, pachysandra's response to cold makes its terminals function like trap doors.

In late fall, a friend of mine transplanted a nursery-grown rhododendron that appeared to be in good health. But on the morning of the first hard freeze, he saw its leaves were wilted, curled, and apparently lifeless. In disgust, he yanked the plant up (with a good quantity of soil still adhering to its roots) and tossed it on the compost heap. When spring came, he was amazed to find that its leaves were again lush and erect and its buds swollen with imminent bloom.

Any plant that keeps its foliage over the winter—like rhododendron—continues to release moisture through its leaves. But when temperatures drop below 32° F, roots are unable to draw moisture from the frozen soil. And because colder air has a lower moisture content—is basically "drier" even at the same relative humidity—broadleaf evergreens risk losing more water than their roots can replace. Anything that reduces the leaves' surface area will retard evaporation—which is why plants *should* wilt when deprived of root moisture: a leaf that droops from its stem, curling in upon itself, insulates its inner surface from the drying air. Pachysandra and rhododendron have evolved a similar reaction in response to cold. Below 32°, their leaves take on the shape of death. But if the temperature climbs above freezing again, their foliage will perk up within the hour.

This frost-proofing response also enhances pachysandra's value in autumn. Its terminals can be effectively buried under fallen autumn leaves. But at the first frost, pachysandra's own leaves collapse downward. Dead leaves settle among the stems, which remain erect. Then when warmth returns, pachysandra's leaves ease up again, pushing the fallen ones aside. After a few weeks of nighttime freezes and daytime thaws, pachysandra's flexing action will have consigned most dead leaves beneath the terminals and out of sight. Any that remain visible until spring are guaranteed to be submerged in the new growth. (An established colony can also swallow cigar butts, small twigs, faded flowers, wine corks, and other small bits of organic refuse.)

Pachysandra's runners are relatively passive and shallow, easily pushed aside. This means that anything you transplant into a pachysandra bed will usually thrive—*provided* its main leaves sprout at least eight inches above the ground, above the level of the average pachysandra terminal. The colony will keep its roots comfortably shaded and mulched with decaying leaves.

In fact, soil conditions inside a pachysandra bed are usually much better than outside. Trapped dead leaves provide humus in very short order, and the probing underground runners loosen up the soil and open channels for oxygen and bacteria. (In the next chapter I'll describe the wide variety of perennials—including regular garden favorites—that can be introduced into a pachysandra bed with no squabbles. In winter, they usually die to the ground, and pachysandra absorbs their dry stalks as easily as it does autumn leaves.)

Nor is there much of a weeding problem with pachysandra. If you want another plant to grow among the terminals, you must introduce it only *after* it's achieved adult size. Any seed falling into a pachysandra bed choked with dead leaves has a hard time sifting down to the soil. Assuming it does germinate, it has an even harder time getting back up again to reach the light. The few seeds that do make it seldom get a good grip in the spongy soil below and can easily be uprooted.

But any *transplanted* adult has roots and stems long enough to pierce through. In the spring, most perennials send up new shoots before pachysandra begins its own seasonal growth, thus eliminating interference at this crucial stage of the growing season. And if their roots spread at or beneath the level of the pachysandra's runners— that is, anywhere from three inches on down—they will have no competition at all.

Every plant has its disadvantages of course, and even pachysandra has a few. In dry or windy spots, its leaves may turn brown at the edges, or it may simply fail to cover. Moreover, the runners from an established colony are quite vigorous, often arising several feet from the edge of the bed. Stray runners can unerringly find the crack between flagstones. When all else fails, they will bore their way up through a solid asphalt driveway. Many garden favorites are simply too low-growing to compete with pachysandra, even in full sun. Violets will survive, but you'll see only outsized leaves (expanded to trap the light) while the flowers remain below, in permanent shade. Wildflowers like trout lily, low perennials like ajuga and *Vinca minor,* and small-growing bulbs like Star of Holland and the more dwarf daffodils should all be grown in the Low Garden, described later.

But there is simply no other plant that thrives so well when left utterly alone: pachysandra may share a few drawbacks with other groundcover species, but its virtues are unique. Pachysandra is now being grown successfully as far south as Columbia, South Carolina, and could probably be grown straight down through northern Florida if its moisture requirements were met. (In the South, I would give it full shade, which is equal to part shade in New England.)

How, then, should you go about planting it? First, decide where you *need* a groundcover most. Consider your steep slopes, isolated spots, the inconvenient corners that make for difficult weeding or mowing, the spotty foundation planting that needs a unifying groundcover—in short, start with places you *already* feel tempted to neglect. Surveying the no-grass spots mentioned in Chapter 3 should give you a good number of likely sites. But don't make the mistake of trying to convert them all at once. Short of an enormous investment, there's no way to buy enough pachysandra to fill a wide bed within one season. So to keep things looking neat during the transition, remove only a narrow strip of grass and plant is as solidly with pachysandra as you can—forming one long, narrow bed that can be widened in succeeding years. This way, it's far easier to weed and tend what will become the "back" part of your bed, and before enlarging it, you can wait until it's moderately under control.

Pachysandra is almost universally available—but in various forms and at various prices. Most expensive of all is the variegated variety of *terminalis* (which also arises spontaneously in many pure-green beds). In catalogs, at least, it looks quite tempting: each leaf is edged in creamy white, but that white edging means that each leaf has less green chlorophyll. And so, variegated pachysandra is more sluggish than the regular green, taking more initial coddling and *much* longer to form beds. This means, too, that it's seldom available in any quantity, at least not at reasonable prices.

Already-established flats of regular green *P. t.* are usually available at nurseries or garden shops. They are also fairly expensive: a single wooden flat of two square feet costs at least $4.95. This is still cheaper than the individual rooted terminals offered in pots and by mail order (which plants also take longer to establish themselves). But since you'll probably want an absolute minimum of fifty square feet of pachysandra, buying all of it at once can easily exhaust your gardening budget.

Yet *P. terminalis* is often available for nothing. You may already have it growing on your property—and an established bed can be raided repeatedly with no ill effects. (As long as the hole is surrounded on all sides by at least another foot of terminals, the gap will fill in within a year, courtesy of new runners.) Your neighbors may see it (rightly) as a welcome addition under foundation planting but (wrongly) as a Green Menace anywhere else, and so toss it out regularly along with the weeds. I've obtained vast amounts of it from people who were extending a porch or planting a new shrub where pachysandra stood in their way.

As long as you have to wait for pachysandra to fill in, however, I'd strongly recommend you invest in the 'Green Carpet' variety of *terminalis*. It's generally available only by mail and more costly than the usual—but more than worth it. 'Green Carpet' has terminals only five inches tall, with smaller, better proportioned leaves of a deeper, glossier green. The ultimate effect is far neater, and makes a far more acceptable foundation for the perennials described in the next chapter. It's only drawback is that its somewhat shallow bed won't absorb quantities of *large* dead leaves. Thus 'Green Carpet' is best underneath trees like black gum, Japanese maple, European mountain ash, and other small-leaved Second-Layer trees. The more sizable leaves of sugar maple, tulip tree, oaks, dogwoods, or cottonwood all need regular *terminalis* to swallow them up.

Pachysandra does spread quickly, but not until it's established proper conditions for itself. Thus if you want an immediate bed, with no visible gaps, place the terminals close together so that the roots are wholly shaded from the beginning. But you can save yourself an enormous amount of work and money by planting them farther apart and letting the runners fill in naturally—it just takes longer. So the following planting instructions are arranged according to how long you're willing to wait for "finished" results.

For the fastest possible bed, buy your pachysandra in flats and lay them in cheek by jowl. Since most flats are of wood that eventually rots, you might consider "planting" them flat and all. But eventually you'll want to introduce perennials—and the seasoned lumber used in gardening flats takes much longer to break down than does a fresh-pruned branch. So the best way is to decant the plants, but very gently; trying to keep them all in a group.

Dig a hole that's equally deep and square. (Use the empty flat as a perfect measuring device.) Then lift up the clump with a piece of cardboard underneath, if possible—the less soil falls from around the runners, the better. Fit it in place. Make sure that the surrounding earth is securely packed before dusting at least a half inch of fresh humus (or a good inch of mulch) directly atop the plants. Finally, water well. Virtually undisturbed roots, stimulated by new soil above and below, will enable the terminals to begin secondary buds immediately. By summer's end, you'll have a bed that looks as if it's been there for years.

But pachysandra can survive far rougher treatment with ease. Almost as effective is to dig it in clumps from an existing bed, along with the surrounding soil. Your trowel or shovel will sever what looks like a deadly number of stems and runners, but a circle of at least nine inches will preserve enough of them to establish the new clump. Digging deeply to about five inches helps the whole clump hold together better (but not much) and also gathers a few extra roots and runners. Don't try for a plug of more than a foot in diameter, however, or the whole thing will crumble apart under its own weight.

Lay the clumps into appropriately sized holes or trenches. Tuck any stray runners in along the sides, and sift the soil over and around them. If it's spring or autumn and the surrounding soil is fairly cool and moist to the touch, you can even forgo watering as long as you pack in the soil tightly enough. Final results depend on how many original roots were preserved per terminal, but the new bed should come back almost as quickly as one planted from flats. (Nurseries often stock flats that have been languishing, with indifferent care, for more than a single summer.)

Remember, though, that as long as you procure pachysandra in clumps to ensure shade for the roots, those clumps themselves don't have to be crammed together. To cover up to twice the area with the same amount of pachysandra, plant rectangular clumps a foot apart. They will fill in the gaps in two years' time. You can leave even more space between clumps and any edging or wall: underground runners surface when faced with an obstacle, and fill in a confined space far more quickly. If you want to have the final bed studded with trees or perennials, plant them *now* in the gaps, so that they can get something of a head start before the pachysandra moves in around their roots.

In the meantime, eliminate in-between weeding problems with mulch, spare flagstones, grass clippings, simply by letting autumn leaves lie, or with strawberry plants. Any regular strawberry bed produces a host of runners that need pruning to increase fruit production of the parent plant. Rather than throw them away, it's more thrifty to tuck small, new plants into gaps between pachysandra. Within a year or two the pachysandra bed will have closed in on the strawberry plants that, being weak-rooted, are easy to pull out. Or, the now fully grown strawberries can be transplanted to a vegetable garden.

To carpet a steep slope, plant the pachysandra in horizontal rows *across* the angle of the slope—and thus at right angles to the gulleys of erosion. Mass your pachysandra toward the top of the slope, because elongating stems will rapidly sprawl downhill. As an added precaution, mulch the bare strips heavily with bark or wood chips to hold the soil in place until runners begin to fill in. Any soil that continues to erode will soon be trapped by a thicket of stems and runners before the runoff has traveled far enough to build up any momentum. Remember that any raised bank dries out quicker than level ground, and water accordingly. Give extra water toward the top: it'll seep downward from there.

To get pachysandra from an existing bed without leaving even temporary holes, uproot single terminals and as many of the attached runners as you can. But don't make the mistake of planting terminals individually. A house I pass on my way to work used that method four years ago, and the separate terminals are still sitting there like so many miniature beach umbrellas. With unprotected bare earth in between, each plantlet will more or less hang fire until a neighbor provides shade for its roots—a kind of Gaston-Alphonse exchange.

The secret is reassembling the plants into clumps again so that the terminals shade the roots. First, sort out the plants, untangling all stems and runners. *Ideally,* your separated plants should have at least a foot of root-producing stem or runner—the more the better. But don't discard any foliage-less runners; they will send up at least token terminals before fall.

Next, dig a hole about six inches wide and four deep. The actual dimensions aren't as important as making the hole's bottom as flat as possible.

Now take one of your single plants and straighten it out so that the roots and runners hang down from the terminals. Hold the stem(s) between thumb and forefinger of one hand, so that the terminals are pointing up and the runner(s) trail down across your palm. (If you have bare runners, count the final three inches—complete with bud —as a stem.)

With your free hand, gently bend each runner around in a circle, one by one, fitting it up in a loose circular knot so it stays put. Runners are very flexible, and gathering them together this way will make the whole assemblage easier to handle. Keep adding terminals, weaving the runners in and around each other, until you have at least six terminals in your grasp, and a loose, flattened coil of runners circling your palm. Then press the coil down *flat* against the bottom of your pre-dug hole. Cover it with dirt, holding the terminals out of the way with your other hand to keep them from being buried. Bend the terminals back over the hole so the runners can receive maximum shade from the beginning; and water.

All this may sound quite complex, but once you've tied and planted a few pachysandra "corsages," you'll get the hang of it. If you want to cut corners, trading a little extra waiting time for immediate transplanting convenience, dig a shallow trench or ditch about a foot long. Align a bundle of runners straight along its length, with terminals protruding at either end. Don't worry if the protruding terminals aren't exactly upright—they usually won't be, but will straighten up by themselves. Pachysandra is remarkably forgiving! But be sure to give unshaded roots an extra helping of mulch—a flat stone or brick will serve the same purpose and can always be removed later.

In hot weather, check newly planted pachysandra to see if it's wilting. A bucket of water will usually revive it completely, if given in time.

If all other sources of supply fail, pachysandra (including the elusive 'Green Carpet') can be rooted quite easily from cuttings. Simply clip the terminal with as much stem as you can, and insert in water—perhaps in a vase, since pachysandra makes a marvelously lush foliage accent by itself. This is also a fine way to salvage those rootless terminals that always break loose when pachysandra is pulled or dug. Moreover, it's a good way to increase your supply effortlessly over the winter months. A terminal plucked in November will be ready for planting in May—or when its roots are three inches long, whichever comes first.

The only problem is that a dormant terminal brought inside in winter will immediately produce new growth and drop its old leaves. But if kept in a sunny window during this transition period, the spindly and pale new growth will become lush and attractive. Once transplanted, such cuttings take a while to spread, but if you plant your bunches closely together, you should have a finished bed in from two to three years.

Pachysandra will always spread more quickly if you keep the roots moist and shaded. If the soil is compacted, clayish, dry, shallow, or subject to strong wind, even established pachysandra will wilt in summer and burn off in winter. In any case, the answer is mulch. Dump a three-inch layer of peatmoss, humus, leafmold, bark chips—anything that's organic and retards evaporation—directly among the terminals. If you want a clump to spread in a certain direction, place a *four*-inch mound to coax it. On a barren, rocky knoll, pachysandra may ultimately need up to eight inches of mulch (in effect, a new soil layer) before it begins to thrive. But this plant simply cannot be overmulched, and will work its way up even if completely buried—this spring, one of my newly planted clumps sprouted vigorously from under half a foot of dead leaves.

In short, where you want more pachysandra, provide more shade and moisture. But unfortunately this formula doesn't work in reverse. When established pachysandra is feeling its oats, it will voyage into even the driest soil. The runners seem to have a mind of their own and will seek out "ideal" moist conditions—often in nearby borders, lawns, or under walks and driveways.

If you need extra pachysandra, just cut off these runners at the point where they went out of bounds. Pull them backward, the way they came, and replant where you want them. Of course, if your bed is that healthy, you can transplant entire clumps from its edge to places where they can be of more service.

To limit pachysandra's growth, remember that its runners are fairly shallow. They can cruise just under the surface for considerable distances but can't dive to any extent. In sun *or* shade, a vertical barrier seven inches deep will stop all runners cold. I prefer corrugated aluminum edging, but don't believe the directions that say it can be hammered down into the soil. The result is a crumpled strip of metal that won't reach two inches deep. I excavate a trench eight inches deep, insert the strip, and replace the soil on either side so that the aluminum is held upright.

By this time, you've probably decided that pachysandra will be ideal under your foundation planting. It is, with two reservations: Anywhere south of Canada, homes made of wood are susceptible to termites. These insects, the size of a grain of rice, resemble ants but are white and lack the narrow "wasp" waist of an ant. Termites need dampness in which to build their nests, so planting pachysandra right up to your foundation creates a nice, moist environment with your floorbeams within striking distance. Dig the ditch I advised in Chapter 7, and *then* plant your pachysandra. It will grow high enough to camouflage the ditch, and you'll hardly know it's there. But the termites will.

A second problem arises if your home uses oil heat. The men who deliver fuel oil aren't always as neat as they could be when connecting the hose, and petroleum is particularly deadly to pachysandra— I've seen one bed, hit with spilled oil six years ago, that hasn't recovered to this day.

Prevention is best. Before the oil arrives, haul out your plastic shower curtain and cover all pachysandra on the route to your delivery pipe. If the deliveries are quite frequent, sheer traffic will damage the pachysandra even if the oil doesn't, so it may make sense to construct a pathway to provide easier access for the deliveryman. Be sure to use a dark material—slate, rounded black pebbles or crushed bluestone—on which oil spills won't show up as dramatically as they would on brick or porous concrete.

Pachysandra sometimes becomes infested with scale insects that, like pachysandra itself, prefer the shady, sheltered conditions of a mature bed. The female lays eggs under her shell, where they pass the winter. In spring, the young wander off, choose an unoccupied spot, and settle down, more or less like barnacles, to feed off the pachysandra's sap. The terminals may still appear quite healthy, but the stems and undersides of the leaves will be spotted with tiny oval bumps of a chalky gray color. The more mobile cottony cushion scales and mealy bugs will apppear as tufts of downy white at the juncture of leaf and stem.

An insecticide is difficult to apply effectively, since you must apply it *under* the leaves of each terminal. Consult your local garden shop for the most lethal (and legal) systemic. But pachysandra beds can survive for years despite a heavy infestation, so this is not a strict emergency unless other plants that are particularly susceptible to scale infestation (e.g., euonymous) are planted close by. (Happily, infected pachysandra will survive transplanting, but the scale insects usually don't.)

In spring, the tops of your pachysandra terminals may be leggy and uneven, spoiling the flat effect for which you planted them in the beginning. But by midsummer, once new growth has become weighty enough to bend the stem, uneven shoots will subside gracefully. Pachysandra also becomes uneven if the bed becomes choked with dead leaves or twigs that support mature terminals and keep them from falling over. You may want to remove the litter for fairly immediate leveling; otherwise, this condition will correct itself through normal decay.

Under the shade of a naturally low-growing shrub such as azalea, terminals can become snagged and supported by the shrub's intricate branches until finally they emerge through the crown of the plant. The easiest solution is to remove the lowest, pachysandra-supporting branches entirely. The elongated terminals, deprived of support, will literally fall back into line. But if you want the invaded plant to remain low, it's best to remove the pachysandra completely, isolating the plant in a wide area of Low Garden (see Chapter 11) that leaves room enough for its branches' future growth.

Pachysandra should be raked as little as possible. A rake's tines can damage many of the shallower runners and will certainly remove much of the mulch a colony needs for its best growth. However, there are places close by the house and under huge trees where an inordinate amount of dead leaves will pile up. Here, some raking is necessary. But first, if you agitate the top of the pachysandra terminals with the teeth of your rake, a surprising number of dead leaves will sink from view. Then, keeping your rake level with the very top of the terminals, you can remove only the *superfluous* dead leaves and not any that are already working their way down to invisibility.

If you find a weed poking through the terminals, take hold of the intruder and pull gently, then relax and give a second, steady pull. It should come up easily, root and all. A good bed of pachysandra keeps the underlying soil in a friable condition and encourages a weed to develop shallower—and more easily pullable—roots. If a weed's stems or leaves break off in your hand, it means that the pachysandra hasn't trapped enough mulch. But once you dig it out, the terminals will close over the gap.

Even before your transplanted pachysandra clumps are erect and healthy, the bed they form is ready to bloom with interplanted perennials—striking and permanent species that are as lush and safely forgettable as the pachysandra itself. The next chapter tells you just what species to use, and how.

10

PERENNIALS FOR PACHYSANDRA

Thalassa Cruso claims that extended beds of pachysandra are "boring." I doubt Ms. Cruso has ever seen pachysandra covering a steep bankside, its staggered terminals overlapping each other like the scales of a fish. But interplanting the groundcover with perennials is the simplest way to relieve monotony before it develops.

Admittedly, annuals—pansies, petunias, zinnias, and their ilk— have the advantage of blooming steadily all summmer. But not only are they doomed to death at the first frost, they also become extraordinarily weedy after about the first of August. This is due to their inbred survival strategy. Since an annual plant will not live out the winter, its only chance to avoid extinction is to produce as many flowers—and therefore, seeds—as possible. Its leaves needn't store up energy for next year's buds; its stems needn't widen to support next season's growth. So in midsummer, petunias often become semitrailing vines, dying out at the center where the first flowers appeared. In August, a zinnia is usually a few bright flowers atop a stalk of withering crud.

The worst example is the annual sunflower, which begins as a stately stalk with Jack-and-the-Beanstalk green leaves. But as soon as the radiant flower has been pollinated, the lower leaves begin dying back. The plant effectively commits suicide to force every bit of strength into the developing seeds. Long before they're ripe, the vast composite disk is already dry and unsightly, ravaged by sparrows and goldfinches if it hasn't already toppled after borers have hollowed the stem. Conscientious gardeners are happy to axe the entire eyesore long before frost.

Although it takes some effort to locate them in catalogs, there *are* perennials that bloom throughout the summer. And when past its bloom, a perennial is likely to remain attractive, simply because it "knows" it has many years of continued life.

What I call a "Pachysandra Garden" is basically an old-fashioned perennial border superimposed on a pachysandra bed—except that it avoids the mess of the traditional perennial garden, while enjoying far more lavish growth of plants whose roots are kept cool and moist all summer. I suggest perennials *only* because anything that grows up through pachysandra's thick stems and dense terminals must be capable of fairly strenuous competition. Any annual as delicate as a petunia just can't make it. Why carve unsightly holes in your groundcover year after year, only to sow the seeds of the scrofulous and doomed? A pachysandra bed interplanted with the right perennials not only *stays* planted, but improves each year with no further effort on your part.

The only errors that can sabotage a Pachysandra Garden are old-fashioned misconceptions of what a perennial garden should be:

1. *A massive display timed to go off all at once*

Horticulturally, the month of May is opening night, Homecoming, and Graduation Day all rolled into one. It's hard not to turn your head without glimpsing a flash of bright petals. However, this display is fleeting, and those tulip beds so often photographed for bulb catalogs usually are utterly barren for the rest of the summer. The trick, then, is finding plants that will bloom in other months too.

2. *Arbitrary all-season color schemes*

The so-called "moon gardens" of England contain nothing but white-flowering perennials. This sounded like a chic idea, so for five years I kept adding only white-flowering plants to a sunny, pachysandra-covered slope. I was always elated to obtain yet another *alba* variety, but always disappointed in the results. The plants did well but, even when in flower, never seemed to ignite the eye. Then, one night as I was leafing through a book of Impressionist reproductions, I realized that *contrasting* colors are what make a flower garden stand out. I'm now leaving the white-flowering kinds where they are, but introducing other colors.

Because perennials predictably bloom at different seasons, it would theoretically be possible to plant a garden whose major colors switched back and forth. Starting with yellow (narcissus), the garden could later switch to white (peony and shasta daisy), back to yellow again (potentilla daylily and black-eyed Susan), and on to white again in fall (chrysanthemum and white snakeroot). (In addition, a number of ornamental evergreens—several chamaecyparises, hinoki cypress, even yucca and heather—come in shocking yellow cultivars.) A proper selection should afford you a continuous display of flowers, highlighted now and again by briefly blooming species.

3. *Extensive specialization in any one or two varieties*

No matter how empty your garden, introducing large quantities of any single plant is always premature. I have this problem in my front yard, where I planted vast quantities of *P. terminalis*. Now that I find *terminalis* 'Green Carpet' vastly more satisfying, the regular *terminalis* is already in place. To establish any 'Green Carpet,' I will have to substitute it slowly over a period of years. You can seldom be sure how a plant will succeed until you've observed it for a year or more under its individual growing conditions. Buying only *one* daylily and watching to see if it prospers gives you time to diagnose other suitable sites and locate other more desirable hybrids.

The reason most gardens look barren is simple: there aren't enough plants. But there are several ways of increasing the amount of flowers per square foot:

1. *Rely on plants that spread and self-seed*

Dicentra exima (bleeding-heart) throws plenty of new seedlings, as do wild geranium and false snakeroot. Other plants like shasta daisy, phlox, daylilies, and tradescantia form ever-widening clumps that make it appear that you were far more generous to begin with.

2. *Stratify your plants above and below ground*

In Honduras, where my father went to pan for gold, the tropical rainforest grew so thickly that when a hurricane passed over, he noticed only rain, a roaring high in the trees, and a gentle breeze at ground level. But under such giant trees grow shade-loving trees of lower stature. Philodendrons, ferns, and other deep-shade-lovers carpet the forest floor. And for the most part, each layer of plants roots in a different layer of soil as well, and so don't compete with each other. In your garden, you can fit additional perennials under any tree or shrub if you "raise" it by high-pruning the lower branches. And a bulb like narcissus can be planted directly below a shallow-rooted perennial like Gaillardia. Result: the same site will bloom twice in succession.

3. *Consider individual growth habits*

It's not simply the plants you grow, but *the combinations in which you plant them* that determines their success and the beauty of your property as a whole. Throughout this book, I class plants not by genus but as the Boxing Commission does fighters—by weight and size. Some dwarf pines and maples are discussed as shrubs in Chapter 7, because that's how they *function* in a garden environment. Spring bulbs are discussed in three separate chapters, according to the height of their foliage.

I've found that virtually any plant will thrive in either a Pachysandra Garden (for perennials from eight inches up), a Low Garden (for anything *down* to three inches), or a Rockery (for anything under three inches). Ultimately, you should perceive any area of your property not as a "flowerbed" or "rock garden" or "hedge," but as a discrete environment reserved for plants of a given size limit. And by associating plants of similar height, you can eliminate a great deal of competition and intermittent weeding.

The simple rule of "tall plants toward the back" is meaningless if, for example, you want to plant a bank with different kinds of phlox. You'll be courting mayhem unless you know that *sublata* is a dense, low trailing plant; midsummer hybrids form tall upright clumps; and the wild spring-blooming *divaricata* spreads loosely and profusely, emerging every few inches. The various specimens would have to be protected from one another! For this reason, every plant in this and some later chapters is identified as one of the following:

SS: *Single-Stalk plants:* New foliage arises from the same spot, only growing taller year after year. If the plant spreads at all, it does so by producing another shoot *directly* next to the main one, so that the plant still appears to be a singleton. *Examples:* jack-in-the-pulpit, tiger lily, allium, crown imperial, and most deciduous trees.

CF: *Clump-Formers:* Plant spreads slowly, with new shoots directly adjacent to the old growth, so that after several years the plant has formed a thick, upright stand. *Examples:* daylily, bleeding-heart, midsummer phlox, Japanese iris, *Lythrum,* most hybrid chrysanthemums, most jonquils and narcissus, columbine and peony.

ODT: *One-Direction-Travelers:* Plant spreads by underground stems or rhizomes, but the new growth is primarily in one direction only (usually toward sunny or less crowded conditions). But old growth tends to die back, rather than rebud. Therefore, a given colony moves from year to year, and may actually wind up several yards from where you planted it. *Examples:* lily of the valley, mayapple, bloodroot, rattlesnake fern, Solomon's-seal.

LS: *Loose-Spreaders:* Old growth continues budding, so that plant advances in all directions. However, new growth arises only at intervals, so that unless the rootstock is contained (as by an edging sunk in the ground), the colony will appear sparse, rambling, and spotty. *Examples:* strawberry, sumac, northern beech fern, Canada mayflower, *Vinca minor.*

TS: *Thick-Spreaders:* Plants advance steadily and thickly in all directions, and should be contained if a groundcover is not desired. *Examples:* dwarf bamboo, pachysandra, most lawn grasses, hay-scented fern, arenaria, veronica, burstwort, most violets.

Obviously, mixing Thick-Spreading plants can be risky—and conversely, introducing a low Loose-Spreader can bind tall Single-Stalk plants together visually.

Virtually all perennials die back in winter. When spring arrives, you'll be faced with an expanse of scruffy pachysandra that hasn't perked up yet. The way to get the show going as fast as possible is with:

Spring-flowering Bulbs

While spring bulbs are perennial, not all are strictly carefree. Most tulips, for instance, need to be dug up yearly and replanted to maintain repeated flower production. It makes better sense to choose bulbs that will gladly increase on their own, multiplying your investment. Watch carefully what the mail-order catalogs say: the verbs to look for are "increases," "multiplies," and "spreads." "Ideal for naturalizing" means only that bulbs look okay when scattered at random.

The following bulbs are the real showpieces of a spring Pachysandra Garden, around which you'll want to arrange the later-flowering perennials. So plant the bulbs first. (Crocus, snowdrop, and other early favorites are too low for pachysandra. See Chapter 11.)

Narcissus (daffodil, jonquil; CF) has leaves that outlast the flowers and do not fade until July. But the foliage must go unmolested if the bulb is to photosynthesize enough nourishment for next spring's bloom. (Some gardeners braid the fading leaves to make them look more respectable.) In a Pachysandra Garden, however, the encircling terminals help support the leaves, making them look as if they belonged there; and when the foliage finally yellows and wilts, the terminals quickly swallow them up. While narcissi need to regrow their roots each autumn, they do so at a depth far below the roots of pachysandra.

Narcissi have been hybridized so extensively that a wide range of colors, shapes, and sizes are available. But not all are equally desirable. So-called "narcissus" hybrids that have multiple flowers per stem are often lanky and frail. For a Pachysandra Garden, look for strains that bear only one trumpet per stem. Another consideration is that most of the "giant" and even standard-size single-bloom narcissi are top-heavy. By the time your planting should be in full cry, spring weather, with its sudden gusts and heavy rains, will have sagged or toppled many flowers. Outsized foliage remains evident until late into the season, so my advice is to go for the smaller narcissi (which also increase more rapidly with less need of frequent dividing).

My particular favorite is *Narcissus* 'Peeping Tom', a *N. cyclamineus* hybrid. In March, just after the earliest crocuses are done, arise flowers of a clear butter yellow. They are never felled by wind or snow, often persisting through really lousy weather and staying fresh and erect until late April. 'Tom' is very widely available. While not a true dwarf as many catalogs claim, it is only half the size of the standard-size 'King Alfred' and other pure-yellow hybrids —making it especially useful for limited, narrow plantings where the smaller but perfectly proportioned flowers make any expanse seem larger by comparison. It arises about nine to twelve inches when most terminals are still matted down from winter, so that at least six inches of each plant is clearly visible.

Like all bulbs I recommend, 'Peeping Tom' multiplies—which is why you should never plant new bulbs in tight groups to begin with. A single 'Peeping Tom' I planted three years ago has since spread, slowly but reliably, to form a clump of eight flowering bulbs.

Various sources specify that narcissi must have good soil, but I find that the *heaviness* of the soil is more crucial than its quality. Narcissi need a good foundation for their fairly hefty foliage and flowers, and a light friable soil may not afford them enough support unless they are planted six inches deep.

Once you've planted 'Peeping Tom', you'll want to add other spring narcissi. Many mail-order firms will offer you "samplers" of up to a hundred varieties. This sounds like a hot idea, but such mixtures look best in a spacious, rustic setting. In a smaller and more formal planting, they produce a disappointing mixture of colors and shapes.

In fact, a few poorly chosen new narcissi can ruin the impact of an existing planting. Last fall, I placed a number of large yellow daffodils at random around my Low Garden, forgetting that close nearby were 'Peeping Tom's arranged in tidy clumps. This spring, the effect was so slapdash that I redug most of those daffodils; now I can again appreciate the 'Tom's without distraction.

The real problem arises when you try any of the many varieties of bicolored narcissi—ones with orange, white, or yellow petals and a trumpet of contrasting color. These varieties usually clash and contrast with one another and always look weird if grouped beside solid-color varieties. I now use one or two clumps of bicolored narcissi, softened by massed one-color plantings, so that the bicolor bulbs stand out as only a minor detail. Otherwise, I've found that separate plantings of a *single* color are most effective. The eye is able to skip from clump to clump so that bursts of similar color unify a yard visually, rather than fragmenting it as different-colored plantings would do.

Unless you have plenty of room, you'll find that a planting of bulbs looks better when it reinforces existing divisions of space than when it tries to ignore them. Limit any one variety to a discreet, already-defined sector of pachysandra, beneath a large tree, along the *full* length of a path, or in one brick-restricted corner. Within those predetermined boundaries, the technique of "naturalizing"—digging holes wherever scattered bulbs fall by chance—is as good a method as any to avoid the rigid one-two-three that makes many single-variety plantings look dull. If you follow this advice and find the effect sparse or monotonous, you can always mix other varieties in later. But it's far more arduous to try and sort out errant bulbs from a mixed planting if the final pattern is too chaotic.

An exception to the one-variety-per-clump-rule occurs with white-flowering bulbs. 'Mount Hood' emerges with white petals and a yellowish trumpet that slowly bleaches to light cream, but other varieties, such as 'Bergen', 'Broughshane', 'Cantatrice', 'Cassata Split', 'Iceland', 'Thalia', 'White Butterfly', and 'White Marvel' are all an unblemished white.

Lacking the carrying power of yellow, a *single* one of these white blossoms will seem lost. But a mixed-variety planting of all-white bulbs has just enough subtle contrasts of texture and form.

By choosing your bulbs carefully, you may be able to plant even a small expanse with as many as a dozen different varieties, each with a different blooming period so as to afford good long-term color while still preserving a coherent appearance. Remember, though, that the pat classifications of "early," "midseason," and "late" are not always reliable. Often a newly introduced bulb will flower earlier or later than it will when fully established. If you already have fairly solid plantings of narcissi, plant new bulbs in a small test plot where you can observe them through at least one year before committing them to your Pachysandra or Low Gardens.

Other Bulbs for Pachysandra Use

Fritillaria imperialis (crown imperial, SS) is a showy and exotic plant for eye-grabbing use. A single lily-like stalk emerges along with the crocus, growing very slowly. Red or yellow flowers don't open until April, but atop them is a topknot of green foliage that adds to their charm. These bulbs don't spread and, to bloom properly, need richer soil and more sun than most narcissi. Because of their size (a healthy plant shoots up to four feet), they look a bit excessive when planted in large groups. I prefer them singly or in groups of two or three, surrounded by solid-color daffodils. The "crowns" are showy if removed to an indoor vase.

Tulipa (tulips, CF) have been hybridized ever since the seventeenth century, from species that originated in Turkey and Southeast Europe. Unfortunately, somewhere in those centuries of hybridizing, tulips lost their ability to renew themselves effectively. The original parent bulb keeps dividing, but the offspring do not increase to blooming size. After a few years, grouped tufts of tiny leaves mark the site where a former single bulb has become six or more bulblets, all of them too feeble to flower.

If very richly fertilized, dug yearly in midsummer, and otherwise nursed (as they are in Holland), these bulbs may reward you. But since pachysandra doesn't encourage this kind of full-scale excavation, it becomes nearly impossible to dig bulbs up again once their foliage has died down.

My personal solution is to skip hybrid tulips entirely. But if you have the time and patience, there are two strategies to coax these costly bulbs into their maximum performance:

1. Plant bulbs in a huge plastic pot of bonemeal-rich, heavily fertilized soil. This makes them far easier to retrieve. Store the bulbs in a cool garage in midsummer, and be ready to replant the pot again in late autumn. (Meanwhile, have some other potted plant handy to plug the hole.) Any small bulb offshoots should be cultivated separately so that only your large bulbs are returned to the same site.

2. Plant them far deeper than is usually recommended. Three years after I bought my property, I was amazed to see tulips I hadn't planted arising and blooming. These bulbs were at least four seasons old, yet they hadn't lost too much of their original vigor. When I dug to investigate, I found that the bulbs were down a *minimum* of eighteen inches—over three times the recommended depth. I've since read that such extremely deep planting is a recognized ploy for getting hybrid tulips to sleep through the warm winters of the Deep South and bloom the next spring. But by itself, this technique is not permanent, for now, two years later, many tulips of this particular planting are no longer emerging at all.

Many of the original tulip species are now being offered as so-called "botanical" tulips. They multiply, continue to flower, and in short do everything a respectable bulb is supposed to. But the foliage of many species tulips is so small that pachysandra will smother them. Leave 'Waterlily', 'Peppermint Stick', and all other species tulips for the Low Garden.

Arranging New Bulbs

When bulbs are in bloom, it's obvious where new plantings are called for. But by autumn, when shipments of new bulbs begin arriving, the existing bulbs' flowers and foliage will have completely disappeared. Unless you can recall *exactly* where your old clumps are, you'll either dig them up by mistake or crowd them with your new selections.

There's one easy way out. In spring, when your existing bulbs are in full flower, select the vacant areas where you want others. Memorialize these spots with painted stakes, plastic swizzle sticks, or other markers that won't rot and are hard to dislodge. In fall, that will tell you that new bulbs can occupy that space without getting in anything else's way. Don't mark where bulbs *already* are, or you'll need several markers to trace the perimeter of an existing planting. Instead, use a marker in the exact *center* of a barren spot. (But be prepared to remove any marker if a later perennial emerges beside it.)

All bulbs mentioned in this chapter are shaped like teardrops: the pointed end is where the leaves will emerge. That end goes up, of course. The other end is usually broad and flattened and may have a few dried-out roots clinging to it. That side goes down. When planting bulbs, *always* have a large pail of leafmold mixed with bonemeal beside you as you dig. Before covering the bulb again, mix an equal part of the leafmold/bonemeal with the removed soil. Even if you've chosen strains that spread on their own, why not give them some extra help? Besides, by mixing in pockets of better soil each time you move bulbs, you are slowly leavening and regenerating the subsoil.

Rescuing and Moving Old Bulbs

No bulb planting is *strictly* permanent. Sooner or later, the clumps they form have to be divided to ensure flower vigor. Besides, you may have decided those 'Thalia' narcissi would look better if shifted over a few yards. Or a previous owner may have scattered a swath of bicolors where an azalea is now overshadowing them. The problem is evident *now*—but shouldn't you wait until the bulbs are dormant before moving them?

Emphatically not! I know it sounds like heresy, but *any* clump of naturally increasing bulbs can be dug up and separated as soon as the flowers and foliage are fully open. The transplanting shock results in only slightly reduced vigor the next spring. I've moved scores of leafed-out narcissi, many in full bloom, and every one of them is now thriving. After all, how else are you going to locate that one 'Peeping Tom' that's strayed into a clump of 'King Alfred'? Too many gardeners make conscientious notes on what to move where later, only to lose the impulse when the motive for the change fades or goes dormant. The only way to improve a garden is to review it month by month and *make corrections at the time*.

Specifically, narcissi should be separated once they have spread to form clumps about eight inches across. But unless you planted the bulbs yourself, you'll have no idea how deep they may be. The more recent offshoots will often be growing out from under the parent bulbs—and may even be lying on their sides. For this reason, dig at least three inches to the *side* of where you see the clump's leaves emerge. This ensures that the actual bulbs aren't lying directly beneath your blade.

Trace each bulb's position by carefully exposing the soil that surrounds the stem. Never try to pull up a buried bulb by its foliage! Loosen the soil beside the bulb with your fingers. Then, when the bulb itself is uncovered, grasp the sheath of the leaves just above it and pull gently. Once the first bulb in a clump is free, it's usually easy to remove the rest by pulling them out sideways. But be sure to free the subsurface leaves first so that they aren't torn in the process.

Should you find that you have accidentally cut a bulb in two, it can often be saved. Regardless of which part has the leaves, find the half that contains the roots—this is the heart of any bulb, from which the upper structures emerge. Cut off any leaves that may be present, and let the bulb heal itself for a week or two in a cool shady place. When a callus forms over the cut, the bulb is ready for replanting—and may sprout again the next year. Cut-off leaves and bulb tops, on the other hand, should be discarded.

Often you'll come across a bulb offshoot that has produced foliage only. Plant it apart from its original crowded conditions, in good soil, and it should bear flowers by the second year. If you find a *colony* that's producing foliage but no flowers, the bulbs are in too-deep shade, have their roots in competition with another larger plant, and/or are not planted deep enough. When in doubt, however, always plant them at a slightly *shallower* depth than you found them originally, since you can always add an inch or so of leafmold later on.

Things get a bit trickier when you go to relocate a very old planting. New bulblets in such a colony are often produced horizontally off the bottom of the parent bulbs. But for some reason, a narcissus bulb is never able to adjust itself the way a corm or rhizome can. It keeps growing in that prone position, twisting its stem around to reach the vertical. Obviously you want to position it right side up this time around. But with the stem twisted into a hook, it appears you either have to break the stem or leave a good proportion of the foliage underground.

You *must* plant the bulb at its approximate proper depth, which for narcissi is four to six inches below ground level. However, it's easy to manipulate "ground level" so that the foliage can still emerge. Figure 34 shows the chief bulb problems and how to solve them.

A. Bulb buried too deep. The easiest to correct. Plant bulb at its proper depth, no matter how shallow by comparison. Just let the foliage sprawl. The pale portion of the leaves that originally lay below ground will be unsightly for only a few weeks, then will fade and disappear. Next year, the new foliage will not flop.

B. Bulb buried too shallow. Again, bulb goes at its proper depth. But fill up the hole only part way, to where the green portion of the foliage begins. At the bottom of their pit, the leaves will still be able to enjoy sun. When foliage fades late in June, fill up the hole completely with good soil.

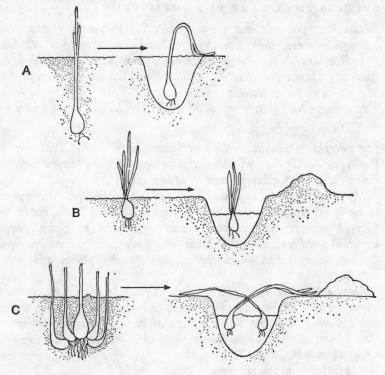

Figure 34

C. Bulb growing on its side. Let foliage emerge from the soil at an angle, whichever way it prefers. When replanting a *clump* of bulbs, point all foliage toward the center of the circle, as shown here. This neatens things a bit and gives the individual leaves that much more distance (from one side of the pit to the other) in which to gain "altitude." Again, fill in the pit when foliage dries up.

Perennials

Whether a perennial is suited to a Pachysandra Garden depends not so much on its eventual height as on how quickly it attains it.

Remember that you originally planted your pachysandra to neaten things up. Therefore, any perennial you plant in it should itself be neat and distinctive—or at least not spoil the effect too badly. This means that you can use virtually any Single-Clump plants, some Loose-Spreaders, only a *very* few Thick-Spreaders, but no One-Direction-Travelers. Avoid sprawling, potentially messy spreaders like baby's breath, most other *Achilleas,* and hybrid goldenrods. Anything that depends heavily on a rosette of basal leaves is also out. I can vouch for the ones that follow: except as noted, all prefer sun or very high part shade.

Aquilegia (columbine; CF) self-seeds very easily. Best for the Pachysandra Garden are the sort that sprout many leaves and turn into a dense hemispherical mound of foliage.

My property has always had plants of this latter type, which seems to be hybrids of *A. vulgaris,* a European species. Their short, fat-spurred flowers vary in color from light pink to pastel purple, borne in such profusion that when about half the blooms are open, the top-heavy stalks begin leaning into nearby plants and across paths.

Standard advice tells you to clip off spent columbine flowers to stimulate reblooming, but with these hybrids, any "repeat" flowers are stunted and about half the size of the originals. So when the stalks have already listed under their own weight, I cut them off clean at ground level. This neatens the plant and encourages new leaves throughout the summer.

Each flower goes to seed rapidly, forming what looks like a loose bundle of small pea pods. No matter how early I clip the stalks, however, a few pods have ripened beforehand, and the small black seeds germinate quite quickly—especially in the sand between pathway bricks. This means a continuing supply of as many new plants as you'll want. The foliage of columbine usually survives well into December and wilts down only after a few snows; it's worth considering as a semi-evergreen accent for warmer climates than mine.

*Arisaema triphyllum (jack-in-the-pulpit; SS; see Color Section) is best grown in a Wild Garden while it's small. But once their stalks get up at least a foot high, jacks positively thrive amid pachysandra. (I planted them every two feet bordering a brick path.) However, hot sun makes their leaves yellow and wilt prematurely. Give them high shade under trees and the part shade in front of taller rhododendrons and azaleas.

Jacks also make a very good cut flower. If *A. triphyllum* is on any state's list of endangered wildflowers, it's because too many people break the stalk *below* where the two leaves come together. Carrying off the foliage dooms the underground corm to malnutrition. If you want both pulpit and leaves for indoor display, clip the pulpit from one plant and a leaf from another specimen. (Always use clippers to remove flowers; yanking will bruise the tissue you leave behind.)

Don't forget that because pachysandra terminals hinder the germination of most seeds, pachysandra-planted jacks won't multiply as they will in the Wild Garden. Let the berries ripen and then remove them for planting elsewhere.

*Dicentra exima (bleeding-heart; CF) is widely offered but still hasn't won the prestige of the old-fashioned bleeding-heart (see below). But to my mind, *exima* is far more versatile. Its flowers aren't as showy and resemble the almost tubular blossoms of squirrel corn, its wild relative; as they fade they often turn a rather garish pink. But *exima* is now offered in the pure-white 'Sweetheart' variety, which in a mixed planting softens the effect of the regular flowers. And unlike other *Dicentras, exima* keeps blooming all summer long. Moreover, it continues to sprout new bluish-gray leaves so that each plant maintains a fresh, healthy look until frost.

Smaller specimens do best in the Low Garden where they can enlarge free of competition and seed themselves readily. But once the plants attain a foot or more, they are wonderful additions among pachysandra.

Dicentra spectabilis (old-fashioned bleeding-heart; CF) is one of the best-loved perennials of the early summer garden. But around June, when its heart-shaped pink flowers fall from their sprays, the plant becomes senile. Its leaves begin to bleach and yellow, looking sickly and unattractive. (Wild *Dicentras* behave the same way, but their annual dieback is speedier and far less messy; *spectabilis* doesn't die back completely until late July.) No matter how attractive *spectabilis'* flowers may be, its prolonged death throes are too obvious for it to be given a solo spot in a perennial bed.

Catalogs now offer new hybrids of *spectabilis* whose flowers hold on as long as early July. But *D. exima* (above) keeps on flowering and producing new leaves straight through October. Since an adult *exima* grows only about half as tall as *spectabilis,* you can combine both in a mixed planting amidst pachysandra. In spring, the taller old-fashioned aristocrat will overshadow its smaller cousin. But when it begins to fade, the more floriferous *exima* is just getting under way to camouflage the degenerating ruins of the larger plant.

If you want extra plantings of existing *spectabilis,* you don't have to buy them. They root very easily from cuttings. In early spring, cut shoots off at ground level and plant them where you want them to grow permanently.

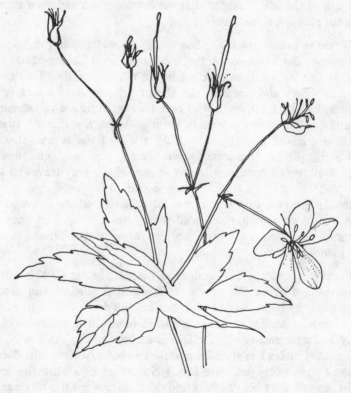

Figure 35

Geranium maculatum (crane's-bill, wild or wood geranium; CF; Figure 35), is a native wildflower that only recently has begun to appear in perennial catalogs. In early spring, palmate leaves arise from a branched creeping rootstock just under the surface. In May come taller shoots with a few side leaves, topped with five-petaled lavender-rose flowers. Once gone to seed, these flowers form the distinctive "crane's-bill" seed pods that in turn dry and curl into a shape like fancy ironwork.

Colonies can be transplanted at almost any time of year, even when in bloom. The foliage wilts almost immediately, but as long as plenty of water is given, *G. maculatum* regains its former freshness within a day after transplanting. Aside from its adaptability to practically any soil or light conditions, wild geranium's real virtue lies in its leaves, which persist throughout the summer, always presenting a handsome clump of foliage up to eighteen inches high. No source mentions it, but at least two subspecies exist (see Figure 36). In one

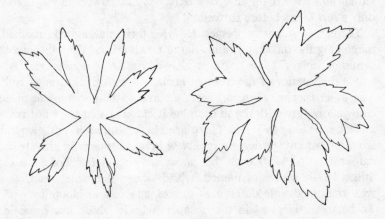

Figure 36

form, the leaf is dark green, finely cut with deep graceful scoops like a Maltese cross. In the second, the lighter green leaf is plumper, with sharper angles between the lobes, and a quilted texture.

The first type definitely makes a better display. In fall, its leaves turn a sudden, lovely red before shriveling. However, one plant of the second type rebloomed fully in late September—a fluke, as it turned out, because the colony did not rebloom again the next year. (This may be a latent trait that could be encouraged through hybridization; if so, *G. maculatum* would become the only American spring wildflower that reblooms.)

Dependably larger and more attractive each year, the plant remains neatly camouflaged among terminals except when its spring flowers or fall color give it away. Clip exhausted flowerstalks to maintain a neat appearance; otherwise this plant is utterly carefree and resistant to insects and slugs.

*Hemerocallis (daylily; CF) is often suggested as the groundcover for banksides and open territory. But when too thickly planted, daylilies become a knee-high thicket of soggy foliage each autumn; the bedraggled leaves remain until new foliage covers them in spring. Daylilies need something to hide them, which make them a particularly good choice for pachysandra.

These plants' only other drawback is suggested by the name daylily. A single plant may stay in flower for up to a month, but individual *flowers* last for one day only. As cut flowers, a daylily lasts only a few hours before shriveling.

There are two native species. *H. fulva* thrives along wild roadsides, mimicking the dazzling orange-flared petals of the tiger lily, another genus entirely (*Lilium*). *Fulva* also comes in a double variety, in which the interior of the trumpet is choked with thick orange ruffles. The other species, *H. flava,* bears a smaller, thinner trumpet of delicate yellow (greenish if you examine it closely) that does not remain in bloom as long as *fulva.* There are also countless hybrids available from almost any garden source. New break-throughs in size or color can cost up to $250 each, but most are only a few dollars apiece. Still, literally scores of named hybrids share the same basic colors, with only negligible differences in size, shape, and blooming period. To begin with, invest in the cheaper hybrids whose low price indicates that they multiply quickly.

Early-, middle-, and late-flowering varieties are available in practically any color, so it makes sense to shop for a full-season selection. If you like pink daylilies, for example, you can have them from a sequence of different plants for most of the summer. But I prefer variety, and would rather see one *Hemerocallis* fading in red while another opens in peach. Avoid the darker shades, however: deep-purple or red daylilies do not carry visually and look rather funereal close-up.

The native *fulva* often sports a yellow streak down the middle of its orange petals, but most hybridizers have bred out this variegation in favor of larger size and color. Only recently have the professionals turned to create variegated or contrasting-centered hybrids. Most are quite expensive, but expect the prices to ease down as the stock multiplies. Some growers are even trying for distinctly atypical blooms.

The very recent 'Mexicali Rose' is a skillful parody of the gladiolus hybrid of the same name. This *Hemerocallis* has much wider petals than normal which blend into a circular ruff centered with pink.

Hybrids listed as repeat bloomers are the ones you should go for first, even if they are a bit more expensive. A new everblooming hybrid, 'Melon Frost', is moderately expensive, but apart from its long duration (allegedly up to two months), the flowers resemble any other peach-colored daylily. And until the roots are well established, the plant blooms only briefly, like any other *Hemerocallis*.

All daylilies arise from sets of underground tubers resembling a dahlia's in miniature, and multiply from shoots emerging from the base of the foliage. Daylilies will grow in shade or sun, but be sure to give more expensive hybrids the sunniest, most fertile sites. Plants shipped in early spring usually have new foliage arising in tight shoots from the nexus of the tubers; ones mailed in midsummer usually have their leaves clipped off about six inches above ground level, but will sprout a few new leaves before frost. New arrivals, however, will not look particularly good until the second year, when they will bloom if planted in full sun. In part shade, daylilies take an extra season or two to establish a decent display.

On a pachysandra-covered slope I grow a series of daylily clumps, including *fulva, flava,* and a broad selection of hybrid reds, pinks, and neon weirdos. They aren't all in bloom at once, and so the display changes from week to week. Planted three feet apart from each other, they look planned and neat (rather than chaotic as clustered daylilies tend to get), and it's far easier to judge the ones I want to move or replace.

Gaillardia aristata, with hybrid strains classified as *grandifolia* (blanketflower; CF) has rosettes of long hairy leaves. The flowers' raised centers are usually brown to black, rough to the touch. The petals are often two-tone, the red at the inside changing abruptly to yellow. *Gaillardia*'s petals narrow to form a tight waist where they meet the central disk, and in some hybrids this trait has been exaggerated so that the petals form an open corona around the center. 'Monarch' hybrids are reputedly the most floriferous. Once planted, any *Gaillardia* will mature within a single season, withstand drought within reason, and cheerfully outperform just about anything else.

The old-fashioned strains should definitely be on your Kill List if you grow them in a standard perennial border. The seeds germinate so prolifically that new plants appear everywhere. Foliage grows rank, smothering smaller plants; enormous roots make it hard to pull the plants loose without damaging their neighbors. However, pachysandra keeps them more disciplined.

Hosta (funkia, plantain lily; TS) is quite frequently used as a border plant for paths and driveways. From July to September, depending on species and variety, Hostas bear tall stalks lined with lily-shaped flowers. The usual color is a dull translucent lavender, with no carrying power unless the petals are spotlighted by a ray of sun. But recently hybridizers have been achieving larger white-flowering varieties—usually more expensive, but the only way to avoid a monotony of sickly mauve. When pollinated flowers ripen to form fat, unsightly seed pods, you can clip off the entire stem—these plants reproduce mainly by asexual means.

Their leaves vanish in autumn, but as long as you have pachysandra to take up the slack, Hostas provide superb foliage accents; the larger ones are particularly striking where a deep green leafy texture is called for. The only hostas I'd use sparingly are those variegated leaves; they look a bit busy if allowed to widen into clumps of any diameter. Interestingly, the "white" variegation—usually a sickly cream—is not always stable. Once when I moved a clump to a new spot in full sun, a pure-green shoot arose and quickly enlarged into a unmottled plant larger and more vigorous than its variegated parent. Evidently, the variegated hosta had been the sport of a larger, healthier-looking strain, and was now reverting to type. Variegated hostas look better if interspersed with normal green-leaf strains or under matching white birches to indicate the borders of a driveway.

Hostas mutate and sport themselves constantly, which is why a single species can have different Latin names. In the days when genuinely new species of hosta were arriving from Japan and China, it was too easy to mistake a wildly original sport like *H. f. gigantea* for a whole new species. (And so it is often listed today, as *H. gigantea*.) Because of this wide variety, you can accumulate quite a selection of different hostas in the Pachysandra Garden, mixing them for maximum contrast with one another:

H. fortunei var. *gigantea,* one of the largest of the clan, is the immense variety of a normal-sized species. Its enormous round leaves reputedly grow to form four-foot clumps, with massive white flowers in July. My young specimen doesn't yet answer that description, but after less than a year of growth, it's already vigorously content, already the centerpiece of an open stretch of pachysandra.

H. grandiflora (or *plantaginea,* or *subcordata*) has enormous four-inch white flowers in late summer. The size, season, and color of the flowers alone would make the plant desirable.

H. lancifolia has leaves too narrow for my taste. The standard lavender flowers disqualify it for extensive use.

H. glauca or *sieboldiana* is an old-fashioned species now widely offered. Though smaller than *gigantea,* it still bears rounded leaves a foot across and tall sprays of two-inch white flowers. You might prefer it over *gigantea* for the bluish gloss of its foliage, peculiar to this species. The best specimen I've seen had been growing in full sun for about twenty years and had a four-foot spread.

Hostas are officially best suited to part shade. However, it seems best to err on the side of too much light, keeping the roots cool and moist under their pachysandra blanket. A further advantage to hostas is that they transplant very easily. Plants shipped bare-rooted as late as July seldom wither at all and, right after planting, will usually produce three or four new leaves. Each plant arises from a stubby rhizome atop a mass of thick, fleshy roots, but offshoots soon branch to form a congested colony. When leaves arise from three or four different main whorls, the branched rhizomes below can be divided—or simply left as is to increase even further. Be sure that each new division has enough leaves to shade its own roots; otherwise it will be unnecessarily retarded. Older plants grown in open soil tend to form a low mound: leaves at the center are almost vertical, while leaves growing toward the sides slant increasingly downward until at the colony's perimeter they brush the ground.

Iris (CF) is largely overrated. The hybrid bearded irises, most commonly offered, are really the least rewarding. Their June flowers are exceedingly brief, and for the rest of the year, bearded iris spreads by itself—but too plentifully when grown in open soil. The rhizomes plow along the surface, and the leaves grow in fans so thickly as to crowd out other perennials. Keeping iris in order means separating the clumps every two or three years, but this is not necessary amid pachysandra. Happily, there are reblooming strains that produce a second stalk of flowers in September and October. The rebloomers I've grown came in rather pastel, watery shades, but now that recent hybridizing has overcome this problem, there's no reason at all to settle for the spring-flowering beardeds.

Avoid the *Iris reticulata* (Dutch iris) hybrids. Since they arise from bulb-like structures, they don't spread rampantly. But their narrow-petaled March flowers are not as attractive as crocus or snowdrops, and the undistinguished onion-like foliage persists throughout the summer.

I. kaempferi (Japanese iris) is fine *if* your soil is extremely moist and rich. Like many unbearded irises, these brightly colored hybrids demand fairly wet roots, or they will fail within a year or two. The enormous flattened petals droop slightly, so that each flower resembles a gaudy silk handkerchief. Like the native American species, their foliage is high and extremely slim, and remains attractive all summer.

I. sibirica (Siberian iris) is undoubtedly your best choice for pachysandra. Foliage is narrow and erect like *kaempferi*'s, but not so tall and therefore less prone to flop over. Flowers are smaller, but still showy. The basic species is white; hybrids now exist in blue, pink, and other pastels, but plants do not flower until well established.

Lilium (lily) is a genus of summer-flowering bulbs that need rich, friable, well-drained soil to a depth of at least twelve inches. My subsoil clay begins at a depth of around three inches, so my lily attempts to date haven't been spectacularly successful. I am now digging deep trenches and filling them again with well-rotted leafmold, hoping for the best.

L. candidum (Madonna lily; SS) has been disappointing for me. Its leaves are wider and of a lighter, richer green than most lilies'; the flowers are pure white. But the bulb must be planted under only an inch of soil (if planted too deep, *candidum* sends up weak mounds of foliage but no flowerstalk). This means that bulbs are easily damaged by slugs, rodents, and a virus that hits *candidum* harder than any other species. All other lily bulbs must be buried at least six inches deep, and *will* grow well if you provide the rich, deep soil they demand. Because they too are vulnerable to virus, it's best not to plant them too closely together, lest disease sweep through an entire planting.

Of the species lilies, the best is *L. tigrinum* (Chinese tiger lily; CF) which blooms with evenly spotted orange-red flowers and survives bitter winters. I've seen old Iowa farms where individual bulbs have

PLATE 8.   A strip of Cultivated Meadow against a redwood fence. From left: butterfly weed (*Asclepias*), daylily (*Hemerocallis*), and a double-flowered hybrid of *Rudbeckia*. (*Tom Andron*)

PLATE 9.   For a more extensive Meadow, use a groundcover of buttercup (*Ranunculus*). The creeping species *repens*, shown here, spreads fast and thickly, but must be weeded back each fall. (*Dennis Yeandle*)

PLATE 10. Butterfly weed (*Asclepias tuberosa*) is the glory of any Meadow. But full sun, rich soil, and several years' cultivation are needed to grow a plant this size. (*Tom Andron*)

PLATE 11.   A Rockery bordering a brick path. From left: dwarf fern, sempervivums (blooming with pink spike), 'Horsford's Dwarf' white pine, *Ajuga metallica crispa,* and a dwarf spruce. In background is an expanse of low sedum and two potted cacti enjoying the summer outdoors. (*Dennis Yeandle*)

PLATE 12.   The Miniature Landscape discussed in Chapter 15. Dwarf
evergreens, sedums, and horsetails surround a "mountain" with a trailing
juniper planted at its summit. The tiny bronze *torii* (Shinto gateway) was
purchased at a flea market. (*Dennis Yeandle*)

spread to form entire beds of *tigrinum* up to three feet across, blooming the last week of July. Other native species have similar flowers, but won't increase quite as rapidly.

Hybrid lilies are definitely more vigorous and disease-resistant than the various species, but to my taste, the flowers of most hybrids have undistinguished form, and the colors are too often garish and waxy. But order an illustrated catalog and decide for yourself. Still, lily bulbs are expensive and demanding, so select only those strains advertised as most vigorous, floriferous, and—in the case of hybrids —disease-resistant.

Liriope (LS) has long, strap-like foliage forming loose tufts. In July and August, it bears short stalks of tiny rose, blue, purple, or (rarely) white flowers. Winter-hardy, it spreads intermittently by underground stolons and soon gives the impression that coarse grass has invaded the Pachysandra Garden. Contain it with a tight circle of aluminum edging.

*Lysimachea vulgaris (garden loosestrife; LS), is an English flower that became an American wildflower after escaping from colonial gardens. But there's nothing "vulgar" about it. From a creeping, branching rootstock, a number of stalks arise each May, bearing almond-shaped leaves. From the leaf axils emerge bright yellow three-quarter-inch flowers centered with light brown. The entire stalk is conical and neat to start with, but in the moister soil of a Pachysandra Garden, the colony becomes tall and thick, the flowers lasting for a full month before finally slowing in mid-July.

One of the very best yellow-flowering perennials, *Lysimachea vulgaris* travels by underground stolons that suddenly turn upward, as do those of mint, to form the stalks. But unlike mint, this is a neat plant. Flowers are not heavy enough to bend the stiff, upright growth, whose leaves remain lush until frost. It spreads reliably but not too tightly, so that errant stalks can be located and clipped before they wander out of bounds. (Do *not* try to pull up unwanted stalks. They are interconnected, and you risk uprooting the whole colony.) Small seedlings of *L. vulgaris* will bloom very late, up to the first week of August, which makes them easier to locate and transplant.

*Lythrum (CF) is a genus of hefty perennials whose hybrids flower in a range of light pink to purple. However, all *Lythrums* are basically similar to *L. salicaria* (purple loosestrife), another raffish

escapee from settlers' gardens that grows in waste places, especially boggy meadows.

L. salicaria is less formal than most named varieties, but still distinctive: an upright, loosely branching plant whose stems are lined with lance-shaped leaves. Reaching seven-foot size in marshy meadows, *Lythrum* tends to be mistaken for a large shrub until early July. Then the plant suddenly "appears" as rose-purple flowers begin opening along the upper third of its branches. Flowering proceeds slowly, from the bottom of the flowerspikes upward. (*L. salicaria*'s rose-purple flowers are quite careless about their petal count: individual flowers on the same spike number anywhere from four to seven.) By late August the very top flowers are in bloom, so that seen from a distance, entire swamps and drainage ditches are washed with misty purple.

Lythrum shouldn't be transplanted until dormant—which in this case means invisible. Desirable *Lythrums* should be scarfed with plastic, therefore, while still in bloom. But even small plants have long, tough roots, and it's vastly easier to take stem cuttings in mid-July.

The *middle* of the stem roots quickest, so make your cuttings about twelve inches below the lowest currently blooming flowers. Trim off side branches as necessary. *Lythrum*'s flowerstalk wilts slightly when cut, but soon straightens up again once placed in a vase. *Lythrum* cuttings look well for a week or so but soon begin dropping their flowers (and later, their lower leaves), retrenching their resources for long-term survival. Cuttings at this stage are no longer vase-worthy, so transfer them to a water-filled jar (indoors or out). Soon you'll notice white roots erupting from the bottoms of the stalks. Add dilute fertilizer. When the roots are about three inches long, the cuttings can be set in pots of damp leafmold. (Since *Lythrum* is basically a marsh plant, set the pots directly in a pan of water to avoid any chance of their drying out.) In late autumn, the pots can be decanted and the plants set where you want them permanently.

*Oenothera pilosella (sundrop; TS; see Color Section) is probably the best of the evening primrose group. The familiar wild biennial *O. biennis* blooms with lanky, four-foot spikes in August, but the perennial *pilosella* is far lower and neater, with deep-green foliage. Its flowers are larger, brighter yellow, and continue to make a good

show for the better part of June, usually coinciding their display with *Lysimachea vulgaris.*

Since the creeping root is rather narrow, transplanted stalks flop over and are hard to support with repacked soil. But plants will definitely bloom the next year and slowly increase into massed colonies. Leaves often turn a deep red in fall. A colony needs thinning only when you decide you have enough of a good thing, or want more elsewhere.

*Paeonia (peony; CF) is a large genus with many species and a vast variety of hybrids, all dependably hardy. They're probably most effective in a Pachysandra Garden that will absorb their decaying stalks in autumn. The cut-leaf foliage is dark green and attractive all summer, however, and the plants spread very slowly. But since the stalks lean after flowering, make sure they don't cast their shade over delicate plantings.

I'm not enthusiastic about "tree" peonies, which take some time to achieve any size. Avoid single-flowered peonies (their poppy-like blooms are rather frail-looking, with tufted yellow centers) in favor of the fully double strains that bear lush cabbages of succulent petals. Doubles abound in every color through yellow to deep red, but my own favorites are those of pure white whose petals are shot through with odd streaks of blood red.

Peonies need rich soil, which the pachysandra litter provides. To assure plentiful flowers, always be sure that the crown of a peony root is planted less than two inches deep. (I plant mine right at ground level, assuming the soil will rise with time.) The tiniest slip of root will produce a leaf the next year; foliage grows larger spring after spring until the plant finally blooms. Meanwhile, the fleshy mature roots (shaped like beige carrots) dig themselves ever deeper. One thirty-year-old clump I transplanted had roots that went down two feet. So digging up an old peony means major excavation—often a difficult task if it has sunk itself in hard subsoil.

Peonies have a few other characteristics that the fastidious gardener may rate as drawbacks. The flowers, particularly the doubles are so heavy that stems often droop or break. Thus it's best to plant peonies on relatively level ground, where the blossoms won't nod off downhill. If opening buds are about to lean, clip them. They'll last nearly a week in water, and cutting the terminal flower often encourages the small reddish buds nestled in the leaves below to develop into late—if smaller—bloom.

No matter what you read elsewhere, do *not* cut back peony foliage until it's utterly died down. Then if you want to be safe, inter it in the Kitchen Compost bin, drowning any insects that may be wintering inside the dry stems. But pests seem to be a very minor problem: I've seen many peony clumps whose foliage was never cut back and which, decades later, are still blooming vigorously.

Phlox (CF) is of several distinct species, each with its own blooming period and best uses. Hybrids stay pretty close to type, so whenever possible, try to determine what your named variety is *of*. The spring-flowering *P. divaricata* and *P. sublata* (creeping or moss phlox) have their place in other parts of your garden, but are too low for pachysandra.

Hybrids of *P. paniculata* bloom from July into August and result in stately, upright clumps that need dividing every five years. (You can postpone this chore by cutting away at the *center* of a clump for new plants, filling the gap with fresh leafmold into which the plant can expand anew.) Most new growth is beset with aphids and a bit of fungus in spring. But the curled and damaged leaves are soon outgrown, and the plants in my garden have never required spraying. 'Mount Fuji', a dazzling white, is particularly long-lasting, but like most white flowers, it needs a nearby fiery red or strong pink counterpart for effective contrast. Avoid blue or deep purple shades, which don't show up well. Also pass by the "eyed" hybrids, whose contrasting centers fail to show up unless the plant is close to the observer. The whole point of phlox is to serve as a stately, colorful sentinel toward the back or center of the Pachysandra Garden.

Also try to obtain the tall May-blooming species *P. carolina*. It never needs dividing or spraying and is hardy straight into Canada.

Physostegia virginiana (false dragonhead, obedient plant, "perennial heather"; CF) is a winner. Neat, closely packed stalks bear fine-toothed green leaves and vertical rows of white, pink, or purple flowers resembling those of the annual snapdragon. The name "obedient plant" comes from the stalks, which easily bend to any shape a flower-arranger desires. All named varieties are compact plants, and their flowers are more showy and opulent than most perennials'. Pachysandra takes care of the rich, moist soil that is the plant's main requirement.

Tradescantia (spiderwort; CF) bears jointed stalks that bear lush, *Hemerocallis*-like leaves. Clusters of buds appear in the crotches of the top leaves, opening singly into showy flowers throughout late June and July. Besides the usual blue and purple, hybrid flowers are now available in white and pink; two or three contrasting shades in close proximity makes the best display. The semi-evergreen leaves remain attractive all summer. *Tradescantia,* unfortunately, is a rather slow grower. It also has tough, shallow, woody roots that are almost impossible to dig without a mattock. However, stems broken off at ground level will root readily in water, offering an easy way to start new clumps without ruining existing ones.

Nurseries sometimes offer good-sized plants in pots, but ones shipped by mail are usually single stalks. Plant these and rooted cuttings in loose soil in part shade to encourage maximum growth. Then when the plant has at least three healthy stalks, the loose soil will let you transplant the clump without tearing it to pieces.

Yucca (Adam's needle, soapweed, Spanish bayonet; CF), when offered, is usually one of the three native Eastern species: *Y. filamentosa, Y. glauca,* and *Y. smalliana.* The last is the "old-fashioned" yucca often found in old gardens or escaped to the wild, but it's also the least desirable as a foliage plant. The leaves are coarse and wide, usually bending under their own weight. Old plants form ragged masses that resemble a clump of daylilies with elephantiasis. The other yuccas—with slimmer, finer leaves—are better beside any outdoor patio, and pachysandra absorbs the older, lower leaves that might otherwise become unsightly. (Variegated and yellow-leaved varieties are also available.)

Yucca's particular requirements are full sun and perfect drainage at the point where the leaves meet the rootstock. The only specimen I ever lost was planted in soggy clay; and for several years my *Y. smallianas* languished amid a groundcover of English ivy that kept them too moist. When I replaced the ivy with pachysandra, all of them shot up and bloomed the second year after: in June, a healthy plant sends up a wildly twisting asparagus-like stalk from the center of the leaves. Eventually the stalk straightens up, towering as high as seven feet, and branches out in a candelabra of waxy white flowers (hence the Southwestern common name for yucca, "candles of the Lord").

Unfortunately, *Y. filamentosa*'s flowers are smaller, greener, and not as showy as the more unkempt *smalliana*'s. Probably the best compromise is to plant *filamentosa* close up, where it looks neater, and *smalliana* toward the back, where its flowers will still show up. But all yucca flowers are definitely worth a close look. Inspection of any panicle will usually disclose a number of ants drawn by the sticky nectar and a few pure-white pronuba moths—the *Yucca* genus' sole pollinating agent. Brush off the insects, and a yucca "candle" makes a stunning cut flower indoors. (Use a tall narrow-mouth vase for proper support.) But yucca leaves are too coarse to look good in such an arrangement. If you want an appropriate foliage accent, cheat and use leaves from the centers of overgrown *Hemerocallis* or *Tradescantia* clumps.

Yucca flowers ripen into melon-shaped seed pods. Eventually the pods split, dropping hard black seeds, and the spike dries out, remaining erect through the winter. Next summer, the leaves begin dying back (the flowerstalk has replaced the central bud that produces new leaves). But the rootstock, still alive and well, begins producing a new series of leaves just to the side of the original rosette.

Perennial Troubleshooting

The plants discussed above are largely trouble-free, but any problems that do arise should be nipped in the bud. If sprays don't arrest a fungus or viral disease, it's usually wisest to destroy the afflicted plant and start over again with fresh stock in a new location.

Many of your taller-stalked perennials may tend to flop over—just leaning, without breaking off. Since this usually happens the first or second season after I've introduced them, I assume it's because the plant hasn't yet developed the strength to grow a wide enough stem. It can also be the result of too much shade, where sun reaches the plant from a narrow angle. The plant then bends, seeking the sun, and may not photosynthesize enough energy to form sturdy stem tissue.

Unless the weight of flowers and foliage actually threatens to break the stalk, I let a leaning perennial fend for itself and hope it will straighten up next year. If the plant's *roots* are being pulled up, though, it needs replanting. While you're at it, check to be sure lumps of hard clay subsoil aren't inhibiting root growth. High-pruning of nearby trees and a barrage of fertilizer in late fall and early spring should also help.

Slugs

A Pachysandra Garden and its adjoining brick paths provide perfect shelter for slugs, but most perennials are not too susceptible to these pests: columbine will only be nibbled; iris and digitalis will be chewed in long, narrow slits. But even if plants survive slug damage, they'll at least *support* these pests until you introduce a really vulnerable plant like dahlia, which slugs will literally eat right down to the ground. It makes sense to keep a slug population from building in the first place.

Slugs like to spend the day in moist, dark places—under leaves, bark, bricks, in between stones. But eliminating their hiding places isn't enough, because they forage far afield at night. Slugs are particularly attracted to recently uprooted dandelions and violets. (Probably wilting softens the plant's tissues, making them that much easier to consume.) So remove such delicacies to the Kitchen Compost or a high, dry spot on the compost heap.

The frequently suggested plate of beer (in which slugs drown themselves) is impractical for sloping or thickly planted gardens. Your main line of defense is a handy box of slug baits, shaped like commercial rabbit pellets. If you have birds or pets in the neighborhood, avoid spreading these baits on open ground. Serve the slugs where they hang out—at the base of stone walls, beside brick walks and edgings, in pachysandra beds and compost heaps—*and* around the base of any newly introduced plant. The next morning, look for unusually large slicks of glossy mucus (which an ailing slug throws off in quantity) as evidence that the baits are effective.

The first application in May should catch young slugs and adults that have survived the winter. But treat an infested area twice to finish off any survivors, and don't shrink from actual hand-to-hand combat.

Slugs are mainly nocturnal, but they also emerge on cloudy or rainy days. To keep my hands clean of their mucus, I skewer them with a long twig, move them to the nearest path, and squish them with a spare brick. The dedicated slug-masher will soon discover that these little molluscs are cannibals. Reduce a few slugs to two dimensions, and others will quickly converge on their protein-rich remains. So if you return to the scene of your killing every fifteen minutes or so, you can count on a new circle of fresh slugs enjoying their last supper.

In late summer and fall, slugs lay eggs that hatch the next spring. You'll find the pearly gray-to-yellowish eggs in masses under rocks and fallen leaves. (In former years I replaced them carefully, thinking they were the eggs of red-backed salamanders, but these rare and delightful amphibians inhabit moist piles of decaying wood. If you uncover eggs in dry territory, they are slug eggs.) The more you can mash now, the fewer adults later.

Cut Flowers

Almost every week, a healthy Pachysandra Garden lets you bring indoors a pleasant assortment of bloom. Cutting flowers regularly prevents them from going to seed, which means more energy saved for the plants, and more flowers next year.

Most vases are designed with formal flower-arranging in mind. The openings are extremely wide, so you either have to cram them with a *lot* of flowers, or resort to devices inside the vase like wire spikes, clay, or Styrofoam—more equipment than I like to keep handy. Yet bud vases are formal, expensive, and so narrow they accommodate only a single flower. That tight fit makes it difficult to add more water—and a double peony can drink up to a half pint of water before it fades. For several years now, however, I've been collecting antique patent medicine bottles in shades of amber, aqua, sea-green, and purple, embossed with irresistible names like WORM DESTROYER, BENBOW'S DOC MIXTURE, and HALE'S HONEY OF HOREHOUND AND TAR. Despite the bottle-collecting boom, these choice specimens still usually sell for less than a bud vase of the same capacity. (The most inexpensive bottles are the "sick" ones, with a limy white film inside from having lain in the earth too long. But when filled with water they become utterly transparent again.) The embossing helps camouflage the stems and refracts water-carried light in elegant and delightful ways. Their wide, long necks made it easy for a tyro like me to arrange up to six sizable flowers attractively and still leave room to pour in fresh water as needed.

Wilted flowers should go directly into the Kitchen Compost—or back into the Pachysandra Garden, if it's slug free. Don't waste the water, either. Now free of chlorine and imbued with sap from cut stems, it's perfectly good for use on the nearest houseplant.

❀ PART THREE ❀

GARDENING BY ENVIRONMENT

11

THE LOW GARDEN

A Low Garden is the spot for all those perennial favorites that are too low-growing to survive among pachysandra. It can also be a site of unparalleled variety: the same square foot of soil can support crocus, snowdrop, daffodil, winter aconite, and species tulips in spring; small violets, veronica, and moneywort in early summer, and *Sedum spectabile* in autumn.

In a sense, a Low Garden is a rock garden without rocks, planted on a relatively flat plain of soil. The only secret is restricting competition meticulously and making sure there's enough light available for all.

Try to position your Low Garden so that it gets sun for at least half the day. Aside from spring bulbs, which arise before the trees leaf out, all best Low Garden plants like sun on their leaves throughout the summer. Remember, too, that unlike pachysandra, these plants' small foliage *cannot* swallow large autumn leaves. Therefore, any trees near a Low Garden should, ideally, be Second-Layer species with particularly small foliage—and high-pruned rigorously. Good choices include:

Acer palmatum (Japanese maple)

Amelanchier (shadblow)

Betula pendula (European white birch)

Crataegus (hawthorn)

Gleditsia (honey locust)

Malus (crabapple)

Prunus (small-leafed plums and cherries)

Robinia (black locust)

Sorbus (mountain ash)

Low Gardens look best on fairly flat terrain. Otherwise, they can be of virtually any size and shape, and are effective even when quite small—for example, along either side of a flagstone walk; thus forming a neat, low avenue that makes the walk itself look wider.

Before you start planting a Low Garden, rid the area of every single blade of grass. But if your Low Garden to be is very deep and wide, consider avoiding a barren, spotty look by strip-planting, just as you would with pachysandra. Cultivate only a two-foot wide strip at a time, as these are little plants! Start at the Garden's front edge and work back toward the center in successive seasons.

If the exposed soil isn't too fertile, spread a half inch or so of leaf-mold right atop it. But this layer of soil should not remain bare for any length of time. A heavy rain will spatter dirt so that it encrusts the stems and lower leaves of your plants. (This is particularly noticeable if your soil is clayish.) So even before you plant, mulch the bare earth with grass clippings. They'll keep the soil moist, workable, and looking fairly neat until your first few plants get under way.

Low Groundcovers are a must. They hold the soil against spattering and also provide a solid background to various plants so that the entire garden appears more uniform. None of the following grows over four inches tall.

Ajuga (TS) is sometimes called buglewort because of its tiny trumpet-shaped flowers on upright six-inch stalks in May. Each plant is a low rosette of crinkled leaves, usually of a deep bronzy hue. Soon after flowering, it sends out runners in all directions. New plants quickly root and consolidate their positions over the summer.

There are several reasons why ajuga fails as an all-purpose groundcover. For one thing, it can't absorb leaves: plants are fairly shallow-rooted and can often tear loose when raked. Ajuga spreads only in spring, so that gaps that appear at other seasons must be filled by transplants. Aphids, dryness, or too much shade can stunt it or make it fail to spread at all.

Ajuga hybrids have either blue, pink, or white flowers and come with several different shades and textures of foliage. Avoid the variegated foliage types, which look too busy when planted *en masse*. But mix plants of at least two different *flower* colors; the more common blue spikes look far better when contrasted with white or pink. White-flowering ajuga has leaves of a lighter green than the blue, so any planting will inevitably show subtle variations of color and texture.

Lysimachia nummularia (creeping Jennie, moneywort; LS) is a delight in a moist, sunny spot—and even in an informal lawn, since this plant is low enough to duck under a mower's blades. Pairs of glossy green leaves appear along long succulent stems. It's relatively inconspicuous, and so surprises you with its yellow, five-petaled flowers that appear in quantity in June and sporadically throughout the summer. Because of its trailing, open growth habit, *L. nummularia* is compatible with the most delicate plantings. Though it tolerates shade, it really will travel in sun, so give it room to venture. As it branches, *nummularia* eventually covers the ground thickly with a flat mat of stems.

Potentilla simplex (LS) is a wild relative of the strawberry, bearing smaller and more delicately cut leaves. It often invades lawns, where you can spot it by its small yellow flowers in May. Since it makes a loose, open series of runners, it's best as a temporary groundcover only, while others in this group are getting started. Other species and hybrids of *Potentilla* exist, but none spreads thickly enough to class as a useful groundcover.

Sedum (TS) comes in dozens of species and hybrids, all with succulent foliage and a thickly branching, fairly low growth habit. Unfortunately, most lose vigor after flowering in early summer. August droughts turn the foliage pale, and the center of any colony usually becomes a tangle of bare stems. The plants are worth using as temporary groundcovers, however: they are so shallow-rooted that they pull up easily to make room for anything else.

Thymus (thyme, LS) is a low, trailing herb that has been recently hybridized for groundcover use. If given full sun, most strains form handsome billowy mats of tiny leaves, blooming with white to purple flowers. However, plantings in my area tend to die back extensively in winter, not regaining their original spread until late the following summer. In any case, thyme grows very slowly, and I can't recommend it except in limited quantities, such as between the stones of a path.

Tiarella cordifolia (foamflower; TS) is a wildflower described more fully in Chapter 12. Like pachysandra, it needs to shade its own roots before becoming wantonly healthy but serves as a superb, attractive groundcover for places too shady for ajuga. The leaves—resembling those of a red maple—grow thickly together. Turrets of white flowers appear in May.

Veronica (TS) is a large genus comprising a bewildering variety of species and hybrids. For Low Garden use, avoid the upright forms known as speedwell.

The wild creeping veronica, *V. persica,* is the only plant I know with asymmetrically colored flowers. Of the four tiny petals, one is white. The petal opposite is blue, and the other two are abruptly divided between blue and white. It's best for part shade: in full sun, *Persica* forms billowy, fast-spreading mats that sweep up and over small perennials. This year I've had to root it out of my Low Garden and rely on the flatter-growing cultivated hybrids whose flowers are all blue or more commonly, pure white, often available in garden centers in early spring. Though they spread relatively slowly, they do so *completely,* even over clayish soil. The dark-leafed stems will crawl over a fallen leaf and set roots through it, effectively "sewing" the leaf down to the ground.

Almost all cultivated veronicas are indiscriminately tagged as either *repens, repandens,* or *radicans.* Choose a plant whose runners are already drooping over the side of the pot, and lift them out horizontally when the pot's soil cylinder is transplanted. If planted when the weather is warmer, veronica may not seem to spread, but with the return of damp, cool weather, the colony will begin spreading actively, often speeding at a rate of an inch a week and continuing on underneath the first fallen autumn leaves.

All the above plants are fairly shallow-rooted, so careful watering is necessary. But even so, it will take a lot longer for groundcovers to fill in than for you to select plants to go among them; so plant your groundcovers first to give them a head start. For a neat, trim effect, use a single variety of groundcover *only*. But to determine which kind best suits your taste, plant several different ones and let them fight it out. Sedum, for example, will find the places that thyme avoids, and potentilla will overrun both.

If one kind seems to do a better job than its competitors, fine: you can always weed them out as the preferable "winner" overtakes them.

BULBS

A Low Garden can be truly glorious in spring, since most colorful and self-spreading bulbs grow best under Low Garden conditions.

Allium (SS) is a wide genus of bulbs of the onion family. Many bear the same loose ball of florets that you see atop ordinary garden onions or chives. But the Alliums' main virtue is that they come into bloom in early summer, when most other spring bulbs are long since dormant. *Allium moly* has relatively large flowers of clear yellow, blooming in early June. But Alliums are now being hybridized for neater form and brighter red and purple colors, and the additional strains are worth trying.

Anemone blanda (anemone, windflowers; LS) is especially useful for the Low Garden. In very early April, daisy-like flowers with long petals—ranging from white through rose and blue to deep purple—are borne on short four-inch stalks. A few *blanda* hybrids are two-toned, with flowers shifting to a second color toward the circumference. (Try to obtain mixed lots, since plantings of all one color—especially blue—are a bit boring.) Just beneath the flower are two deeply cut, fern-like leaves that provide a nice touch of green when the petals drop. By June, the leaves have faded too and quickly disintegrate. Anemones seldom seed themselves, but the corms increase slowly over the years.

Crocus (LS) arises from sturdy gladiolus-like corms, producing bright flowers early in March. My only quarrel with this genus is that unlike most other spring flowers, crocus does not have a strong stem.

Instead, both the bud and the emerging grass-like leaves (each with a white stripe down the middle) are enclosed in a whitish sheath that extends up from the corm to just above ground level. Sharp winds will capsize them, and hard frost ruins the petals, reducing them to the consistency of wet cellophane.

Species crocus (including the so-called "snow crocus") bloom earlier than the norm and with smaller flowers, which can make them something of a disappointment. Invest mainly in the large hybrids of solid colors. Deep blues and purples don't always show up unless massed in wide drifts, so begin with the large whites or yellows. But mixed plantings of crocus always look spotty and awkward. Plant a single variety in a clump about a foot wide, and let it contrast with nearby colonies of different colors.

Individual corms should be planted about three to four inches apart—to cover as much territory as possible, and because they will slowly divide to form small clumps of their own. In addition, crocus seeds itself readily. The seed capsule is produced exactly at ground level, where the leaves join the underground sheath. Yet the seeds evidently disperse themselves some distance; each March a few new blossoms erupt in odd spots in my lawn where I know they couldn't have been planted originally. But like narcissus, crocus can be moved in full bloom, while you can still be sure of the color. (Bulbs growing in *very* loose soil can usually be hauled up by the sheath without damage.) Bulbs should be replanted three to four inches deep; if the sheath is longer than that, let it flop. The leaves will be properly supported when they emerge next spring.

Eranthis hyemalis (winter aconite; TS) arises in March with stems seldom more than four inches tall. Atop each is a yellow, buttercup-like flower with six wide petals and beneath it, a ruff of small green leaves that expand after the flower fades. Once established, winter aconites form a spreading colony that carpets the ground in drifts of yellow. But by June, the leaves have faded and rotted away.

Since winter aconite arises from a flattened tuber, not a bulb, it's particularly vulnerable to drying during shipment. Unfortunately, tubers are seldom mailed in plastic bags that would preserve moisture, and so usually arrive in an advanced state of desiccation. Plunge the wrinkled tubers in water as soon as you can, and leave them to soak a few hours before planting. Even with this emergency treatment, only about half will recover and bloom the next spring, so to ensure a dependable display, buy twice as many as you think you'll need.

When you go to plant them, you'll note that some tubers have a small circular depression on one side that bears a few tiny hairs—which are former roots. But most tubers are like free-form raisins, offering not a clue as to which way is up. But when tubers are planted horizontally, (as they "officially" should be) the law of averages assures that at least half will be buried upside down. To be safe, plant all your "blind" tubers on end, so that the main axis is vertical. That way, all your plants will be 90° out of kilter, but new growth can easily manage a right-angle turn. (When the plants begin spreading and self-seeding, the second generation will be properly aligned.) Recommended planting depth is two inches, but I'd plant tubers only two inches apart rather than the recommended three. Any plant that crowds itself naturally seldom minds company from the beginning, and a closer planting assures fewer gaps if some of your tubers don't survive.

Winter aconites don't take well to transplanting in full leaf. But dormant tubers are very hard to locate, and moving them while they're up at least assures that they'll be pointed in the right direction. It's worth the risk: dig a wide, deep ball of soil around the roots, as large as you would when moving a regular perennial.

Galanthus (snowdrop; CF) is an absolute staple of the Low Garden. In very early March, up come the leaves of blue-green or olive, depending on the species, followed by flower stalks, each topped with a single bud that nods on its stalk like the lantern of an old-fashioned lamppost. The flowers themselves almost seem to be permanent buds —tiny little eggs of pure white without apparent seam or crease. But on a warmish afternoon, the three petals will flare outward to resemble a limp airplane propeller. You must pick a flower and turn it upside down to glimpse the narrow, green-tipped tube that encloses the flower's reproductive organs. Only by looking straight up the tube can you see the yellow pollen-tipped anthers. Snowdrop stems are so highly succulent that you can mash them in two between your fingers. (This makes picking easier, but be sure you've reached down as far as possible into the welter of leaves before breaking the stem loose.)

It seems incredible that any flower can withstand repeated nightly freezes with no damage, but such highly elastic tissues are better able to survive a sudden plunge into the teens. By April the flowers stay open continuously. The ovary behind the petal swells into a plump minature watermelon. Under its weight, the stem slumps to the ground and the capsule eventually bursts open, distributing new seeds a few inches away from the parent bulb.

There are a number of different *Galanthus* species. *Single-flowered* ones include:

Galanthus nivalis, the common snowdrop usually sold by mail, has named varieties with larger flowers: 'S. Arnott' has rapidly multiplying bulbs; 'Straffan' can produce two separate sets of flowerstalks before going dormant; 'Viridapicis' has spots of green at the end of each petal.

G. elwesii (giant snowdrop) is worth getting for its large (up to one inch) late winter blooms. This species prefers drier soil than most snowdrops and increases more slowly by division, though seeds germinate readily.

G. ikarie latifolius has medium-sized flowers and particularly wide, glossy blue-green leaves.

G. plicatus (Crimean snowdrop) has thinner, daintier upright foliage and narrower petals than most snowdrops, making it most appropriate for neat and formal surroundings.

Double-flowered snowdrops are all varieties of *nivalis* and show up better at a distance than the single forms. 'Lady Elphinestone' has large petticoats of white touched with tiny brushstrokes of yellow; 'Ophelia' is pure white. But unfortunately, neither is as fast spreading as the single *nivalis*.

Because these bulbs increase over the years, do *not* plant them in tight groups or you'll soon wind up with overgrown clumps that need dividing. Plant single bulbs every foot or so. As with many other bulbs, newly planted snowdrops often arise a bit later than their established counterparts. The bulbs need time to grow and multiply, but when they do, you can see a marked increase each spring. One colony has at least doubled in the five years I've been observing it, and the lushest, most appealing planting I know—with stalks up to a foot—has been in place for at least twenty years. These thick, freeform clumps may be inappropriate for extremely formal garden spots, but *Galanthus* spreads attractively among rocks, in the crooks of a brick path, and under deciduous Second-Layer trees such as birches. Such colonies will feature taller plants toward the center, and will not need dividing at all until you want to borrow some of the outlying offspring for planting elsewhere.

Interestingly, this is one bulb that's *supposed* to be moved while still in leaf, rather than while dormant. This means getting your trowel ready about mid-March: when snowdrop foliage fades, it breaks down very quickly so that even large colonies are hard to locate.

Muscari (grape hyacinth; TS) has masses of thin stems and a stalk that bears small, roughly circular blue flowers in a mass resembling an inverted bunch of grapes. It qualifies for some kind of award as the hardiest of all spring flowers. I've transplanted bulbs from a clay path where they had been baked, parched, and trodden down for at least a decade. The foliage was stunted and crushed, but the bulbs were fat, obviously vigorous, and rapidly dividing. Another time, I came upon a matted tangle of bulbs washed in by the tide on the shore of Long Island Sound. Both foliage and bulbs were puckered from their prolonged salt water bath and apparently dead, but just out of curiosity as to what they were, I planted them. The next spring, they flowered robustly: grape hyacinth! Any plant that can take this kind of abuse is not something you should admit to a narrow planting in the hopes that it'll stay put. Colonies of the common *armeniacum* spread very rapidly by division and by seed and can form wild, trailing tangles of foliage that engulf smaller bulbs and perennials. Now I have massed all my grape hyacinths in a single area where they compete against each other, rather than attempting to colonize the rest of the garden.

One reason for its vigor is that after lying dormant over the summer, *Muscari* usually reawakens around September and sends up a second set of spindly leaves to give the bulbs an extra shot of photosynthesis before spring. Provide an extra dressing of humus and fertilizer for congested clumps. New bulblets will squeeze themselves above and below the parent layer; but as long as everybody's roots can obtain equal nourishment, the flowers increase proportionately. *Muscari* is now offered in a pleasant grabbag of species and varieties, and you can pack several together for a varied, intriguing display.

Muscari armeniacum is the common deep-blue grape hyacinth most frequently sold. Leaves are narrow, thread-like and sprawling— easily the least attractive foliage of the genus. The variety 'Heavenly

Blue' has lighter-colored flowers than the norm. Since this is the species that produces fall foliage, I beg gardeners to watch their beds for a possible fall blossom. If so, you may have a mutant bulb that will rebloom in autumn—a real horticultural break-through.

M. botryoides has thicker leaves and larger, more spherical florets. The white variety *album* is lovely, but the leaves are of a much lighter green, and the plant as a whole less vigorous and slower to spread than most of the genus. Give *album* its own site, or it will be smothered by its blue brothers.

M. comosum (the giant grape haycinth) is probably your best bet: lavish, showy bloom and foliage that is more restrained than the smaller *armeniacum*'s. In the variety *monstrosum* or *plumosum,* flowers are exploded into hair-like petals so that the flowerhead resembles a swirl of blue cotton candy.

M. latifolium has broad, attractive foliage like that of a snowdrop: the bottom florets on each head quickly fade to a very deep, dull blue.

M. macrocarpum is much larger than most *Muscari,* but the flowers (on stems to ten inches) are a pale yellow that shows up well only when interplanted with regular blues.

M. tubergenianum has darker florets toward the top of the well-formed, square-topped spike. Leaves are trim and erect, making it by far the neatest *Muscari.*

Narcissus (daffodil; CF) has a number of six-inch dwarf to miniature species that are appropriate to the Low Garden. (Their bulbs are often surprisingly large, however.) A few of the odder ones are discussed later in the Rocky chapter, but for Low Garden use, don't omit *Narcissus jonquilla* and *juncifolius*. Their tall, grass-like foliage is attractive in itself. Then in very late May, when most narcissus have quit, each bulb blooms with a series of small yellow flowers, each with a short trumpet and wide, oval petals. The entire display lasts up to two weeks—a long time for such a late-flowering bulb—and the upright foliage remains attractive until it fades.

Scilla sibirica (Siberian squill, star of Holland; TS) is the most rewarding and delightful of all spring bulbs. From the center of two or more glossy, sharp-pointed leaves ascends a spray of six-pointed flowers of the deepest, clearest blue. The largest plants never measure more than eight inches tall, and so even wide colonies give an air of perfect proportion and delicacy. In New Jersey, *S. sibirica* is in riotous bloom in late April, but at the same season, I have seen it up and in ready bud in a frosty garden in Elmira, New York. Cold weather, even snow, does not trouble the flowers at all, and the leaves and stems are sturdy enough to withstand high winds.

Even in the poorest soils, this plant increases tremendously. An established colony, when raided for bulbs to transplant elsewhere, will be found crammed with the tiny worm-like leaves of seedling bulbs, many of them no larger than a pinhead, working their way down to the proper depth. Thus squill is another bulb you shouldn't plant in clumps to begin with. Insert one every six inches or so, and within a few years they will fill in their gaps automatically.

Tulipa (tulip; CF) hybrids are too tall and short-lived for the Low Garden. But not so the species tulips, of smaller size, but of good form and color. Most of these "botanical" tulips will multiply and self-seed.

Tulipa clusiana (lady or peppermint stripe tulip) has petals streaked with white and red. The thin, hair-like foliage permits planting in close clumps, but be sure to provide good, deep, rich humus if you want it to multiply.

T. eichleri has broad, squat flowers of bright crimson, but foliage is sprawling and messy. To camouflage it, interplant with Siberian squill or grape hyacinth.

T. kaufmaniana (water lily tulip) flowers early and is by far the best species, combining low habit, thick petals, and bright color. A host of desirable hybrids are now being developed, not all of which spread as readily as the original species. Mixed lots can be a bargain, but for a better display, be ready to separate the bulbs later into groups of a single color.

T. princeps has the broad, alternate leaves typical of most hybrid tulips. The flowers are also the most "hybrid-like" of all tulip species: the overlapping petals are red, streaked with white, opening to pure red within. Unopened buds are very plump and almost flat at the base. Yet the entire plant is less than a foot tall.

T. tarda has narrow, yellow petals edged with white, opening into a not-too-showy flower that resembles that of a large *Allium moly*. Foliage is neat and strap-like and, as the name implies, the blooms appear later than most species'.

T. turkestanica blooms dependably and self-seeds easily, forming large seed capsules. But the flower itself is disappointing. Although several are borne to a stem, they are small and don't show up at all in the welter of other, brighter spring flowers.

T. violacea is small, but its globular flower is a striking lavender-red. The thick, narrow foliage is a deep green. Plant it by itself in a partly shaded, sheltered area with excellent humus where it doesn't have to compete with showier tulips.

T. whittallii has cup-shaped, orange-yellow blooms resembling an enormous crocus. Foliage is thin and neat—more delicate than *kaufmanii,* and a good companion to that species.

Autumn-flowering Bulbs

. . . can be grown successfully in Low Garden, but are something of a disappointment. Because late September and early October are drier and warmer than March and April, fall-flowering blossoms seldom endure as long as their spring counterparts.

Colchium (SS) is only marginally attractive. In spring, a large tiered mass of green foliage arises. But no flower appears, and the leaves usually take a good amount of abuse from slugs and insects before they fade late in June. Then in mid-September, huge buds emerge on white, weak, fleshy stems. Those that don't collapse under their own weight elongate at varying angles to open in pale lavender crocus-like flowers about eight inches tall. At best the color is washed-out, fading back toward white at the stem and making a fairly poor show. Bulbs dug in the summer (as most commercial colchiums are) can be left unplanted on a windowsill. They'll bloom—as the frequent advertisements say they will—but should be planted immediately thereafter to assure roots for next spring's leaves.

Crocus (LS) includes several fall-blooming species and hybrids, most moderately attractive. But they are somewhat lackluster in comparison with spring strains, spoil very quickly, and are effective only if planted in full colonies. (A loose grouping of fall-blooming crocus invariably looks like a local mistake, similar to the few azalea buds that always fall for ambiguous autumn light and burst into premature bloom.)

Galanthus nivalis var. *reginae olgae* is an autumnal snowdrop, pure and simple.

All fall-blooming bulbs should be interplanted with spring-flowering species. This way, the former will not look so barren in spring when their flowers fail to appear. It might make even better sense to ring any fall-flowering bulb with a few *Muscari armeniacums,* which sprout autumn foliage and help the leafless blooms look as if they belonged. (In spring, *M. armeniacum* throws up flowers that will assuage any bloomless foliage in the vicinity.)

Planting and Arrangement of Low Garden Bulbs

Because all bulbs in this section are virtually permanent, they should be positioned with some care. For proper design, my main rule is to *duplicate existing plantings of bulbs of the same species.*

Let's say you already have two or three tight clusters of snowdrops, each two feet apart. When you introduce new *Galanthus* bulbs, they too should be spaced two feet apart from the originals—and from each other. If you have a bed of white crocus, new bulbs of that color should be added to the perimeter, not scattered throughout the garden. If you want an existing bed to remain small, then build a similar, matching colony some distance away. Each *color* of bulb should have a pattern all its own, and that pattern should relate to the *entire* expanse of the Low Garden area, even if that "pattern" means spacing individual bulbs two to three feet apart. This way, bulbs that bloom at different times will present succeeding patterns of their own as the spring weeks pass, without causing visual confusion.

Thus, because winter aconite and *Narcissus triandrus* bloom at different seasons, the two can be interplanted without harm. The same is true of bulbs that bloom at the same time but at different *heights:* taller *Narcissi* can be interplanted with the much lower *Scilla sibirica.* But intermingling these bulbs is effective only if you keep a watch on *color.* (The Impressionist painters discovered that the eye best responds to a display of two colors that contrast sharply.) For example, blue squills look good beneath yellow miniature narcissus. But match two different narcissus of slightly different shades, or crocus of more than two contrasting colors, and the eye reads the conglomeration as muddy, and somewhat lacking in true sparkle.

Quite often I get "bonus" bags of short-lived hybrid Darwin tulips along with my fall bulb order. I plant them in the Low Garden, but have to expect that they'll give out eventually. So after setting them twelve to eighteen inches deep, I fill their hole to within six inches of the top and plant a new layer of species tulip or some other colonizing bulb. Most of these will bloom before the Darwins emerge from below. Thereafter, they'll camouflage the Darwin foliage. And when the hybrids finally die out, that planting site will be permanently bulb-infested and provide never-ending spring color.

If you need extra bulbs from any existing planting, remove them from the *center* of a colony where they're least noticeable. However, if old bulbs at the center have grown to patriarchal size, removing the outlying small fry will keep the clump lush and neat. Tuber plants like anemones and aconites need a ball of soil about the roots, but all *bulb* plants can be moved bare-rooted, even in full bloom. This is fortunate, because there's no way to correct an unsatisfactory pattern, spacing, or color arrangement except when the bulbs are actually in flower. (Cool spring temperatures seem to minimize transplanting shock.) Although flowers may fade quickly, the bulb will have ignored the insult when it arises again next spring.

All spring flowers are attractive when cut and brought indoors. I keep the smaller ones in old-fashioned cobalt-blue Bromo-Seltzer bottles, usually available inexpensively at flea markets. For a nodding snowdrop, place a small circular mirror under the vase to help you see *inside* the flower as well. But be ready to replace spring blooms after a day or two. If they seem long-lasting outdoors, it's only because the cool weather preserves them. (This was dramatically proven during the record 90° temperatures that hit the Northeast in April 1976. Many emerging wildflowers and daffodils wilted within twenty-four hours.) Higher indoor temperatures so accelerate the flower's metabolism that they usually wilt in two or three days, while flowers of the same colony may not have even fully opened.

SHRUBS

Since you want to take in your Low Garden with a single glance, any shrubs it comprises should either be very small or so fastigiate and upright that they don't block your view.

Buxus microphylla nana compacta is an extremely dwarf boxwood that eventually grows to form a rounded bun 8 inches tall. Flowers are insignificant, but it makes a far more attractive, dependably evergreen border than *Teucreum,* which is widely advertised for that purpose.

Rhododendrons: a number of rhododendron and azalea species seldom grow taller than 15 inches, always spreading wider than high. Except as noted, flowers are purple to lavender. Therefore, first try to obtain the differently colored varieties marked with an asterisk, later filling in your gaps with the easier-to-locate purple-flowering types:

Rhododendron fastigiatum (upright and good for marking borders)

R. flavitum (yellowish cream flowers)

R. gumpo (white flowers—plant is very low and spreading, and should be given room to form a semi-groundcover)

R. gumpo roseum (pink flowers)

R. keleticum* (more compact and congested than the above species)

R. macrantha (pink flowers; form very low and spreading)

R. obtusum japonicum* (very low and spreads up to three feet in diameter)

R. racemosum (prolific pink flowers)

R. radicans* (prostrate, seldom grows taller than five inches)

R. ramapo* (open, twiggy, but stands shearing)

R. ramapo album (white flowers)

*R. 'Rosebud' (rose-pink flowers; a hybrid Gable azalea)

R. rupicola*

R. 'Watchung' (a cultivar of *R. ramapo*)

Rosa (rose): can make splendid additions to a Low Garden. Use any of the "miniature" roses now widely offered by mail.

When miniature roses were first sold a few years back, they

claimed to have been developed from plants grown as windowbox subjects in Switzerland. I supposed that if they grew in the Alps in the first place, they must be winter-hardy, and so I planted my first miniatures outdoors—with a bed of good leafmold but no winter protection.

Their foliage wilted alarmingly at the first frost—but then, so do most roses'. The next spring, however, they sprouted thick buds of new growth and flowered constantly from late May onward. Although the *flowers* are miniature enough, the plants themselves often reach 18 inches and up with proper nourishment; their upright canes allow them to be planted quite close together.

New hybrids are constantly being developed, and are far too numerous to mention here. However, any catalog will give you a wide selection of acceptable candidates. Restrict yourself to those described as most floriferous, and avoid ones with especially tiny flowers—they won't show up well at a distance. Make sure you have a basic color range of yellow, pink, red, and white before duplicating any of your colors.

PERENNIALS

Aquilegia (columbine) is too rampant in most of its hybrid forms. However, *A.* 'Biedermeier' (CF) forms a tight, round 12-inch ball of foliage. In May, flowers—of white, pink or deep bluish lavender with white centers—arise thickly on short stalks that do not droop even after they go to seed.

A. canadensis (SS) is a tall and upright native American species, with really good form and color. I first saw its bright red and yellow harlequin's caps in riotous bloom on the broken rocks of a Catskill cliff. (*Canadensis* cannot tolerate shade, and so will not succeed in the shady Wild Garden.)

All columbines self-seed, particularly in the sandy seams of brick paths. But if you also have larger hybrids in your Pachysandra Garden, you won't know *whose* seedlings these are until they bloom. Therefore, have a test bed of rich, sunny loam where seedling columbines can be quarantined until they identify themselves. The most desirable plants can then be transplanted to spots of honor; losers can be swapped or discarded. (High on the Kill List are those with nodding flowerstalks, muddy color, and lanky foliage.)

For more dependable results, collect the seed of columbines you know you like. A columbine flower ripens very quickly into a crown of small capsules like tiny vertical peapods. Simply break off a corner of one capsule to see what gives. If the seeds inside are black, the whole flowerhead can be snipped off. If they're green, visit the plant again the next day—the day after, they may be ripened and scattered.

Sow the seeds in your test bed. New plants will often emerge by August, or certainly the next May. They will bloom when they attain about eight inches. Hybrid strains can produce a wide range of surprises, but depending on the proximity of other plants, species *canadensis* seedlings will be more or less true to form.

Chrysanthemums (CF) provide spectacular color in September and October when most other perennials have shot their bolts. But for me, this late bloom conceals a number of drawbacks: chrysanthemums remain visually inert for the best part of the summer, often becoming thin and weedy. Some gardeners pinch off side buds for larger, better-shaped flowers, but this only guarantees that the plant itself will become untidy and probably require staking. Normal-sized chrysanthemums tend to flop in heavy October rain, but specially pinched stalks flop absolutely.

Flowers (especially the white and light yellow shades) become "stained" with purple blotches after cold nights. New shoots are vulnerable to slugs and fungus, and old lower leaves frequently wither to an unsightly brown. But if you buy budded mums in autumn, all too often the shoots fail to "break" again the next spring. This probably has something to do with their nursery cultivation. Most sources agree that mums like a humus-rich soil. Yet I've yet to see a garden-center mum that wasn't potted in pure clay. These plants are probably propagated in greenhouses where humidity and mass fertilizing make soil quality less important. Mums form their buds when the light becomes longer, and plants are easier to shade when kept indoors, of course. But greenhouse conditions aren't the ideal environment for any would-be hardy plant.

I prefer the cushion mums for their naturally neat look—they give a lavish show of small blooms, whose tightly crammed stalks more or less support one another. Also try to locate *species* chrysanthemums that haven't yet learned to be fussy, as well as recent Far North hybrids that are exceptionally hardy and vigorous. (Plants that survive cold can usually survive other adverse conditions.) Buy them from mail-order firms in spring or early summer. Within the dark box, the new growth becomes soft and succulent, but when set out in full sun, quickly perk up and increase. Newly planted mums will usually bloom earlier than their established counterparts, so clip dead flowers promptly to return strength to the leaves.

After a hard frost, a mum's stalks shrivel but remain standing like winter weeds. For appearance's sake, you should clip them off about November. Strew the stubs with a light straw mulch. Mums that have survived the winter should be strewn with poison baits in spring to forestall slug damage.

Digitalis (foxglove; SS) is best known by the hybrids of *D. purpurea,* an overweening border plant that sends up five-foot stalks of lovely trumpets mottled with ringed spots of darker color (see Color Section). Though most *purpurea* hybrids are biennials, they will seed themselves in a Low Garden. Lower, and less likely to topple after blooming, are the dependably perennial species *grandiflora* and *lanata.* Neither grows above three feet, but both bloom with *purpurea*-size flowers. Such foxgloves are the best perennial for a steep bankside; use ajuga or veronica as an underplanting.

Fragaria vesca (European or woods strawberry; CF) is usually marketed by its French name of *fraise de bois.* Unlike other strawberries, these are clump-forming plants that produce no runners at all. Foliage is neatly arranged, as if a handful of strawberry leaves had been jammed in an underground vase. Flowers appear intermittently all summer, ripening into small, conical berries with a tart, fresh taste. For this reason, *fraise de bois* should be within easy reach so that the sometime crop can be gathered—and be protected from slugs that will hollow out a ripening berry. Dividing clumps too often weakens them and reduces berry production—about one division every four years not only gives you more specimens, but preserves their health and vigor.

Heuchera sanguinea (coralbells; CF) bear tall sprays covered with tiny flowers of red, pink, or white. They are airy and delicate, but fail to show up effectively at a distance. More desirable, however, are the rosettes of low-lying, maple-like leaves that eventually spread to form a four-inch groundcover. At this point, the flowerstalks are crowded enough to support each other effectively; and mixing several different colors makes a better display. Good soil and sun are necessary, however, for vigorous flower production.

Hostas include a number of CF dwarf forms perfectly suited to a Low Garden. Rising just above the groundcovers, their loose rosettes of thin leaves remain pleasantly in bounds. Flowerstalks are shorter and less floppy than on full-sized plants.

H. lancifolia, with especially narrow sword-like leaves, has several good hybrids to its credit. (*Lancifolia* X 'Louisa' is an especially desirable *white*-flowered dwarf with variegated foliage!)

H. venusta minor has slightly wider leaves than *lancifolia,* but borne so loosely that a plant doesn't look well until it's been established for a few years. Flowers are typically pale lavender. There are too many other hybrids and varieties in these smaller sizes for me to list individually, but most catalogs list a hosta's leaf size along with the color of its flowers.

Dicentra exima is best for pachysandra. However, it will not seed itself among the terminals, so keep at least one plant in the Low Garden, where *exima* seedlings can arise. Although the foliage of young plants is slug-susceptible, seedlings quickly develop a thick fleshy root that helps them withstand transplanting shock and drought. Two-inch seedlings moved to a good locale can often reach blooming size before the end of the summer.

Potentilla (TS) comes in a number of spreading forms that are supposed to form low, prostrate mats. But most die back at the center and become leggy. *P. verna nana* forms neat narrow clumps with sporadic yellow flowers all summer.

Primula (primrose; SS) leaves are borne in flat rosettes, close to the ground. Fairly shallow-rooted, they can be happy in a fairly thin layer of good soil. More importantly, they keep producing new leaves regularly until frost, so that small plants usually increase in size over the summer, remaining fresh and crisp-looking while nearby perennials are starting to look bedraggled. But their neat growth habit keeps them from interfering with even the most delicate adjacent plantings. Blooming primroses offered in garden shops in May and June are invariably hybrids. Take your pick of the colors you like best; but only one of each. Individual plants will eventually form clumps that can be divided.

Hybridizers have done wonders with the various strains, though the more sophisticated plants are available only from specialized nurseries. Especially stunning is the Gold Lace Polyanthus, whose very dark petals are edged and striped in a light color that makes each single petal look like two. There are also a number of species *Primulas,* which—though not as exotic or large as the hybrids—are still worth collecting because they will self-seed. Generally, rarer kinds are available only in seed form, but you can buy plants of *P. vulgaris* (the English cowslip) that blooms early with tightly held flowers of rich creamy yellow. In all, a careful selection of different plants can assure you a succession of bloom from March through late June; and a varied and charming Low Garden can be entirely constructed using no other perennial. Primroses don't look good when massed, as so often illustrated; I prefer them studded every six inches or so throughout a low carpet of veronica.

Plants sold in wood or plastic flats are often growing in hard clay; plant them bare-rooted. This will make the flowers fade more quickly, but it's absolutely necessary for them to get established properly. Too tight a growth habit means a plant is too dry or is getting too much sun; but a plant that leans to one side with floppy, outsize leaves and scant flowers is asking for more light.

Viola (violets; TS or LS or CF) bloom only in early spring, when they are outclassed by bulbs. Moreover, most are thick spreaders, which rules them out as companion plants. Existing stands of violets are worth preserving, however, because they host caterpillars of the fritilleries—brown butterflies whose underwings are plated with gouts of bright silver.

A very few native violets are single-stalk plants, providing handsome accents even when not in bloom. My favorites are *V. fimbriatula* and *V. saggittata,* both of which produce lance-shaped hairy leaves throughout the summer after their lavender-rose flowers fade. Use them to fill small gaps between primroses.

A Low Garden can also be planted with many of the plants described in Chapters 14 and 15, but the species above are best suited to this kind of environment. Each year I try a few new species, only to haul them out again when they become invasive, unkempt, or dead. Increasingly I'm limiting my plantings to cultivated veronica, moneywort, primroses, and miniature roses, all unmatched for neatness and dependability. So start with the best and easiest before you begin experimenting.

If your Pachysandra and Low Gardens are separated by a path, it's fun to line up plants of the same genus so that one side of the walk is bordered with large species and the other with smaller ones. To one side of my main brick walk, emerging from the pachysandra are enormous hostas, blue Siberian iris, and *Lysimachia vulgaris.* In the Low Garden "across the road" are their smaller counterparts—dwarf *Hosta lancifolia, Iris verna,* and *Lysimachia nummularia.* Each set of counterparts blooms at about the same time with the same color, and it's easy to make comparisons because the relative proportions are maintained throughout the growing season.

Except for hostas and the larger primroses, be sure all your perennials lie well outside the perimeter of any colony of fast-multiplying bulbs like *Galanthus, Muscari,* or *Scilla,* whose emerging growth can hoist smaller plants right out of the soil! To mulch delicate plantings, use grass clippings. Take a good wad of fresh clippings in one hand and shake vigorously. A rain of narrow confetti will sift down between your plants, and whatever falls atop them will soon dry up and be blown aside.

If it's properly positioned, any Low Garden plant should grow fully upright. Primroses are the most responsive to lack of light, but if you find *any* plant emerging with its foliage at a distinct angle to the ground, it's being shaded by some tree or shrub that needs to be pruned higher. Afflicted plants invariably face *away* from the main source of shade, so the culprit should be obvious.

This doesn't necessarily mean the plant needs direct sun, however. Many times I have found plants growing tall and upright in what seemed to be heavy shade. But straight above them, there was always a gap in the trees that revealed a patch of blue sky. Conversely, I've seen many plants in full sun that were leaning away from a tree, wall, or hedge that blocked their "view" of the sky. In fact, many of my small trees used to lean *toward* the white-painted east wall of my house, ignoring the actual sun (they straightened up only when the house was finished in a dark aluminum siding). Evidently plants depend heavily on *reflected* light, and not on just the sun's direct rays.

Whenever it snows, never miss the opportunity to inspect your Low Garden. Most of us think wrongly that snow is a mask, a blanket, a disguise. Quite the contrary: it shows you more clearly what was there all along in terms of pure form. Erasing small details, it emphasizes the primary lines and angles—the corners of your stone and brick paths, the placement of small shrubs. The heavier the snow, the more clearly your garden's strengths and weaknesses reveal themselves.

Last night, as I write this, there was a five-inch snowfall; tonight a half moon presided over the landscape, letting me see clearly that my weeping thread-needle cypress looked downright silly beside the Miniature Landscape. I saw where a stretch of Low Garden could be continued to follow a path's outline, shrinking in width until it became a narrow border, and where a line of advancing pachysandra—already forming a crested wave just beyond a brick pathway—ought to be forestalled with edging. It would have taken me months of summer observation to pick out these same flaws and relationships. Anything that looks wrong in a winter snowscape *is* wrong, and should be corrected as soon as the ground thaws.

The only remaining problem with a Low Garden is that its tidy groundcovers make a perfect spot for errant seeds to germinate. A great many will be the welcome offspring of desirable plants nearby; so each spring, I tack up a notice on the office bulletin board offering dogwood seedlings (among others) at twenty-five cents apiece. Even if you're not a Scotsman like I am, weeding your garden is infinitely more pleasant when you're being paid for nearly every scoop of the trowel.

In short, try to get some value from your unwanted extras. And should there be a vacant lot in your neighborhood where people dump garden rubbish, examine it carefully for free discards you can cart home. I have found crocus, *many* different narcissus, ajuga, domestic strawberry, grape hyacinth, daylilies and pachysandra growing happily among discarded weeds and grass clippings. The varieties weren't always what I'd have chosen personally, but they were free—and many are quite welcome now that they've reached maturity.

12

THE WILD GARDEN

Growing native American wildflowers on your own land has a certain reverence, a hush, a thrill. These are the flowers cited by Hawthorne and Thoreau; whose silhouettes were stitched into samplers and painted on Pennsylvania "Dutch" *fractur*. Their blooms have a reticent grace that few longer-blooming perennials can match. Yet many species are genuinely endangered—because, in all fairness, these plants often make life particularly difficult for themselves.

The great majority of wildflowers are fleeting: they sprout, flower, and often wither long before the summer has reached its peak. Thus it's practically impossible to locate and save them should bulldozers come romping through during the other ten months of the year.

When the first spring leaves of a tree or shrub are broken or nibbled off, it can always generate replacements. But a ladyslipper, trillium, or troutlily has no new leaves ready to go until the *next* spring. So if these leaves are damaged, the plant is usually set back severely. Nor is most wildflower seed airborne like a dandelion's or a thistle's. Instead, a species like bloodroot reproduces by small black seeds that usually fall at the foot of the plant, extending the species' range only by inches. I know of vast stands of some endangered species, but they are almost always the result of slow asexual propagation, not of self-seeding.

Unfortunately, many wildflowers have yet another self-destructive trick up their sheathes: they demand a far lighter, richer, clay-free soil than most gardens afford. Several of the extremely desirable beauties will not grow at all except in highly specific soils (Indian pipe in deeply shaded decaying leaves and twigs; pink ladyslipper in dryish pine straw or oakleaf litter; partridgeberry in the shade of *small*-needled evergreens). But the forest itself is by no means an ideal environment for these relatively small plants. Even if animals and insects steer clear of them, the ecology of a forest is constantly changing—and not always for the better. I have seen trilliums degenerating under hemlocks that were casting too much shade, ladyslippers trapped in the coils of greenbrier like butterflies in barbed wire, troutlily bulbs forced to the surface by the expanding roots of a beech. *If* you can duplicate the right mixture of soil and shade, your garden is probably a far safer place for wildflowers. But to preserve them, *you must help them to thrive*. Otherwise, you are simply investing time and money toward their eventual extinction—on your land and in the nation in general.

Where should your Wild Garden be? Somewhere where it can remain forever, because the plants do best when left unmolested.

The best choice is a spot where wildflowers bloom to begin with: where troutlily mobs a leaf-strewn forest floor; beside an outcrop of bedrock that's upholstered in mosses and ferns; where a veteran jack-in-the-pulpit broods over the fading blossoms of wakerobin trillium. But in the wild, you must keep nature from *un*doing what it has so graciously provided. Keep trees pruned of dead wood that can break off and crush your plants. (Have your tree work done in winter, when there's frozen soil or snow to cushion boots, ladders, and falling wood.) In summer, remove weeds, seedling trees, and shrubs; block pachysandra, creeping ferns, and grass. Arrange fences or shrubs so that children don't see that sector of ground as the shortest distance between two points.

When starting a Wild Garden from scratch, this is also the main consideration: keep it out of the way. If you decide to devote a portion of your property to wildflowers for easier maintenance, under no circumstances should it be on a hilltop or sun-baked area where water drains away on all sides (though such sites are appropriate for Cultivated Meadows). Most wildflowers like a soil that never dries completely, but is still deep enough not to get boggy after prolonged rain.

One way to keep your ground fairly moist is by providing shade in exactly the right seasonal doses—strong in early spring when wildflowers are sprouting, deeper in summer when sun-loving weeds are germinating.

When a catalog describes a given species as "shade-loving," look again and see if the plant is described as growing in evergreen woods. If so, it *is* a shade lover: pines and hemlocks retain their foliage all year, so that the light beneath them is consistently dim. But when most wildlings emerge in early spring, they receive the almost full sun that streams down through the still-leafless branches of deciduous trees that are naturally high-pruned by competition. In April the sun is at the same angle and intensity that it will be later in August, so these plants are expecting—in fact, demanding—a pretty strong dose.

To grow your flowers properly, you'll usually want conditions to be even a bit brighter than in the average forest. If truly enormous wildflower colonies thrive where summer shade is quite deep, I suspect it's not shade these plants enjoy as much as protection from Dog Day heat. Note that a great many wildflowers bear the species name of *canadense,* meaning that Canada comprises good part of their range. They are used to cold winters, but more importantly, cool moist summers. After I noted how "shade-loving" perennials often seem content in sun as long as their *roots* are shaded and moist, I began studying published photographs of arbutus, lady-slipper, and trillium, which are said to abhor full sun. A good many photos of these wild plants show them thriving in an expanse of obviously open sunlight that's so wide it must be direct for at least three hours. This made little sense until I scrutinized the companion plants in each illustration. I could usually make out ferns, sedges, and moss, which grow where the ground is moist. Therefore, a wildflower with its roots in cool, damp soil can make use of extra sun.

Your Wild Garden, then, should be a low-lying area shaded by Second-Layer trees. If you don't have any Second-Layer trees growing already, you'll have to plant them and until the trees have reached at least ten feet, hold off introducing any but the easiest Group A wildflower species. Since a Wild Garden should never be raked, your Second-Layer trees should be small-leafed ones like hedge, trident, and Japanese maples, ironwood, hornbeam, gray and black birch. In a Wild Garden that's more or less square or circular, smaller plants toward the center will be lost to view—perhaps lost permanently if you can't reach them for weeding. A rustic stepping-stone path will provide easy viewing and keep visitors' feet in the right places.

Very strong winds gust throughout April and May. As a result, wildflowers often get their blossoms prematurely stripped, and the taller-stalked ones like bloodroot and trillium are broken over. A windbreak of arborvitae or rhododendron is needed. If the border of your Wild Garden is also the border of your property, then your windbreak can also serve as part of your privacy hedge.

Soil

Few gardeners realize how deep forest loam can be. I was once called to fight a forest fire ignited when a stand of hemlocks was struck by lightning. When our team arrived, the fire was smoldering through layers of humus whose moisture had evaporated under the heat of the surface flames. In one spot where this subterranean blaze had broken through to the surface, it looked as if a giant cookie cutter had neatly removed a section of soil almost a foot deep. Clay and sand do not burn, of course; plant matter does—so in this particular forest, the leafmold must have been at least twelve inches thick. On the Jersey Palisades, I have seen pink ladyslipper orchids thriving in five inches of oak leafmold atop clay, but those top five inches were *pure* leafmold—no pebbles, no air pockets, no worm burrows.

The simple method of not raking up autumn leaves will give you a halfway decent layer of leafmold in several years' time, but I'm assuming you'd like to speed things up. Therefore, start piling leafmold *atop* your existing soil. And keep at it, as much and as often as you can. (Because most wildflowers are best planted in fall, spread your leafmold deeply no later than June, letting it settle and further decay for at least three months.) An inch deep is good for crested iris; two inches for a good-sized false Solomon's-seal. But at least four to five inches, allowed to age for at least a year, are required for a native orchid or a thriving trillium colony.

I've grouped the following species according to how easy they are to grow. No matter what your soil, the ridiculously easy Group A wildflowers like mayapple and can be introduced immediately. As soon as you have loose humus that's fairly free of clay, foamflower and all the Group B plants can come in. If they begin spreading, you'll be asssured that your soil is improving. But not until you have dependable summer shade and deep black humus should you attempt any of the more exotic C's—yellow ladyslipper, trilliums. The acid shade-lovers of Group D are the very last to go into any land being prepared for them.

Group A: Wildflowers for Almost Any Soil

Arisaema triphyllum (jack-in-the-pulpit; SS; see Color Section) is one of the real workhorses of the wild. A young jack sends up a single three-lobed leaf that can be mistaken for hepatica. On an older plant, the stalk is wrapped in a mottled purple sheath, and *two* leaves emerge, approaching the size and deep green of shagbark hickory's. Between these two leaves is the "pulpit," or hooded spathe, and inside it the "jack" or spadix, the sexual portion of the flower. (There are at least two subspecies of *A. triphyllum:* ones in which the white pulpit is striped with green, and another striped with purplish brown.) The pulpit lasts for at least three weeks; later, grotesque oddly shaped berries, each the exact shade of day-glo red plastic, develop along the spadix. The leaves are usually retained through August.

Jacks tolerate a wide range of soils. I've found good-sized ones in swampy bogs and in loose, dry sand piled by a road. The only conditions a jack can't tolerate are deep shade, poorly draining clay soil, and winter flooding. But in part sun and protected with a deep leaf-mold mulch, I've seen twelve-inch plants grow to three feet in as many years. In the wild, jacks often grow in strangled clumps where a parent has dropped its berries. One such clump I found yielded one blooming adult and twenty-seven seedlings. When planted separately, at least four celebrated their independent status by blooming the next year.

Happily, they can be transplanted in full bloom without taking umbrage. The stem ascends from a narrrow corm resembling an onion, with short white roots like those of a daffodil, so you don't have to worry about digging widely around a plant as long as your spade goes deep enough. And because jacks are corm plants, they'll stay exactly where you put them. Any new plants that appear will be shallow-rooted seedlings, not offshoots, and since their young corms will not have had a chance to dig too deeply, they can be transplanted without disturbing the parent's root system.

Jacks are vulnerable to romping chipmunks and squirrels who often break the succulent stems, so I try to plant them up against fallen logs and in other conspicuous but protected spots. Once a jack has grown to a height of two feet or more, it can be moved to a partly shady spot in the Pachysandra Garden, where it should continue to thrive.

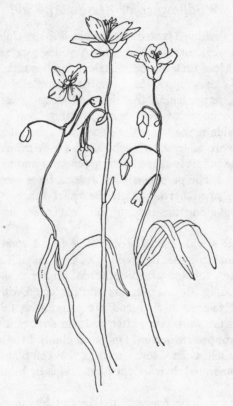

Figure 37

Claytonia rosea (spring beauty; CF; Figure 37) forms tufts of lush, succulent leaves and masses of lovely white to pink flowers on stems to eight inches. Plants arise from a fat, shallow bulb that can be moved while the plant's in bloom. Situate them at least six inches apart and they will seed themselves widely, growing more beautiful and plentiful each year. By June, the leaves fade and decay, making room for other plants.

Epipactis helleborine (no common name; SS) is the only orchid to claim the title of weed. It even *looks* a bit weedy: a tall plant to four feet, its tall flowerstalk and not too-showy leaves greatly resemble ragweed and any other hundred or so gulch-runners. But if you look closely, you'll see the typical orchid flowers, staggered in rows and in widely variable tones of brown and purple, green and white.

This is an orchid I can guarantee will grow for you, because it's not an American native, but a European import. Since its first reported appearance in Syracuse, New York, in 1879, it has spread to virtually all sections of the country. I've seen it growing on the tromped-over clay banks of Lake George and along the raw bull-dozed subsoil of unpaved roads. It's so new as yet (and to a non-orchid lover, probably so unspectacular) that it's not listed in any catalog. Meanwhile, feel free to collect it from the wild. I have not transplanted it myself, but the roots are reported to range deeply. Chances are it will respond well to being moved along with a large ball of soil, and won't mind dryish conditions as long as you give it part shade. With all other terrestrial orchids acting temperamental to a degree, it's a delight to have one whose manners are downright uncouth.

Geranium maculatum (crane's bill, wild geranium; CF)—see Chapter 10. Keep plants toward the back of the Wild Garden so that they don't mask more delicate, low-growing species. It's good for a wide range of sun and soil conditions, but full shade causes sparse, weak-stemmed foliage and no flowers.

Iris cristata (crested iris; TS) is probably the easiest to grow of the native American irises. It doesn't need extra dampness as do many species, just part shade and protection from slugs. The deciduous leaves arise from very pronounced knuckle-like nodes on a rapidly spreading fan of rhizomes which, in a healthy few years' time, can carpet several square feet with neat six-inch tufts of foliage. Proportionately small (and unfortunately short-lived) flowers appear in May. An *alba* variety is available and should definitely be planted beside the regular blue *cristata* for maximum clout. Lay out the rhizome network about an inch deep, with the latest nodes facing in the direction you want them to spread, and mix a bit of sand with the humus used to cover them. *Cristata* seems to appreciate a well-drained soil, since the only plantings I've lost were in distinctly soggy, clayish ground.

Figure 38

Podophyllum peltatum (mayapple; ODT) is the easiest wildflower to grow, and one of the more spectacular. In spring, just about the time trees are budding, you will notice olive-green structures, glossy as oilcloth, mushrooming out of the soil (see Figure 38). Each resembles a cross between a furled umbrella and a hibernating bat. (Picked and placed in water, they will continue to expand, just like their rooted counterparts outside.) More often than not, the "bat" will have a head—the bud of the flower to come. Blooming stalks develop two leaves, as shown. The bud, held at the fork of the two leaf stems, enlarges to hang down between them. It soon opens into a flower of five white petals (the variety *roseum* is pink). However, these showy flowers are soon pollinated. The flower sketched in Figure 39 was just about to lose its petals, as the ovary before them

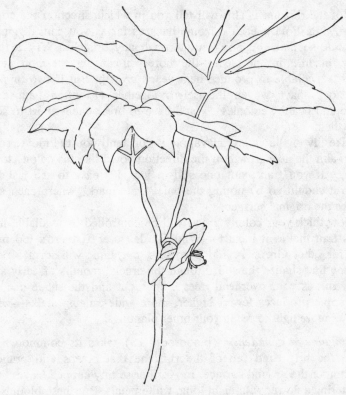

Figure 39

swelled. Over the summer, this "apple" continues to expand into a golf-ball-sized yellow fruit.

The underground rhizomes, about a half inch thick, seem utterly oblivious to soil conditions. I have seen stands flourishing in almost pure clay, and the specimens pictured were gathered from the dry bankside below an asphalt road, where the rhizomes lay in full sun beneath soft-drink cans and old beer bottles. Probably the best time to move mayapple is in late August, right after the leaves have wilted. But the plants can also be moved in early spring when the new growth is emerging, and this way, you know *exactly* where the tips of the rhizomes are—each is producing one of those distinctive umbrellas.

Dig at the site of that season's growth with a trowel, and expose one of the rhizomes. This will tell you in which direction the colony is growing. Follow each rhizome back as far as you can, digging to the *side* so that you don't cut through any branches. Try to keep your rhizomes in one piece—the more you can dig, the more stored food is available to produce next year's growth. But if two or more rootstocks have woven themselves together (as often happens in large and healthy colonies), you'll have to break them apart to separate them.

Like lily of the valley, mayapple is constantly on the move, so always aim the new growth in the direction you'd like the colony to advance. If you transplant one still in leaf, it's easy to see just how deep it should go by noting the pale "watermark" where each stalk broke the original surface.

How thick your colony grows will be controlled by available light. This trait makes it ideal for Wild Garden use: If there's too much sun for other Group A and B species, mayapple will form a dense colony that shades the soil through the crucial months of early summer. But as your overhead trees branch out and the shade deepens, mayapple produces fewer, higher, more wide-ranging stalks—which allows more light to reach your other plantings.

Sanguinaria canadensis (bloodroot; TS) takes its common name from the bright-red sap of the rhizome that creeps and branches just under the ground surface. In April arise tiny cupped leaves, each sheltering a flower with eight long, white petals. But these blooms are not likely to last more than a day. *Sanguinaria*'s petals are extremely fragile, and the light brush of a visiting bee is enough to break them off even before they have opened fully. (A double variety is rather widely available. Since there are up to two dozen petals per flower, this *flora plena* strain is not likely to get knocked bald quite so quickly.)

After the petals fall, the leaf elongates and unfurls. In one shady, moist corner of my Wild Garden, bloodroot leaves approach dinnerplate size, with a quilted texture and the outline of a shallow-notched lilypad. A healthy planting will increase each year. But if leaves arise in congested masses each spring, it means your soil hasn't got quite enough leafmold or is too dry: the rhizomes aren't able to spread enough for the colony to get out of its own way.

Smilacina racemosa (false Solomon's-seal, Solomon's-plume; ODT) is superior to the true Solomon's-seal (Group B, below). Certainly it's easier to grow; I've seen it flowering and multiplying in hard clay. In appearance, the plant is almost identical to ordinary Solomon's-seal: a single nodding stalk up to three feet long rises from the ground at an acute angle. Along it appear alternative almond-shaped, heavily veined leaves. The crucial difference is in the flowers. True Solomon's-seal has small and fairly inconspicuous bell-shaped flowers hanging the length of the stalk, while *Smilacina* features a dazzle of white florets in a raceme at the very end. The flowers are far more showy, and in late summer ripen into quarter-inch berries of mottled reddish purple.

Like mayapple, *Smilacina* grows from an underground rhizome—stubby, gnarled, and rather dry-looking. This is where the plant stores nourishment, and an unbroken rhizome will ensure a good-sized stalk the next season. Bury it an inch deep in good leafmold-rich earth. If the plant is in leaf, tamp the earth down carefully and lay a small rock atop it so that the weight of the stalk doesn't pry the rhizome loose.

Ferns for Group A soil:

Ferns for a Wild Garden should include only single-clump-formers that won't smother your flowers. Begin with *Dryopteris marginalis* (evergreen wood fern) and *Polystichum acrostichoides* (Christmas fern). Both will remain green long after December when other ferns are crisp and sere, and tolerate intially poor soils if given extra moisture in midsummer.

By the time all Group A wildflowers are *actively* spreading, Group B selections should be able to hold their own.

Group B: Wildflowers
for one to two inches of pure humus

Asarum canadense (wild ginger; TS) bears purplish-brown bell-shaped flowers that seem made of suede leather. Borne at ground level, they are usually hidden in the past fall's dead leaves, so enjoying them means bending down and doing some careful excavation. However, I grow this plant for its foliage alone. The four-inch heart-shaped leaves stand atop single stalks, covered with a fine fuzzy pile reminiscent of an African violet's texture.

A. europeus (TS) forms tight clumps of glossy round foliage. It's best suited to the Low Garden (see Chapter 11), but makes a nice accent and contrast with:

A. shuttleworthii (evergreen ginger; TS) resembles a giant sharp-lobe hepatica (see below). Far darker in hue than *canadense, shuttleworthii's* leaves look best when interplanted with erect wildflowers like jack-in-the-pulpit. Like *canadense,* the flowers are practically invisible.

Erythronium (LS) is a large and pleasurable genus, represented in the Northeast by *americanum* (adder's tongue, dogtooth violet, troutlily). In very early April when trees are still bare, single tongue-like leaves emerge from the forest floor. Each is of a satiny olive green mottled with darker spots of brown. Occasionally two leaves arise together, and between them a stalk with a nodding, lily-like flower. On the inside, the six petals are a bright yellow tinged with orange. The outside of the petals is a beige or warm gray, but since the petals are sharply reflexed, the inner yellow is visible and striking. The common name "dogtooth violet" comes from the plant's bulb, which is oblong and slightly discolored, much like a dog's tooth. After its leaf yellows and decays (about June), the bulb sends out meandering little rhizomes of ghostly white. Knobs at the ends develop into new bulbs. In virgin woods, troutlilies spread by this method to cover as much as an acre.

While the plant is supposed to relish good leafmold, I have seen it coming up with thin, unhappy leaves, not blooming, where the loam is deep and rich. But I have never seen *Erythronium* growing so richly as in a scrubby area of brush beside a parking lot. The leaves were fat and plentiful, with frequent flowers. Here, sapling trees had been cleared, chipped up, and dumped in a pile six inches deep. The lushness of their growth in that woodchip pile may hint at some saprophytic source of nourishment—that is, perhaps *E. americanum* depends on a fungal or bacterial alliance. This could explain why it doesn't always do well in good *rotted* humus, where soil-decay organisms are less active.

Thus, I would suggest you plant your troutlily bulbs with as much raw leafmold, twigs, and other coarse vegetable matter as possible. Bulbs are available from catalogs, but visit any woodland colony and you're sure to come upon a few bulblets running themselves aground on a stone or tree root. Bury them as shallowly as they were before to avoid interring too much of the leaves—the bulbs will soon be digging their own way deeper.

A number of other species and cultivated hybrids are available for mixing with the native *americanums*. The European *dens canis* has flowers of weak lavender that are probably the least striking of the genus. However, a good many of the *Erythroniums* imported from Holland have been hybridized from our own Western species, popularly referred to as fawn lilies. For the most part, they bear taller, wider, lighter green foliage and flowers in pastel colors atop longer stalks. (They also bloom more dependably.) By the time your soil has reached Group C status, they too will have spread themselves enough to begin making a real show.

Hepatica acutiloba (sharplobe hepatica; CF) has dark glossy semi-evergreen leaves with three pointed lobes, as if someone had sharpened an outsize clover leaf. Small—and in my opinion, not terribly attractive—pale pink to bluish flowers are borne in very early spring. However, the leaves themselves form distinctive clumps.

Hepaticas shipped in spring always seem to arrive waterlogged and decaying, so order by mail only in the autumn, well before new growth is getting ready to emerge. (Dormant plants are less likely to have a great deal of sap in the foliage.) Plant the crowns a bit above the soil level and then making up the difference with a micro-mulch of grated maple leaves to reproduce these plants' natural environment—sugar maple forest.

Maiathemum canadense (Canada mayflower; TS) has a thin yellowish rhizome that trails along just under the leaves of the forest floor and sends up a series of single leaves of a rich glossy green. Every so often, two leaves will emerge and from between them, a tiny raceme of white flowers (see Figure 40). For some reason, Canada mayflower seems to thrive only when crowded in extremely close quarters—between two tree roots or narrow slabs of rock. It particularly enjoys being allowed to trail through the raised hump of an osmunda fern or between the fissures of a natural rock path.

It's seldom offered by mail, but sods of a foot square can very easily be lifted from individual woodland colonies. Cut the turf carefully on all sides, so that rhizomes leading to and fro are broken off cleanly—otherwise they will start pulling loose as you lift the clump. Set the entire toupée down where you want it, and sift good soil—leafmold is too light—among the leaves. Add water and more soil,

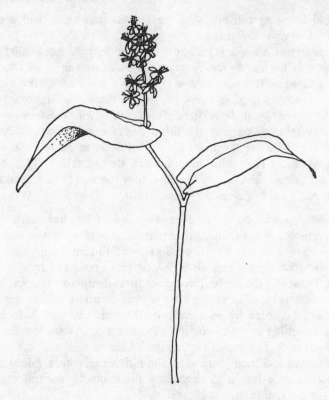

Figure 40

alternately, until you can no longer see the original surface of the tuft, but so that the leaves aren't buried. As long as it remains securely anchored, the colony will invade the surrounding soil within a year, permanently binding itself to your property.

Tiarella cordifolia (foamflower; TS) is an attractive ground cover. Again, to keep a Wild Garden's soil in proper shape, you must maintain a year-round light mulch of dead leaves. But since the wildflowers themselves appear so briefly, you'll want foamflower for hiding the ground litter. The semi-evergreen leaves are hairy and pale green, closely resembling a wild grape or maple leaf in shape, borne on short stems. In late May and early June, a six-inch spike of white flowers arises from each plant. Foamflower then more or less settles in for the summer, spreading itself by thin surface runners.

Like many other wildflowers, it spreads and blooms better when given good shade in summer: one particularly lush specimen in a photo I've seen is blooming in really deep gloom. However, foamflower will tolerate almost full sun. One colony of mine has lived in a dry, sunny expanse since I planted it: the flower racemes are short, but the plants are spreading well. When quite robust, the leaves reach a height of about eight inches, so be sure to keep it segregated from anything smaller.

Ferns for Group B conditions:

These include the deciduous osmunda ferns: *O. cinnamomea* (cinnamon fern) and *O. claytoniana* (interrupted fern). Since the B wildflowers are mostly low-growing and spreading, the upright growth habit of these tall single-clump ferns will give your garden greater stature.

Group C: Wildflowers
for three to four inches of pure humus

Cypripedium spp. (ladyslipper orchids; SS) are the showpieces of any Wild Garden. Your only problem is achieving the proper soil conditions. Most of these plants have extremely shallow roots, which means that deep soil isn't a must. But what's there must be perfect—and retain moisture all summer. Many other wildflowers go dormant well before the end of July, and August drought makes no hardship for plants that are already estivating. But wild orchids retain their leaves well into October. If you have healthy bloodroot that retains enormous leaves well into September, orchids should do well close by.

C. calceolus, often touted as the easiest to grow, is a fairly variable plant; authorities disagree whether the yellow ladyslipper is *C. calceolus* var. *pubescens* or just *C. pubescens,* a species all its own. But in all its forms, this is the only orchid with long, markedly twisted petals that set off the pouch with remarkable elegance.

C. japonicum (Japanese ladyslipper) is offered only sporadically; in one catalog that does feature it, the photograph clearly shows a clump of *C. reginae* (see below) to which *japonicum* is similar. But its foliage is pleated, giving an effect rare among orchids. A generous pink pouch is set off by showy green sepals.

C. montanum (mountain ladyslipper) is taller than *pubescens,* with chestnut-brown sepals framing a white pouch. It ranges along the Pacific Coast from northern California to Alaska, in a wide range of environments from deep moist shade to dry mountainside, without too much difference in the vigor and size of plants. Because of this versatility, it seems a good bet for the Eastern Wild Garden as well. But *montanum* is largely native to well-drained brushland, and a bit of extra sand in the humus and good half-sun are probably a good idea.

C. reginae (showy ladyslipper) bears a pouch the size of a small lemon, with color ranging from pure white through almost bright red, borne atop a sizable plant covered with downy hairs. I nestled mine just to the north of a stand of arborvitae; its roots lie at the bottom of a bankside heavily mulched with oak leaves and grass clippings. Scratching at the dead leaf litter quickly turns up light, moist grains of humus the texture of peatmoss. *C. reginae* can take more sun than I give it, as long as its roots are moist. A new grass mulch applied after each mowing of the lawn adds nitrogen and promotes dampness.

Because all *Cypripediums* are so drastically rare in nature, never try to obtain them except by mail. Ironically, some of the very people who offer these plants are themselves part of the conservation problem: they collect plants from the wild and ship them off in such damaged condition that they quickly succumb. I suggest you buy only from nurseries who raise these wildflowers themselves, even though I have not been able to find one that doesn't ship its orchids barerooted, in plastic bags! Most experts agree that a *Cypripedium* resents having its roots disturbed, and shipping dormant *potted* plants would certainly increase the orchids' survival chances.

Loss of a single plant usually means poor soil or damaged stock. But the sudden dieback on an *entire* clump points to outside interference: rodents, squirrels, or possibly disease. If your locale is mole-infested, definitely grow all terrestrial orchids in a chickenwire basket sunk in the earth.

Dicentra canadensis (squirrel corn; CF) has flowers closely resembling those of old-fashioned bleeding-heart. The foliage is ferny and more delicate, and not very long-lasting. This species is not listed widely in catalogs, which may indicate some cultural difficulty: it needs practically full shade during dormancy in summer, and very deep and fertile humus.

D. cucullaria (Dutchman's-breeches; CF) is more delicate-looking than *canadensis*. Rather than Netherland pantaloons, the flowers remind me of a white, horned headdress set on a tiny yellow face. The light gray airy foliage lasts only a month before yellowing. But with proper Group C conditions, the plants form thick layers of foliage studded with bloom.

Hypoxis hirsuta (yellow star grass; CF) is of the lily family, but more closely resembles a tuft of sedge whose narrow leaves have been tied up into a tight bundle. In early June, it erupts with a series of three-quarter-inch flowers of six petals of startlingly bright yellow. *Hypoxis* requires part sun or very high shade, moisture, and a soil that's deep, spongy, and slightly acid—that is, composed of oak and other hardwood leaves, not pine needles. It doesn't form large clumps, but will self-seed.

Polygonatum (Solomon's-seal; ODT) is a genus currently in some dispute. Various sources list the giant Solomon's-seal as *P. canaliculatum, commutatum,* or as a variety of *biflorum*. But most species including the *latifolium* and *multiflorum* of the Old World are largely similar: all bear inconspicuous greenish flowers hanging along the stem. Though *Polygonatums* will grow well under Group C conditions, I'd advise them only as contrasts for *Smilacina racemosa* (false Solomon's-seal, above) which they closely resemble.

Streptopus (ODT) is a genus worth substituting for *Polygonatum*. Smaller than the Solomon's-seals, these plants have extremely similar structure, including pendant flowers. But there the resemblance ends. *S. amplexifolius* (mandarin) has petals distinctly ruffled and curved at the edges, which makes them extremely decorative and appealing. *S. roseus* (rose mandarin, rosy twisted stalk) has flowers of winning pink that far outclass the dull greenish teardrops of the *Polygonatums.*

Trillium (SS) is a large genus, but *grandiflorum* (large white trillium, snow trillium) is the one to start with—easily the most rewarding and easiest to grow. From a vertical bulb-shaped rhizome rises a single stalk with three leaves, each resembling a dogwood's. Above the leaves is a single flower with three narrow green sepals and three wide, deeply veined white petals with ruffled edges. (Do not confuse with *T. nivale,* also called snow trillium but far less showy.) The plump, pale beige rhizomes should be set two to four inches deep in fall. They need a deep, moist, friable soil in which to sink their roots. The leaves welcome any light conditions up to part sun.

After *grandiflorum,* most other trilliums are somewhat of an anticlimax:

T. cernuum (nodding trillium) has a stalk and leaves similar to *grandiflorum*'s, but the flower is far smaller, varying in color from greenish white to pink, and hangs below the leaves like a mayapple's. You have to crouch to appreciate the flower or else plant *cernuum* a good distance from the path, where it can be viewed in profile.

T. cuneatum has bluish green leaves dramatically mottled with olive brown, making it a good companion for troutlilies. The deep purple petals are tall and upright, resembling the miter of a bishop. This is a Southern species, but grows in the North in sheltered locations.

T. erectum (purple trillium, red trillium, stinking Benjamin, wakerobin) is widespread enough to have garned a number of common names. Reflexed sepals are prominently displayed, giving the flower the look of a reddish troutlily. Foliage is wide and attractive, preferring shadier conditions than *grandiflorum.* The white variety of *erectum,* commonly called wax trillium, should be planted beside the regular red form for comparison's sake. Otherwise it looks like a down-at-the-heel *grandiflorum.*

T. recurvatum has thin reddish petals that twist in on themselves, as if the flower were afflicted by aphids. Unless you're a trillium buff with your better species absolutely thriving, I'd pass it by.

T. sessile (toadshade) is the ugly duckling of the trilliums, resembling a stunted *cuneatum.* The roundish leaves are mottled fairly nicely with brown, but the flower is either a sullen purple or yellowish green. The petals are held so upright that the flower remains closed, like a gentian's. The variety (or according to some sources, species) *luteum* has yellow petals.

Trilliums do spread, however slowly, by new rhizomes. But until your *grandiflorum* has begun adding new stalks to its spring display, it's poor economy to introduce any "difficult," "rare," or "seldom-offered" trilliums. Chances are they won't outperform the more common species.

Group D Wildflowers

. . . require at least four inches of acid, moist, but well drained soil. Scrape up fallen evergreen needles, which under established plantings often form a semi-rotted layer about half an inch thick. Pile them about four inches deep in a flat, low-lying (but not swampy) area, and mix with equal parts of pure leafmold, with perhaps a trace of peatmoss. Still, this soil must be constantly replenished, and you need the fairly constant year-around shade that only evergreens can provide—plus the *absence* of floppy, deciduous leaves that can smother many of these small plants.

See Chapters 5 and 6 for good small-needled evergreens to use. If your space is limited, use balsam fir primarily, and then stud the intervening ground with hemlock seedlings. When they begin to shade out the balsam firs, they can be cut off at the roots, one by one. You can attain maximum soil richness by adding a *Quercus borealis* (northern red oak) and a *Pinus strobus* (white pine) to the selection, and introduce mountain laurel or rhododendrons to the west to serve as windbreaks.

Remember that any evergreen should be allowed to branch as much as it wants until it's about twelve feet tall. When it reaches that height, high-prune. But be sure to avoid leaving gaps of sunlight that will bake your plants. Any well-rooted pinestraw or oakleaf mulch you can cart in meanwhile is all to the good.

Chimaphila maculata (pipsissewa; SS) is a real aristocrat of the shady acid forest. Thin glossy evergreen leaves—like those of an elongated holly—are borne on short, woody stems. Each leaf has sharp-pointed lobes, and the main veins are outlined in creamy white. It bears buttercup-like flowers nodding from a short, straight stem, but needs a rich, moist leafmold to do at all well, and seems to be dwarfed in proportion to how many droughts it has to suffer.

Clintonea borealis (bluebeads; CF), as its Latin species name implies, is a Northern plant. The leaves remind you immediately of a phalaenopsis orchid—two (sometimes three) glossy light-green oval leaves sprawl along the ground. In May, their center sprouts a stalk whose several yellow flowers later ripen into bluish berries—hence the common name. To see it in its real glory, visit the Keene Valley State Park surrounding New York's Mount Marcy. There, blue-beads spread by underground rhizomes, forming colonies of an acre or more. But this area is a virtual rainforest, and deep watering during late summer seems vital for a healthy bed.

Cornus canadensis (bunchberry; TS) is unsurpassed for loveliness. A miniature relative of the familiar dogwood tree, *canadensis'* three-to four-inch stems bear a circle of four to six typically dogwood-like leaves. In June, each rosette of leaves blooms with a white bract. This is one plant that makes me wish I lived some hundred miles farther north. It simply will not tolerate hot summers—a warm afternoon is okay, but July and August nights had better be cold enough to make you want a sweater. Given enough cool and acid loam, however, bunchberry forms huge carpets, flowering later and later with increasing altitude, so that by climbing some of the higher peaks, you can come across bunchberry still in bloom as late as July.

Cypripedium acaule (pink ladyslipper; SS) is "stemless" in that its two or three oval leaves arise directly from the ground. However, the characteristic pink "slipper" arises on a stiff, hairy stem up to eight-een inches tall.

C. acaule is one of the commonest wild orchids in the Northeast, yet it's notoriously difficult to transplant. The answer in part seems to be that established *acaules* can weather the droughts of late summer as other orchids cannot. Knowing that *acaule* is native to dry pine woods, most gardeners try to give it similar conditions. But *acaule* must not be allowed to dry out for the several years it takes the plant to establish itself. The blooms on plants growing in dry soil are distinctly smaller and less colorful than those of plants I've seen growing in damper conditions, so I suspect it should be planted in a damp spot from the start.

Begin by planting a clump of fastigiate white pines. Their dead needles will fall in a fairly discrete circle, providing the rotting pine-straw necessary for this ladyslipper. When your trees are in place, spade down six inches or so between them and replace the soil with oakleaf mulch, rotted pinestraw, and a touch of grass clippings *stirred in,* rather than just piled on top. Plant mail-ordered stock in autumn, with the roots just about an inch below the surface, water thoroughly during dry spells the next year, and hope for the best.

Gaultheria procumbens (checkerberry, wintergreen; LS) resembles a miniature mountain laurel. Small glossy evergreen leaves are borne on flexible woody stems that arise from a creeping rootstock. The plant blooms with small, pinkish bell-shaped flowers. Try to grow it beneath evergreens that cast a high shade. *Gaultheria* is also an excellent choice beneath mountain laurel, because of the similarity of the leaves.

Goodyera pubescens (rattlesnake plantain; SS) is a terrestrial orchid that bears a relatively insignificant stalk of tiny white flowers. It's desirable mainly for its dramatically variegated, semi-evergreen foliage that arises in a rosette from a creeping rootstock: each leaf is a deep glossy green, on which the veins are marked in white. *Goodyera* doesn't necessarily demand Group D conditions—I have seen a specimen holding its own in the corner of a shady lawn—but since the plants get smothered so easily by fallen leaves, a small-needled evergreen overhead offers safest shelter.

Hepatica americana (roundlobe hepatica; CF) is similar to *H. acutiloba* (Group B) except that its leaves are rounded off, resembling a clover's, and its roots prefer a slightly more acid soil. Use *americana* on the fringes of your Group D planting—hepatica spreads naturally and will eventually seed itself into the exact mixture of soil it prefers.

Lycopodium spp. (club moss, ground pine, princess pine; LS) is a most attractive giant moss, sprigs of which are often found in brandy-snifter terrariums. But these are simply cuttings that—unfortunately—will never root. Vast amounts of club moss are collected each year for Christmas decorations, and as a result, these lovely plants are increasingly rare in the wild. *Clavatum* is the smallest species, with sprigs only about three inches high; *obscurum* is the largest, with fairly hefty upright branches up to ten inches. But my favorite is the middle-sized *complantum* (ground cedar), whose five-inch foliage is arranged in arcs that resemble the growth of seedling arborvitae.

All club mosses arise from a slender, scaled runner that trails just below the soil surface. Frustrated collectors often pull up twelve feet or more of runner without coming across viable roots. Your only hope is to either grow your own from ripe spores collected from the "clubs" or—as I have—obtain a section of a newly rooted colony from a wildflower specialist.

Mitchella repens (partridgeberry; LS) is a tiny evergreen vine that roots as it trails. Leaves are round, borne in pairs along the stem; color is deep green with the central vein usually brushed with lighter green or white. Partridgeberry blooms with a pair of waxy, trumpet-like flowers that later ripen into a *single* red berry about the size of a small pea. Ripe berries remain on the stem for some time, and it's not unusual to find blooming colonies that still bear the fruit of the previous season. *Mitchella* is happy in a fairly wide spectrum of soils, but the leaves are so tiny—the largest about a half inch across—that they can be easily smothered by deciduous foliage.

This is another plant used to garnish brandy-snifter terrariums—but fortunately it roots readily and will probably survive until late spring when you can move it outdoors permanently. But plants shipped by mail are usually barerooted. Dig a narrow trench in the soil and fit the stems lengthwise. The small, weak roots usually emerge in bunches from the stem between leaves; make sure they're buried under a mound of leafmold mixed with sand. Then use small pebbles or pairs of twigs crossed at an angle to hold the stems flat against the ground. Plants usually begin spreading the next spring. I lost one of my best *Mitchella* plantings to squirrels, so you might want to cover yours with a hood of wire mesh until they cover any temptingly bare soil.

Trillium undulatum (painted trillium; SS) is the most spectacular of the genus. It is similar in size to *grandiflorum,* except that each undulated petal is brushed at the base with streaks of purple-pink that usually form an "eye" in the flower's center. This trillium likes more moisture as well as extra acidity; it's often photographed growing among seedlings of balsam fir, and so I assume it will do well beneath a planting of the mature trees.

Introducing New Wildflowers

While trailing or spreading plants can ease themselves into more acceptable territory, a stationary SS plant such as jack-in-the-pulpit, ladyslipper, or trillium has to make do with existing conditions. But since soil acidity, drainage, sun, and pockets of moisture and fertility can vary enormously over a small area, the odds are not good that any one spot will be perfect for the new arrival. It's best to buy several plants and put them in different apparently suitable locations. This trial-and-error technique at least ensures that any one species will have the widest possible range of advantages your property has to offer.

Of course most wildflowers look best when clumped together, but wait until the second spring has come and gone. Then if any specimens aren't doing well, you can move them closer to the ones that are succeeding. But if *all* specimens of one species cash in their chips, wait a year or two until your soil improves.

Before you admit failure, remember that individuals of the same species often have vastly different emerging times. I once moved a large clump of mayapple and distributed the rhizomes to a number of different spots. Each spring, those growing on flat terrain have fully extended their leaves before those on a shadier slope have even broken the surface. (The latter colony is just as healthy, however.) This may be due to local soil temperatures, but one on my most vigorous jack-in-the-pulpits doesn't arise until its smaller neighbors a few feet away are already finishing bloom. But a plant that blooms with spindly and reluctant blooms after its third winter should definitely be relocated. (Again, a sluggish plant will usually do better next to a winner of the same species.)

No matter how good your Wild Garden soil is, you should make a constant effort to deepen and improve it. Broadcasts of grass clippings will help the soil retain moisture through the summer; but smaller, delicate wildflowers need a mulch of leaves over the winter, particularly if your snow is infrequent or scanty. Regular-size dead leaves can smother them, however. Get hold of some heavy plastic sheeting or curtain liner, a piece of galvanized wire mesh, and a bushel of old, dry leaves that have lasted at least one winter. Rub a handful of these brittle leaves briskly over the mesh, and the plastic will catch the fragments of minced leaf that sift through. This micromulch is ideal for any newly transplanted wildflowers.

One final problem: the seeds of weeds, trees, and grasses will find your ever-improving soil an ideal site for germination. My answer is to lay a few small half-rotted tree limbs between the plants in late spring. Later in summer, I can wade into the garden across this "log jam" without crushing anybody's roots.

13

THE CULTIVATED MEADOW

Many of our taller, most spectacular wildflowers prefer full sun all summer long. Denizens of meadows, banksides, open fields, and roadsides, few of them bloom before early summer, and many keep on flowering until cut down by frost. Most importantly, they have a broad tolerance for drought and poor soil, and are often so vigorous they have earned the name of weed. It makes sense to give them an environment all their own, where they receive *full* sun. A Cultivated Meadow can be any size you like. But I'd place any such environment toward the perimeter of your property—for close-up viewing, you'll want the relatively lusher and neater Pachysandra or Low Gardens.

You shouldn't need to add fresh humus unless the existing soil is utterly wretched, but extra mulch is necessary at all seasons to help retain moisture. This means grass clippings "dusted in" spring and summer, and a light sprinkle of chopped leaves in fall, as soon as the plants die down.

Meadow Groundcovers

Acres of full-grown grass waving in the breeze, studded with daisies and poppies, is an attractive sight. But unmowed grass tends to look messy on a small scale. In place of grass, you'll need a quick-spreading groundcover—tall enough to discourage weeds, but low enough to allow any stalked, upright plant to make it through easily. Employ real ground-huggers that would be unruly almost anywhere else.

Dennstaedtia punctilobula (hay-scented fern) is a delightful sub-stitute for grass. The light green feathery fronds (up to two feet) are borne in loose bundles. This fern is a Loose-Spreader that eventually produces a solid mass of fronds that are, however, still yielding enough to let most tall stalks emerge without conflict. The delicate leaves often scald in the heat of late summer, withering to a brittle brown. Watering during the days of drought should forestall this, but the stems of fronds pluck loose easily, and so a small colony can be neatened up in a jiffy.

Dicentra exima (bleeding-heart) is best in the Pachysandra Garden, but very large specimens will hold their own in a Meadow. They look particularly well grouped with sensitive fern (see below).

Equisetum (horsetail, scouring reed) is ungainly but exotic. A primitive relative of the ferns, it arises from a creeping root in coarse branched plumes up to several feet tall, depending on species. The leaves are only vestigial, represented by tiny dark-brown streaks around the central trunk.

There are quite a few species. The best for Meadow use grows from six to eight inches tall and often appears in profusion on dry embankments and along railroad tracks. In sunny, rich soil, it often emerges from its rootstock in eccentric tufts that look like something a kindergarten class dreamed up with pipe cleaners. But even so, it never grows thickly enough to trouble more delicate plants. Its root-stock is fairly shallow and can be stopped by aluminum edging, so a contained tuft of horsetail might be intriguing as a Low Garden ac-cent. And since it's technically a weed and hardly an endangered species, you can dig all you want.

Hieracium spp. (devil's paintbrush, field hawkweed) forms loose, flat rosettes of hairy light-green leaves. New plants are constantly arising from surface runners and from branchings of the underground root system, so that plants eventually cover the ground rather thickly, though enough gaps are left so that some weeding will be necessary. From late spring to early summer, each rosette sprouts long hairy stalks topped by bright dandelion-like flowers.

H. aurantiacum has orange to red flowers and spreads with great rapidity. All other common species are yellow: flowers of *H. pratense* and *H. venosum* are about the same size as *aurantiacum*'s, but for best contrast, try for *H. bombycinum* with even larger yellow flowers. A mixture of several strains makes for a better display.

Onoclea sensibilis (northern beech fern, sensitive fern) is a loose-spreader that will tolerate clay and full sun, emerging with lush uncut fronds of a light blue-green color that rather closely resemble those of the indoor rabbit's foot fern. Make sure that *O. sensibilis* is in full sun; otherwise its fronds tend to arise singly, which spoils their effectiveness.

Ranunculus (buttercup) forms flat rosettes of deeply cut, fern-like foliage above a fat, pale rootstock. Buttercups are semi-evergreen and in late May and June provide a series of rich golden yellow flowers gleaming in the sun like porcelain. The branched stems are so succulent that a pinch frees them. Each flower lasts only a day or so indoors, ending in a sudden cascade of dropped petals.

The two common roadside species, *R. acris* and *R. repens,* both have fully double varieties that you should try to secure if possible. *R. acris* self-seeds to form loose clumps, while *R. repens* (see Color Section) spreads quickly by surface runners to form enormous colonies. In fact, *repens* has become a serious weed for me, spreading into shady Wild Garden and sunny lawn with equal vigor. Mowing doesn't deter it, so plants have to be uprooted one by one.

Veronica persica (see Chapter 11) is a fast-growing wild veronica that dependably fills the gaps other plants leave. Most Meadow plants are so much taller that it can't smother them.

Vinca minor (myrtle, periwinkle) bears pairs of glossy dark-green leaves on lengthy stems that root intermittently as they trail over the ground. This plant is frequently offered as a groundcover, but it takes an exceedingly long time to spread, and seldom grows thickly enough to stifle weeds. It does best in moist ground; allow it to twine its way among other, taller plants that will give it considerable shade.

It's usually easy to get some clippings of *Vinca* from a neighbor. Bury the *entire* sprig about a half inch deep, with only the last inch or so protruding from the soil. New roots and leaves will begin to arise in a month or so. The flowers of nursery-grown stock are almost invariably blue, but mail order firms now offer white, red, eyed, and *flora plena* varieties. Since plants do take a while to establish themselves, start with a wide variety of different types. If one does better than the rest, you can either let it take over or send off for reinforcements of the laggard strains.

Any of these groundcovers will do well by itself, but you can combine them for a more varied, natural effect. Of course, some adjustments may be necessary: hawkweed will not tolerate any companion higher than veronica. And when buttercup foliage thins out, shortly after blooming, colonies of hay-scented and sensitive fern will slowly encroach themselves. But since a rustic, carefree look is what you're after, why not let the best plant win?

Upright Meadow Perennials

Most of the following plants will not bloom until at least the second year following their introduction. Thereafter, be on the lookout for any that have begun seeding themselves.

Allium (SS) are bulbs of the onion family; the larger "Persian" hybrids, with their enormous purple or blue flowerheads, look best in a Meadow. Their June flowers will provide some color while other Meadow plants are just beginning bloom.

Althaea (hollyhock; CF): perennial hybrids produce foot-high clumps of quilted, semi-evergreen foliage and tall, sturdy windproof stalks laden with hibiscus-like flowers. Single varieties are more attractive than the doubles, and a group planting of several colors offers the best effect.

Asclepias spp. (milkweed; SS) has single stalks up to five feet tall that arise from an underground rhizome. The leaves are plump and not particularly attractive, but the plant is worth growing for its dull-rose flowers, borne in sprays somewhat like those of mountain laurel.

Milkweed pods are the size and shape of young cucumbers; on crisp October days they split to release their seeds, each with a collapsed silk parachute that's teased outward by the drying wind. More importantly, milkweed is the sole food for caterpillars of the monarch butterfly, a spectacular insect whose large orange wings are veined with black.

Asclepias tuberosa (butterfly weed; CF; see Color Section) is a close relative of milkweed, but far more aristocratic and desirable. Long-lived orange flowers are borne in dazzling sprays that contrast beautifully with the neat, narrow foliage—and attract more than their share of butterflies. These plants demand fairly good soil and moisture and are a bit finicky in establishing themselves, so when taking stem cuttings or ordering roots by mail, get at least a half dozen. At least one should survive and slowly spread to form a breath-taking clump.

Chicorium intybus (chickory, cornflower; SS) survives even in the cracks of cement sidewalks, thanks to its long, thick taproot. The denim-blue flowers and loosely branched structure give it a pleasantly rustic look. Your main problem is obtaining it in the first place. The plant becomes recognizable only when the flowers appear in late June—a poor time for transplanting. Hot July is just ahead and chickory, throwing most of its midsummer energies into flower production, is ill-equipped to produce new roots and leaves. Collect seedling plants whose roots haven't yet dug deep into the hard subsoil; or the seeds themselves.

Chrysanthemum leucanthemum (oxeye daisy; CF) resists cultivation. Its long-stalked (to two feet) flowers in June and July disguise the fact that the semi-evergreen basal leaves are ground-hugging, seldom getting up more than four or five inches and easily overshadowed by taller plants. Therefore, daisies occur most plentifully in short-grass meadows and along steep banksides where drought prohibits competition. But even in good soil, daisies often die back in winter; protecting them with low groundcovers of field hawkweed or veronica is probably the best solution.

Cirsium spp. (thistle; SS) is sometimes cited as a component for "old-fashioned" gardens, but is not worth growing. The plants are unkempt, and the prickly leaves are lethal if you try to uproot them by hand. Destroy thistles with a shovel driven into the soil at an angle so that it cuts the taproots at a depth of two to three inches.

Digitalis purpurea (foxglove; SS; see Color Section) is a biennial, but seeds itself dependably enough to produce a persistent colony. The seedlings' small rosettes of quilted leaves quickly enlarge when moved into nearby full sun. In fairly moist, good soil, they produce tall (up to six feet) stalks of lovely flowers unmatched by most other perennials. *Digitalis'* stalks can grow as tall as hollyhock, so be sure that the two plants are separated for an effective display. Let exhausted flowerstalks remain until frost so that seeds have a chance to ripen and self-sow.

Eupatorium purpureum (Joe-Pye weed; SS) has arching, heavily textured leaves borne along a colossal, imposing single stalk up to eight feet, capped in July and August with a flattish head of tiny flowers. Their color varies from muddy grayish purple to a delicate shade the color of old pink velvet. Find one with particularly attractive bloom and mark its stalk with a plastic scarf for transplanting in late autumn. Since Joe-Pye weed can get large, set it well to the back or center of your Meadow.

Eupatorium rugosum (false or white snakeroot; CF) is a far more cultured-looking relative of *E. purpureum*. The plant forms a clump of fairly neat stalks lined with attractive heart-shaped toothed leaves. In September plants become really spectacular, blooming with frothy heads of tiny white flowers that show up very effectively against the plant's deep-green foliage. Nevertheless, one *E. rugosum* is all you need. The plant seeds itself prodigiously, and soon you'll have new plants coming up in a wide variety of places. As long as full sun and room are available, they will succeed in any soil, and transplant with ridiculous ease.

Helianthus (sunflower; SS to LS) has certain perennial species, all neat and some growing to ten feet and more. If your Meadow is fairly moist throughout the summer, *H. decapetalus* and *H. salicifolius* (willow-leaf sunflower) will thrive. For dry sites, use the tall *H. maximilianii, mollis,* and *rigidus*. Most sunflowers are single-stalk plants with deep roots that make transplanting difficult; therefore, it's best to start them from seed if possible. Be sure to *bury* seeds beneath some low groundcover so that they aren't eaten by birds before they can sprout.

Hemerocallis (daylily; CF) looks good in a Meadow, but eventually must be separated before it spreads to form clumps that can squeeze out other plants. In keeping with the entire Meadow's natural look, I'd begin with the native *H. flava* and *H. fulva.*

Lilium (lily; SS) isn't advisable unless your meadow soil is deep and fertile. If so, a spot beside your more upright plantings will suit many of the native lilies, of which *L. pomponium* (Turk's-cap lily) is probably the most spectacular. Other native lilies need more moisture than your Meadow is likely to offer. *L. tigrinum* (tiger lily) is also a good choice, though it eventually forms clumps that can throttle other plants.

Malva moschata (musk mallow; SS) is an English escapee. In spring, highly cut palmate leaves arise from a deep taproot. From late June to frost, it blossoms with short-lived, two-inch, hibiscus-like flowers of pure white or rose pink, several tones darker than wild geranium.

The cultivated *M. alcea fastigiata* seems no more fastigiate than *M. moschata,* and all mallows need Meadow conditions to do their best. I originally planted this plant amidst pachysandra, where part shade and excess moisture made its stems lean and sag. With bright sun and dry soil, they straighten up and are far more satisfactory. Over the winter, mature *Malvas* often retain evergreen tufts of tiny leaves atop their stalks and are ready to make a real leap when spring comes. The deep taproots discourage successful transplanting; they do seed themselves plentifully.

Monarda didyma (beebalm, oswego tea; LS), a relative of mint, arises with characteristic square-sided stems and opposite leaves, spreading to form loose stands. In late June and July, each stalk is topped with a single flower whose brilliant red petals flare out from a central disk, resembling comic-strip drawings of an explosion. A second, tiny flower often arises from the center of the original.

Phlox paniculata (CF) has tall stems, dark green opposite leaves, and late summer flowers that have been hybridized into every shade from clear white (e.g., 'Mount Fuji') through deep purple. In bright sun most phlox towers up to six feet, and looks best in a sea of black-eyed Susan (see below).

Phlox seeds itself sparingly, but creeps by underground runners to form large clumps that will need dividing every four to five years. Overgrown clumps may have a few odd-colored stems at their perimeter, but these are freshly seeded plants that are regressing to the hybrid's original parent colors, not sports as some sources suggest. Move these mavericks to a site of their own.

Potentilla argentea and *recta* (cinquefoil; CF) form fairly dense, two-foot shrubby mounds with small five-petaled flowers all summer. *P. recta*'s are larger, with petals of a yellowish cream, a nice contrast to the usual pure-yellow flowers of *P. argentea* and other hybrids. The compound leaves resemble horse chestnut's in miniature, usually with five main lobes—hence the common name.

Rudbeckia hirta (black-eyed Susan; SS) grows wild on dry slopes where it gets the least competition from grass. Its leaves are narrow and upright; showy flowers are borne all summer but most abundantly in July. Though a biennial, this species seeds itself readily enough, spreading into wide masses that make a nice contrast with hay-scented fern.

Strictly perennial species include *R. lacinata,* whose fully double form (golden glow) has flowers that resemble succulent zinnias. *R. speciosa* and *R. triloba* (coneflower) have raised central disks that give the flowers a coarse appearance, most attractive when grown among *R. hirta* for contrast and comparison.

Solidago (goldenrod; CF or LS) comprises over a hundred wild species and scores of natural and artificial hybrids. It's sheer coincidence that hayfever victims begin sneezing in late summer and fall when the goldenrod blooms: this plant's sticky pollen is not airborne and thus seldom causes nasal distress. The real allergetic culprit is ragweed, which blooms inconspicuously at the same season as goldenrod and wafts its pollen into the air.

Since individual goldenrods vary so widely in size, vigor, and color (from deep rich gold up through pale creamy yellow), make your selections directly from the roadside. Stalks arise from a perennial rootstock that survives transplanting well, but many species are loose-spreaders that colonize large areas without ever producing an effective display. Choose only those plants that are forming clumps.

The main drawback with wild goldenrod is that the lower leaves usually wither and brown off in late summer and need another low-growing plant to camouflage them. Hybridized *Solidagos* offered by mail have overcome this drawback, however. Along with improved flower density, they usually form tighter, neater clumps than their wild counterparts.

Tussilago farfara (coltsfoot; LS) blooms along with the earliest crocus. Lemon-yellow petals surround a bare central disk of matching color. These flowers are supported by scaly, succulent stems that resemble the flowering stalks of sempervivums, and at a distance, the clumps of bright-yellow flowers look exactly like early dandelions. Again like a dandelion, the coltsfoot stalk remains low until the flower is pollinated, then elongates dramatically so that the seeds can be broadcast over a wider range. In April appear the first of the "colt's foot" leaves—large (up to twelve inches across) with scalloped edges and dusted with a velvet gray sheen. These leaves continue to arise all summer in clumps from a deeply ranging underground stem. When transplanting, dig at some distance from the flowers or leaves so as to retain as many roots as possible.

A Cultivated Meadow will also accommodate vigorous and upright selections from the Pachysandra Garden, as long as you can provide some extra water during the droughts of midsummer. Overhead sprinkling tends to beat down these plants' upright stalks, so use a low soaking hose if at all possible.

Once established, a Cultivated Meadow is gratifyingly permanent. The fickle daisies and Susans may come and go, but most species will dig their taproots ever deeper, seeding themselves plentifully so that you'll have no trouble filling in your gaps. Though most will be content to grow in clay, the better your soil, the better their display. You should mulch blooming plants with fairly copious amounts of partly rotted compost every few weeks, and they will automatically adjust themselves to the new soil level. For a neater look in winter, clip off dead stems and flowerstalks and *bury* this litter in the compost heap. The hollow pith canals of "weed" stalks can harbor a wide range of hibernating insects, pupae, fungus, and disease bacteria that you won't want to awaken in the Meadow next spring.

14

ROCKERIES

A wide number of perennials have such compact growth and profuse flowers that they're justly referred to as "rock garden gems." But most gardeners forget that it's the sculpture of the enclosing rocks in which they're exhibited that pleases and attracts. No matter how rich or rare your plantings, visitors are likely to pass them by unless your setting is comely in itself. The term "rock garden" puts the emphasis on plants; a *Rockery* is attractive even before it's planted.

Any good Rockery tries to re-create the appearance of a naturally exposed layer of bedrock. Therefore, you can hardly do better than to begin with the real thing. Your property may already feature a number of Rockery sites that have escaped you until now:

I. Exposed Bedrock Outcrops, such as emerge from a lawn or other fairly flat area, are the easiest to manage. The very top of any outcrop is usually fairly solid, hard stone that has resisted centuries of weathering. But running through it may be veins and pockets of softer stone that have become "rotten" from exposure. Such rock is usually so fragmented that working with a hammer and chisel, you can scrape loose fairly sizable chunks of stone. (Don't use a sledgehammer for such operations; the vibrations will usually fracture the solid rock that you're trying to preserve.)

To allow enough water to collect for a birdbath, for example, my father carefully excavated a pool in a large outcrop and to deepen it still further, edged the "basin"'s lower rims with cement. (To make any concrete "corrections" blend in better, mix the cement with fragments of the rock you've removed.) Following the grain of the rock allows you to hollow out long, fairly narrow slots. Try to excavate them as deeply as you can, because it's here that most "rock garden" plants will thrive. Such "ravines" usually wind up with at least one open end. If so, block the end with small walls of fitted stone fragments.

II. Hidden Bedrock Outcrops are a great deal more common than you'd think. Quite often a developer's bulldozer reveals a large swell of bedrock within a foot or so of the soil surface. If he doesn't have to blast it to make way for the house's foundation, this whaleback of solid rock usually winds up buried under the lawn, where it seldom leaves enough room for healthy grass roots. Each summer, you will see the grass beginning to die and form a predictable shape.

In any case, the solution is remarkably simple. Strip the grass on all sides until the rock's main dome is wholly exposed and you have followed its slopes at least eight inches deep into the soil on all sides. Then carve new eight-to-twelve-inch "walls" in your turf that go straight down until they reach bedrock. Edge those walls with a cement, stone, or brick curb wide enough to support the outside wheel

Original soil level

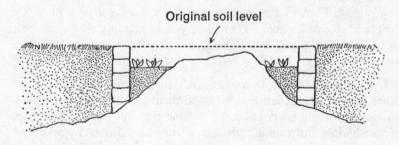

Figure 41

of your lawnmower (Figure 41). Add soil within, and you'll have a neat-looking outcrop with a lush encircling border of plants—far more attractive than if you tried to bury it and hope that it would disappear.

III. Free-Standing Boulders occur frequently in former glacial areas. Although not directly connected to the underlying rock, they are often too massive to move without a bulldozer—and impossible to camouflage. So think of boulders as garden sculpture; plan and plant *around* them.

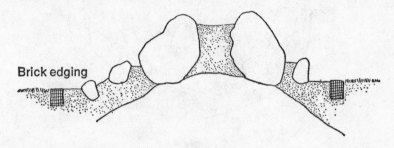

Brick edging

Figure 42

If the boulder is resting on exposed bedrock, you will have to add soil around it so that you can grow plants right up against its faces (Figure 42). But a boulder resting in soil needs only a bit of excavation around it to lighten and enrich the surrounding soil.

If you don't like the color or texture of a sizable boulder (schist and sandstone are rather uninteresting), spruce it up by applying Boston Ivy, a small-leafed plant that will hug the stone's surface. Plant the roots outside the boulder's direct shadow—*not* under or against it, or the plant may receive too little moisture. In a few years, even a large boulder will be completely swathed in tendrils. Errant runners can be easily trimmed off.

This trick works especially well with isolated, upright rocks over five feet tall. If you have a number of smaller boulders lying around, gather them into one spot. Pack the crevices between rocks with good humus, and build small Poor Man's Stone Walls to unify the composition (Figure 43).

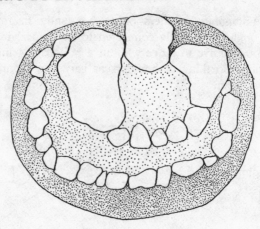

Figure 43

IV. Exposed Ledges—Natural or Artificial

A hillside faced with naturally exposed seams of rock probably comes closest to reproducing the native habitat of alpine plants. In Figure 44, water drains in the direction of the arrows, but because the seams of rock are deep and narrow, the contained soil remains moist even in fairly hot weather.

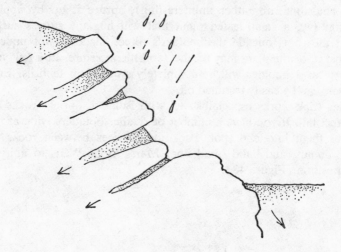

Figure 44

The problem comes if the seams of your rock slant upward from the cliff face. Water won't run uphill, and plants introduced into the fissures will seldom survive. You must carve off as much loose rock as you can, import new soil, and reset the stone in a "false" cliff that resembles the slabs in Figure 44. As with a natural steppingstone path, rocks should be buried almost level with the slope of surrounding soil.

V. Sunken Amphitheater

Many rock garden experts advise building a "dry wall"—a very wide stone wall with a core filled with soil, as in Figure 45. However, notice the patterns of drainage (see arrows)—you must pour a great deal of water into the top for enough to reach plantings at the bottom. If winters are cold, frost will penetrate the sides as well as the top, and only plants with roots long enough to reach the central core will be assured of protection.

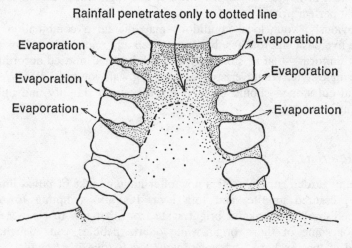

Figure 45

What you want is a bankside with a *single* exposed face, as in Category IV above. If your land is utterly flat, build *down* rather than up. The inner slopes of the sunken "amphitheater" Rockery in Figure 46 are naturally watered by runoff from the surrounding lawn.

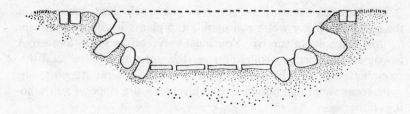

Figure 46

Such a structure's depth more or less depends on the depth of the underlying bedrock, but the larger the amphitheater's slopes, the more impressive and healthy its plants will be. Consider at least one set of stone stairs for access to the bottom "floor," which needs be just roomy enough for you to turn and admire your alpines. Enlarged still further, an amphitheater could become a sunken patio with a central pavement of flagstones, lawn furniture, and high slopes that provide almost perfect privacy.

Obviously, your local conditions may dictate a combination of these five basic approaches, but try to keep any one Rockery looking fairly uniform—that is, stones always look better if massed according to a single style. Whatever style of retaining wall you use—PMSW or formal cut stone—should be used throughout to simplify and unite the entire structure.

Materials

Many garden supply centers now offer large chunks of pitted limestone, fissured granite, and tufa lava. It's also tempting to use crushed marble, chunks of bright agate from that trip to New Mexico, or some of those bright-white quartz pebbles your daughter found at the seashore. But unless your local stone is of similar appearance, such imports stand out blatantly. Your Rockery should be composed of *natural*-looking rock, letting the *plants* provide the variety and color. Rocks dug from your own land are more likely to match each other—and the existing bedrock—than ones brought in from a quarry or stoneyard. Even if your land is rock-free (a mixed blessing!) a trip to a road embankment or construction site will supply you with more effective stones than any you could buy.

Depending on what you turn up, you may want to use certain natural rocks shaped by weathering as bits of "found" sculpture. In New Jersey, for example, the glaciers have left behind numerous lumps of Triassic sandstone whose softer spots have weathered out, leaving empty sockets. I often set them on end as small-scale menhirs, rising from the ferns and pachysandra. (Remove any artificial statuary so that more subtle rocks can display themselves to best advantage.) I once found an extraordinary stone, roughly shaped like a shark's head, with "teeth" of massive crystalline quartz. It works as a Rockery ornament only because its grain and texture match the bedrock outcrop on which it's placed. A rock that matches its companions will always be an asset, but if it's too wildly different, it functions as bric-a-brac.

Soil

Rockery soil has little chance of being replenished with natural litter. Small spaces can't accommodate more than a token mulch, and the plants you'll be growing are too tiny to contribute much of their own detritus. Therefore, the soil you add to pockets and crevices should be fairly rich from the start.

But texture is important too. Many choice Rockery plants naturally grow in a *scree*—a deep pile of rotten rock and stone chips formed at the base of eroding cliffs. Such a soil is extremely heavy, slow to dry out, and provides excellent texture for tiny roots to grip on. The problem is that it's almost impossible to transplant new specimens into such a solid, scratchy medium. Any of the Rockeries described above will drain very well indeed, so your only worry is how to keep the soil from heaving. Mix in a bit of builder's sand and a good quantity of sharp gravel. These rock chips weight the humus down, providing a rough texture through which roots can squeeze and anchor themselves. Rains and frosts will shift and settle new soil, and plants introduced prematurely will heave and sink along with it. Your newly added soil must pack down *thoroughly* into the spaces between rocks, so wait at least six months before planting.

You should prune the limbs of other trees in the vicinity so that your plants get as much morning and afternoon sun as possible. At the high altitude where alpines grow, the sun is strong, but the air quite cool. At the lower altitudes where most of us live and garden, the sun is weaker but *hotter:* at high noon, sun can heat rocks until they're painful to the touch and communicate heat deep into the earth. Several times I've moved small rocks during July and August and found the soil beneath them steaming.

The fact is, most rock gardens don't have enough rocks. Even deep soil will tend to dry out unless the surface is covered *solidly* with small stones that retard evaporation. Again, the best source of suitable size rocklets is your own property. Whenever you dig holes for new plants, carry along an old plastic flowerpot into which you can toss small stones and pebbles. Wash them clean of any clayish subsoil and press them into the soil of your Rockery as if you were building a cobblestone path in miniature. These rocks can later be removed if plants begin encroaching on them, but in the meantime, they'll form a perfect cosmetic mulch for exotic specimens, providing sheltered cracks where their seeds can settle and germinate.

Plants for the Sunny Rockery

Literally hundreds of different plants are possible for Rockery use. If the following list seems short, it's because most so-called "rock garden" plants are wanton thick-spreaders and quickly get out of control. I restrict the Rockery to plants that cannot withstand competition, that need full sun and grow delicately and diminutively. (Remember, you want to *compliment* your rocks, not camouflage them.)

Bulbs

Snowdrop and grape hyacinth tend to multiply rampantly and squeeze out other plants. A very few bulbs are suited to tight spots:

Anemone blanda (Greek anemone, windflower) is a good Low Garden bulb, but the multipetaled flowers of blue, white, pink, and purple are a superb spring contrast against unchanging stone. The flowers and leaves fade soon—enough that intervening plants will not be shaded out.

Crocus—especially the smaller species and "snow crocus"—are good for Rockeries. But plant them only in sheltered crannies where their flowers will not be blasted by spring winds, and where their narrow, grass-like foliage won't get in the way of other plants.

Muscari album (white grape hyacinth) has shorter, more erect foliage than the blue strains. It's also less vigorous, thereby preserving a neater appearance. New bulbs seem to appear a short distance from the parent, rather than forming congested clumps, and the foliage does not resprout in autumn.

Narcissus have several miniature species that are quite exotic. *N. bulbocodium* has tiny threadlike petals and a shallow, gaping, bowl-shaped trumpet. *N. cyclamineus* is a slightly taller dwarf whose petals are swept straight back from an unflared, cylindrical trumpet, as if blown back in a high wind.

Both of the above blossoms are so radically distorted from the norm that they look freakish unless grown in thick, multiple plantings. I prefer *N. minimus* (or *nanus*)—a daffodil of perfect proportions, but with stems only three inches high and a flower not more than an inch long. The bulb is fairly large, as is the case with many narcissus miniatures.

Perennials

The following plants—a list compiled from specialized catalogs, as well as from my own observation—are appropriately tiny for Rockery use, but flowers are proportionately huge. The height in each case refers to the foliage only; flowers are sometimes borne on significantly higher stems.

Ajuga is too vigorous a groundcover for the restricted Rockery: small runners will spread out over the bare stone and, if they cannot find soil in which to root, will die back over the winter. However, *Ajuga metallica crispa* is far more compact than the normal *A. reptans*. The leaves are of the familiar bronzy-purple but are wider and crinkled up like crushed foil. Unlike most ajugas, *A. metallica crispa* spreads very slowly, eventually crowning its site with a mound-shaped welter of wrinkled leaves somewhat resembling a miniaturized rhubarb. Stunted blue flowers appear in spring.

Alyssum (basket of gold) is a loose, sprawling plant that looks ratty once its flowers fade. Old colonies produce ragged, semi-woody stems. Hold out for the smaller strains: *A. sardicum; A. saxatile* (including the varieties "Dudley Neville" and *flore pleno*); and *A. wulfenianum*. All grow to no higher than 4", with characteristic yellow flowers.

Androsace chamaejasme (rock jasmine): tiny 1" spreading rosettes, yellow flowers.

A. sempervivoides: 3" sempervivum lookalike—green rosettes, pink flowers.

Armeria maritima (sea pink) forms an impeccable low mound of thin evergreen leaves. In May each tuft sends up dozens of circular balls of small flowers on long, succulent stems. Try to get *Armerias* of different colors—common strains flower in white, purple, red, and shades of pink. Though *Armeria* will seed itself, cut back the flower-stalks as soon as the petals start to fade to neaten the plant and divert energy back to the foliage.

Bellis spp. (English daisy) is less hardy than catalogs would have you believe. Flowers are daisy-like, but like some chrysanthemums, tend to discolor prematurely. 'Dresden China' has 2" rosettes, double pink flowers.

Bellium minutum, another daisy-like flower, grows 1" high. Flowers are pink, streaked with white, but plant is not reliably hardy.

Campanula (bellflower) has a number of tall, leggy species and hybrids that should be avoided. However:

C. aucheri (4") is neat and will enjoy part sun.

C. cochleariifolia or *pusilla:* (1½") a mound-forming bellflower; flowers blue or white.

C. dasyantha, or *pilosa* (1")

C. elatines (3"), usually listed by its variety name of *garganica,* is particularly prolific and easy to grow.

C. muralis, or *portenschlagiana* (1")

C. parryi (2")

Campanulas are often hard to transplant, so give several specimens of each a choice of different sites to ensure that at least one survives.

Celmisia petiolata: narrow spear-shaped leaves in clumps: white daisy-like flowers.

Daphne petraea or *rupestris:* (6") evergreen mound smothered with waxy pink trumpets.

Dianthus (carnation) tend to be leggy and flop over; the centers of old colonies become sparse and die out. Restrict yourself to the smaller, mat-forming species and hybrids:

D. 'Ariel' (2")

D. alpinus: to 2"; cushion-forming

D. arenarius

D. brevicaulis

D. myrtinervius: (½")

D. peristeri: (2")

D. 'Prince Charming'

D. 'Rose Cushion': thick blue-green 1½" mats

D. 'Tiny Rubies': 1" spreading tufts

Most *Dianthus* like a sweetish soil, and the rarer alpine strains demand it. Therefore, mix the removed soil with a spoonful of crushed limestone before transplanting.

Erigeron aureatus: 2" clumps of deep-green narrow leaves, golden daisy-like flowers.

E. mucronatus: rampant 1½" spreader; white or pink flowers on 6" stems.

E. pulchellus: the native American species, produces ground-hugging rosettes of leaves never more than a half inch off the ground, and diminutive daisy-like white flowers with gold centers. It likes full sun but is impartial to soil: the plants I collected were growing in eroded reddish clay under the dripping eaves of a Catskill hotel. Unfortunately, the plant is not perfectly hardy, but under sheltered conditions, individual plants form thick rootstocks and later, colonies. Flowers are produced throughout the summer, the stems lengthening when more moisture is available.

Erodium chamaedryoides: 3" mounds; red, pink, or white flowers

Geranium subcaulescens splendens: 4" trailing stems, pink flowers

Geum makes a good Pachysandra or Meadow plant in its normal, large sizes. But *Geum* X 'Waight Brilliant' is a small (3") mound of deeply cut leaves bearing orange flowers on 6" stalks until frost.

Hosta lancifolia minor: heart-shaped leaves about ¾" across in loose rosettes 1½" high. In July, a flowerstalk up to 8" arises with a few bluish-purple blooms. Seed should be collected in the hopes that even tinier sports may result.

Iberis (candytuft) blooms beautifully in spring, but the woody stems are sprawling and nondescript the rest of the year. (For full-size candytufts, hold out for 'Autumn Snow', a variety that reblooms in fall.) The only true miniature is *I. saxatilis:* a 3" trailing candytuft, with white flowers.

Iris commonly used in rock gardens are simply not satisfactory. The dwarf iris sold in garden shops have short-lived blossoms of muddy color, and their foliage is even more shapeless than that of taller strains. *I. reticulata* (the so-called "Dutch iris") bloom in late winter, but otherwise contribute nothing by way of foliage accent.

I. cristata lacustris is an extremely dwarf 4" iris forming thick mats.

Opuntia spp. (prickly pear) is the only cactus native to the American Northeast. In July and August, the flattened pads bloom with wide, showy flowers ranging from light yellow through orange to deep red, depending on the individual species or hybrid. *Opuntias* should be planted *only* in a Rockery, since without containment, they spread widely and erratically, with broken-off pads rooting to form new colonies. One true miniature is *O. erinacea utahensis,* a 3" prickly pear with yellow "desert waterlily" flowers.

Opuntias bear clusters of small, particularly irritating hairlike spines that break loose in anything—cloth, leather, skin—that brushes them. Yet they're so tiny that they're difficult to see, even when you can *feel* just where they're at. Thus, when transplanting this cactus, it makes sense to use a pair of old canvas garden gloves. (The gloves will wind up bristling with a rusty-colored five-o'clock shadow, and will probably have to be discarded after.) Plant *Opuntias* with plenty of rock on all sides, possibly on a fairly high elevation to keep them away from visitors.

This cactus can be de-spined without injuring it or you. Watch for new pads to begin sprouting. When they're about half-grown, you'll notice they're studded with short, green cone-like structures. Unless removed in time, each will dry and ripen into a cluster of spines. Hold the pad securely with a pair of pliers, so as not to break it loose from old growth and carefully rub or clip loose the succulent pods.

Oxalis lacinata: 3″ clumps of cut leaves smothered with showy pink to lavender flowers

Penstemon pinifolia: 3″ mats, red flowers

Phlox kelseyi: 2″ mats, deep-violet flowers

P. sublata (creeping or moss phlox) is a vastly more common species that trails over the ground, forming dense mats about three inches deep. In April, colonies are literally covered with flowers, ranging from pure white to deep purplish blue.

Unfortunately, creeping phlox's few virtues are usually balanced by drawbacks. The plant is not a dependable groundcover—it spreads erratically, rooting weakly along its stems, and unless it gets a good amount of moisture, new growth tends to die back. Because of its thick eventual growth, it will smother smaller plants. But the phlox itself can't stand competition: the least shade makes it grow lankily, with only intermittent bloom. In fact, its leaves are so tightly compacted that older colonies often seem to smother themselves, and their sharp, prickly leaves makes nearby weeding a painful chore. I'd restrict *P. sublata* to deep, narrow pockets of soil where it can't spread any wider than a foot and will maintain itself in neater shape.

Potentilla cinerea: prostrate evergreen foliage; yellow flowers

P. fruticosa 'Medicine Wheel Mountain': 2″ prostrate, yellow flowers

P. nitida: 2″, pink flowers

P. verna nana: 3″, yellow flowers

Rosa (rose): Ideal for the deeper, moister pockets of a Rockery are the Miniature roses—but pick a color that shows up well at a distance. One particularly apt Rockery subject is the new full-size 'Red Cascade', a prostrate climbing rose. Planted atop an outcrop, its weeping canes will travel *down* over the bare rock, eventually reaching lengths of about six feet. This habit makes it a cinch to prune, and a rockbound rose is extremely easy to fertilize and spray.

Saxifraga (saxifrage): These plants are a specialty to themselves, but a great many demand a sweet, limy soil. Two of the smallest are:

S. izoon baldensis: 1″ gray rosettes and white flowers

S. caespitosa emarginata produces ½″ mats of leaves—again with the outsize-stalked white flowers that are a saxifrage trademark.

Sedum is a large genus of basically handsome succulents, most of which thick-spread into wide mats of foliage. However, the effect is not permanent. After they flower in July, most strains remain weak and stringy-looking for the rest of the summer. Plant them in narrow crevices where they can obtain moisture even on hot days, and where they can spread without endangering other plantings. A more formal effect is achieved by separating different sedums, but interplanting them is the only way to assure a solid cover.

Flowers can be white, yellow, or from light pink to deep red; different colors usually flower at slightly different seasons. Roughly similar sedums are sold under many different names, so order about a dozen different ones and decide among them once they begin to grow. Probably the neatest species is *S. spurium*—sort of a succulent parody of pachysandra. Round flat leaves are borne in rosettes atop a trailing, brown-skinned stem. Frequent watering and mulching with screened leafmold will keep the new shoots thick and upright.

S. spectabile is a giant single-clump plant. Beginning in late July, the tip of each stem flattens into a wide plateau of tiny flowers. Old-fashioned hybrids of *spectabile* have foliage of a rather watery chartreuse green, and their flowers—in varying shades of dull pink—fade quickly. Recent hybridizing has vastly improved the leaf color to bluish green, tightened the shape of the clump and extended the life of the flower: 'Autumn Joy' has broccoli-like heads of deep red that last a bit over a month. The variety 'Stardust' has white flowers for contrast to the reds and pinks.

There's no need to divide your larger clumps, since *spectabile* propagates easily from cuttings. In June, break off one of the larger stalks and leave it in a cool, dry place until its end heals. Remove all leaves from one side of the stalk and wherever you want a new clump, lay it flat in a shallow ½″ trench, burying it about halfway as if it were a fallen log. Within a week, buds in the nodes of the leaves will expand into new stalks, with new bunches of roots developing just beneath them. The result is a modest, elongated clump that you can either separate or leave to grow as is.

Sempervivum spp. (hens 'n' chickens, houseleeks, live-forevers) roughly resemble miniature artichokes, with rosettes of small succulent leaves above fat taproots. Larger rosettes regularly produce new plants until they form a tightly jammed colony. Foliage colors range from every shade of green and red into combinations thereof.

The main drawback to sempervivums is that they bloom! The entire rosette elongates vertically into a single stalk with widely spaced leaves. At the top is a branched spray of thickly petaled, usually bland-colored flowers. The flowers themselves are very short-lived and soon fade or rot—or both. The extra sap that opens the flowers also increases their weight, so the stalk almost invariably flops over. Then the entire plant dies and decays, leaving a vacancy that neighboring sempervivums are slow to enter.

Another problem is that sempervivum taproots have very little holding power. In open soil, a good portion of any sempervivum colony usually gets heaved by frost. They seem more secure when competing against others of the same species, or when given a tight, narrow crack of rock in which they can brace themselves. New plants can be anchored most easily by pressing a small stone deeply into the soil. Pull the stone out, lay the new sempervivum's root in the depression, and gently replace the stone. The youngster will begin almost immediate growth.

Always be sure to weed sempervivums carefully and regularly. Grass seed often slips in between the members of a colony and sinks roots that, when pulled out, can often pull the sempervivums along with them.

About a hundred original species have been extensively hybridized, but many named strains look almost exactly alike. To ensure a wide visual variety, order the sample collections some mail-order nurseries offer to new customers. But two species—and their hybrids—are particularly desirable for Rockery use:

S. arachnoideum (cobweb or spiderweb houseleek) is smaller than most, and its younger, central leaves are roofed with a mat of cottony white fibers. The plants show up particularly well, seldom flower, and are best for filling up thin cracks and gaps between larger sempervivums.

S. globiferum makes little flat spheres of tightly wrapped scales of bright chartreuse. New plantlets appear as tiny "berries" over the entire surface of the mature parent. When about the size of a large pea, they often break off, quickly taking on a ruddy tinge that makes them easy to spot. Since these free-rolling plantlets have no roots as yet, make a pit by pushing a hard pebble into the soil and fit the sempervivum into this socket. *S. globiferum* very seldom flowers, and so its thronged colonies, overlaid with a layer of young, make an effective permanent groundcover for short stretches.

Silene acaulis grandiflora: 1½" mat-forming elongated leaves; rose flowers

S. alpestris: 2" evergreen mats; white flowers

S. caroliniana or *pensylvanica* (catchfly, firepink) has been one of my all-time favorites ever since I found it growing wild on the shores of Long Island Sound. The root is massive and deep, supporting a low tuft of narrow deep-green leaves. In May and June, it bears phlox-like flowers ranging from lightest pink to almost full red. It flourishes best in the layers of "rotten" rock underneath weathered outcrops where—surprisingly—it doesn't mind being swept with salt water during an occasional hurricane. Young plants are best transplanted before their roots become enormous and cumbersome.

S. wherryi: tight 4" mounds; pink flowers

Solidago minuta: 3" goldenrod (do not confuse with *minuta* varieties of other goldenrod species)

S. multiradiata 'Pony Mountain Strain': 2–3" colonies

S. spathulata nana 'Medicine Wheel Mountain Strain': (2–3")

Viola (violet): Most species bloom only in spring, and most of the large- to middle-sized ones are rampant spreaders. A few species, however, preserve a neat and huddled habit.

V. arenaria blooms all summer with light-purple flowers.

V. fimbriatula's adaptability makes it a fine violet for Rockery use. I first came upon it as a colony of tiny 2" plants blooming on a sunny outcrop. After being moved to a more fertile expanse of humus, they enlarged into plants with spear-shaped leaves fully six inches long. One plant was utterly razed by chipmunks, yet within a month it had sprouted a new set of leaves and was the same size as its unmolested counterparts. Yet, while this violet *enlarges,* it does not *spread,* and packed down between sempervivums, its rose-purple May flowers show up to best advantage. Seed germinates readily to form new plants.

V. hederacea: roundish leaves form 4" mats, with white flowers marked with purple.

To obtain these desirable gems, you must usually write off to one of the several mail-order firms that specialize in these tiny plants. Your Rockery should remain a privileged preserve for your particular favorites only; it's better to have only two or three superb specimens among the rocks than a solid bed of humdrum laggards that you tend to neglect.

Dwarf Conifers

Dwarf conifers are an entire field in themselves, and you can fill even an enormous Rockery without ever duplicating a specimen. The ones I recommend for Rockeries never grow above 2 feet even after ten years or more of healthy, unpruned growth. Some have developed from mutant seedlings, but the majority have arisen as "witches' brooms"—sudden genetic anomalies that arise spontaneously on otherwise normal plants. When such a witch's broom is large enough to provide material for grafts and cuttings, a new variety can be propagated.

Dwarfs look far better in combination than they do singly, and should be carefully arranged for best visual compatibility. First plant your "groundcovers"—the prostrate cultivars that slither over bare earth and rock. Then come the bun-shaped dwarfs, and lastly, a few upright strains to give scale and stateliness to the entire planting. Particularly attractive types are starred.

I. Prostrate Forms: should be obtained while still very small. Larger specimens often creep over the sides of their pot and harden off in that position. Planting them in flat ground means either bending the branches *very* carefully back to horizontal or cutting them off—a bad choice in either case. Plant where they have plenty of room to cascade downward.

Cedrus deodara prostrata (deodar cedar)

  *C. libani sargentii (cedar of Lebanon)

Juniperus communis hornibrookii (juniper)

  J. c. saxatilis

  J. c. 'Silver Lining'

  J. horizontalis admirabilis

J. h. 'Bar Harbor'

J. h. *Douglasii*

*J. h. *glauca*

*J. h. *glomerata*

J. h. *lividus*

*J. h. *procumbens*

J. h. *pulchella*

J. h. *wiltonii*

J. *procumbens*

*J. p. *nana*

J. *scopulorum repens*

J. *squamata prostrata*

J. *taxifolia lutchuensis*

Picea abies inversa (Norway spruce)

*P. *pungens prostrata* (Colorado blue spruce)

Pinus densiflora prostrata (Japanese red pine)

P. *sylvestris* 'Hillside Creeper' (Scots pine)

P. *thunbergii prostrata* (Japanese black pine)

Pseudotsuga taxifolia fletcheri (Douglas fir)

Sequoia sempervivens nana pendula (dwarf redwood; prostrate despite the "pendula" designation)

Tsuga canadensis 'West Coast Creeper' (hemlock with large needles and not sun-shy like *T. canadensis* 'Cole's Prostrate', which must be grown in part shade.)

While still small, any prostrate tree can be trained upward in fastigiate fashion like a *pendula* (see Chapter 6)—though obviously on a smaller scale. This is especially effective if you have at least three prostrate evergreens of different species. Train one of each's central leaders up for a foot or so, then let it cascade back down. The effect is like that of a fountain with several different jets of varying texture.

II. Globular: The vast majority of dwarf evergreens form small buns that are broader than high. The following do not spread excessively and have trim, attractively congested foliage.

Abies balsamea 'Hudsonia' (balsam fir)

**A.* balsamea nana

A. koreana 'Compact Dwarf'

Chamaecyparis lawsonia ("false cypress"): Almost all *C. lawsonia* varieties are good bets; many resemble tightly globular arborvitae and come in a surprisingly broad range of foliage colors—whitish, yellow, blue, and blue-green.

VARIEGATED:

C. l. duncanii	*C. l.* albospica
C. l. 'Elwood's Pygmy'	*C. l.* albovariegata
C. l. filiformis compacta	*C. l.* aureovariegata
C. l. forsteckensis	*C. l.* 'Fleckellwood'
C. l. gimbornii	*C. l.* 'Fletcher's White'
C. l. 'Green Globe'	*C. l.* 'Gold Splash'
C. l. minima	*C. l.* 'Snow Flurry'
C. l. minima aurea	
**C. l.* minima glauca	
C. l. nana	
**C. l.* nana albospica	
C. l. nana glauca	
**C. l.* nidiformis	
**C. l.* pygmaea argentea	
**C. l.* tamariscifolia	
**C. l.* tharandtensis caesia:	
(closely resembles a blue juniper)	

**Chamaecyparis obtusa coralliformis* (hinoki cypress)

C. o. intermedia

C. o. juniperoides

**C. o.* lycopodiodes

C. o. nana: tight, globular hinoki cypress

C. o. nana gracilis: a more upright, fast-growing variety

C. o. pygmaea: hardly a pygmy, but a flat-topped bun with reddish twigs exposed

**C. o.* repens

Chamaecyparis pisifera nana aureovariegata

    C. p. squarrosa intermedia: a perfectly smooth mound of semi-weeping gray-blue foliage.

*Cryptomeria japonica bandai-sugi

    *C. j. globosa

    C. j. jindai-sugi

    *C. j. monstrosa nana

    *C. j. nana albospica

    *C. j. spiralis

Juniperus squamata pygmaea

*Picea abies capitata

    P. a. maxwellii

    *P. a. gregoryana parsonii

    *P. a. repens

*Pinus mugo pumilo

Tsuga canadensis 'Birds Nest'

    T. c. 'Brandley'

    T. c. 'Jeddeloh'

    *T. c. 'Jervis'

    *T. c. nana

    T. c. 'Von Helm's Dwarf'

This list is only a sampler of varieties I've actually seen, and hardly exhausts your options: one single mail-order firm lists over fifty dwarf sports of *Tsuga canadensis* alone. When confronted with an unfamiliar variety, it's best to make your selections according to the plant's mature size, which most of the better dwarf dealers provide on their price lists ("1' tall and 3' wide at two years," and so forth). Planting in a restricted environment, of course, will often stunt them even further.

Since keeping these globular specimens fairly low is the whole point, high-pruning is not called for. But prune any branches that are actually sweeping the ground. You should be able to see the trunks on all your trees, so as to be able to check on rate of growth, need for mulch, extent of winter heaving, and so forth. Chamaecyparises in particular often have interiors matted with dead, brown foliage—

an unsightly haven for insect pests. Such trees usually benefit from what I call "open pruning"—removing all interior dead wood and redundant or superfluous limbs. Open pruning also makes the specimen more recognizably a tree, and often gives the illusion of greater size.

III. Upright Conifers: The following are usually more fastigiate than normal evergreens; often more brightly colored. Though some attain good size, they are invariably neat and compact at any age.

*Chamaecyparis lawsonia 'Bloom'
    C. l. 'Grayswood Pillar'
    **C. l.* 'Witzeliana'

*Cupressus sempervierns gracilis
    **C. s.* stricta
    C. s. 'Swane's Golden'

*Juniperus communis compressa (Irish juniper)
    J. chinensis 'Kaizuka Variegated'
    J. scopulorum 'Grey Gleam'

  Picea glauca conica (Alberta spruce)

*Taxus baccata standishii

*Thuja occidentalis spiralis

This group virtually never needs pruning as long as full sun is provided. But again, be sure to bare the first three inches of trunk.

Plants for the Shady Rockery

It's true that most desirable alpines demand full sun, but others will allow you to grow a perfectly lovely Rockery in almost full shade.

Groundcovers:

Arenaria balearica (sandwort) is the only shade-loving species of the genus, good for carpeting open patches.

Asperula odorata (sweet woodruff) has rosettes of thin leaves borne one atop the other on short stems no taller than 8″, topped in spring with sprays of white flowers.

Asplenium georingianum pictum (Japanese painted fern) is slow-growing, but eventually fills crevices with a thick mat of elongated triangular leaves, each a light grayish green and variably banded toward the margins and veins with pink, gray, and lighter green. Though it rises later in spring than most ferns (and even later in a cool and shaded environment), it produces new fronds all summer.

Asplenium platyneuron (ebony spleenwort) is a dependable single-clump fern. Its neat little fronds get up to 18 inches, borne in tight sprays.

Polypodium vulgare (common polypody) can grow in very shallow soil, such as the humus skullcaps of large woodland boulders. When moisture is scarce, the leaves furl themselves up and apparently wilt, opening again with the next rain. This desiccation can be avoided by growing it in deeper soil.

Tiarella cordifolia (foamflower) is a dependable wildflower that quickly covers moist, shady spots (see Chapter 12). The Oriental species *T. polyphylla* and the Southern *T. wherryi* are extremely similar.

Veronica persica makes a good trailing groundcover for shady areas, increasing far more quickly than the species listed above.

Viola blanda has elongated oval leaves of a clear, light green. In April it bears tiny white flowers, their lips decorated with threads of dark purple, atop disproportionately high stems, so that flowers teeter twice as high as the leaves.

Tsuga canadensis 'Cole's Prostrate' (SS) is not strictly a groundcover, but the only conifer that must have shade. It will weep down the face of a rock like a green waterfall, but is also attractive on flat ground, eventually forming a series of low mounds a foot or two across; old branches drop their needles to reveal smooth gray bark.

Perennials for the Shady Rockery

Many guides suggest woodland wildflowers as good Rockery choices, but as we've seen, most of them begin going dormant around May. You'll welcome the transitory appearance of *Clitonia* (spring beauty), but for a more permanent vertical accent, use jack-in-the-pulpit: the leaves remain in good condition until August.

Convalaria majalis (lily of the valley; ODT) is a classic garden staple. Pairs of leaves arise in early spring, often bearing between them a spray of small bell-like flowers. *Convalaria* is sometimes recommended as a groundcover for open areas, but it's a one-direction-spreader, allowing weeds and grass an easy entry. Restricted to a Rockery, however, lily of the valley continues to double back on itself, getting thick enough to bloom noticeably.

The standard old-fashioned white *C. majalis* has outsize *gigantea* and *flora plena* varieties. The recently introduced pink variety is *roseum*. New leaves and flowers arise only from the "pips" or terminal buds. Give them a bed of well-rotted leafmold at least 4″ deep. Continued mulch and dried manure late each autumn will help them spread and increase flowers.

Iris cristata, a wild dwarf iris seldom more than 5″ high, does best on a raised Rockery where slugs are infrequent.

I. gracilipes forms a uniquely neat clump of drooping grass-like leaves, attractive in themselves. The flowers, of lavender or white, resemble the blossoms of *kaempferi* in miniaturized form.

I. verna is similar to *reticulata* in bloom; the leaves later grow to 5″. The rhizome is very shallow; plant in a deep pit with rock sides that will contain it in a tight clump.

Rockery Care

Try to plant all new stock in late spring or early fall, when weather is cool and the plants can sink new roots easily. But unfortunately a great many rock garden nurseries ship plants in June, when temperatures and sun strength are at their height. Use a lawn chair or bushel basket to shade newly planted arrivals during their first few days.

In July and August, Rockeries should be watered at least once a day—first when the morning dew dries off, around 10:30 A.M. Use the very lightest spray your hose nozzle will attain. A five-minute sprinkle will last the plants through to the afternoon hours. A second five-minute sprinkle at two o'clock will cool off the plants' leaves and the heated rocks around them.

15

MINIATURE LANDSCAPES

Outside my father's kitchen window, a stunted juniper cascades into space from the bare summit of a tall mountain. A deep gorge cuts beneath the mountain's east slope, revealing rocky palisades on either side. Last summer, a sizable avalanche washed out one side of the gorge, so my father rebuilt it. While he was at it, he relocated a couple of small hills and transplanted some full-sized trees so that the distant horizon presents a better silhouette.

It wasn't too great a chore! As the gnat flies, this alpine vista is only eighteen feet long. The distance back to the "horizon" is a little over seven feet. All its flourishing trees and perennials are *natural* miniatures that will never grow much larger—and are as easy to relocate as ordinary Rockery specimens (see Color Section).

Such a garden would seem to be the result of meticulous planning, but actually, this one *evolved* out of a coincidence of the right opportunities: a neighbor of ours was building a swimming pool. The excavation dynamited loose a great quantity of dark crystalline bedrock, most of it in hefty and eccentric chunks that were dumped along a waste stretch of roadside. One we examined looked just like a sheer cliff face topped with an overhanging escarpment. Lovely—except that like a Hollywood stage set, it was a mere façade of stone some six inches thick that couldn't stand upright on its own. But we found two other flatish stones that when fitted against it made a free-standing (and remarkably convincing) "Mont Blanc," its face seemingly polished by ice and snow. Moreover, the slabs left a space between them that could be packed with soil and planted to give the effect of a highland forest.

We already knew the Japanese tradition of *bonkei*—wide, shallow pots in which small rocks and artificially dwarfed trees give the illusion of extensive landscapes. But such creations need constant care and watering the year around. Could we construct an entire landscape in slightly larger scale, using *naturally* dwarf evergreens that would never grow out of proportion? Why not! There were plenty of extra rocks to work with. Mounding and sculpting loose soil resulted in gorges and valleys that looked surprisingly natural when planted with appropriately tiny plants.

Only recently did I learn that the first gardens commissioned by Japan's shoguns were similar miniature landscapes—three-dimensional replicas of famous scenic views of the Inland Sea. From *The Japanese Garden: An Approach to Nature:*

> A portion of the traditionally white-gravelled courtyard was converted into a pond, representing the sea, with a pebbled shore about it. The pebbled variety was called *suhama,* literally "gravelled seashore"; if stones were used, they were called *ariso,* or "rocky beaches."

Somehow, re-creating an alpine landscape presents even more of a challenge than duplicating a rocky beach. Part rock garden, part dollhouse, part stage set, a Miniature Landscape changes from week to week as its flowers bloom and fade, as its trees increase and its goundcovers spread and self-seed. Few quests are quite as compulsive as the search for *just* the right plant to complete a given cranny. And I've already made enough mistakes and rewarding discoveries to offer some ground rules.

Location:

A Miniature Landscape (hereafter abbreviated as ML) *must* be in full sun. The ML's rugged terrain casts a surprising amount of shade, and most of the micro-size plants you'll want to grow need an unobstructed view of the heavens.

Since a ML is intended to represent a fairly extensive vista, it should be situated where it's easily and *consistently* visible from inside your house. (My father's ML directly adjoins a patio outside the kitchen window; mine appears in the angle of a brick path outside my front door, where it's also visible through a picture window.) To give a greater illusion of distance, it should *not* be backed up against anything. My father's ML is built up against the edge of a cliff. The ground just behind it falls away quite abruptly, so that beyond his "horizon," the eye sees only an indeterminate vista of empty space. Failing that, you need some bland, nondistracting visual boundary to stop the eye so that it ignores what is beyond in favor of more proximate details.

The perfect ML should appear to have been carved out of *normal* reality—and so be doubly dwarfed by what lies around and beyond it. When visitors see my ML for the first time, they usually remark, "What a shame you had to put that brick pathway so close! It ruins the effect." But after repeated viewings, I like the bricks more and more *because* they remind me that what I'm viewing is artificial. They help me appreciate the illusion all the more. (Meanwhile, on a strictly practical basis, such nearby paths afford me easy access for care and weeding—and also let the curious visitor see how it's done.)

Construction:

Any ML should be higher in back than it is in front, so that the surface is "raked," just like a stage set. This affords an illusion of greater depth by duplicating one of the traditions of Oriental landscape painting: the effect of distance is achieved by a convention in which a "far" object is depicted *above* a "nearer" one even though both may be nearly of the same size. The same effect can be achieved in three dimensions, as long as your ML—again, like a stage set—is basically oriented toward a single viewing angle. By happy coincidence, my land already slopes upward from the foreground of my ML, so that for me, a raised background is not strictly necessary. However, a rise of at least a foot is called for if your ML site is on flat terrain (see Figure 48, below).

The back of your ML won't generally be visible, but it's the most important single component. This part will support a great weight of soil, and if it's not perfect to start with, you may have to uproot years of work in order to repair it. Thick and solid is the key: brick is too flimsy, but concrete blocks cast for patio use would probably be acceptable. Best of all are *very* large, straight-edged stones that can be fitted carefully together so that they won't budge.

This back wall should be straight and fairly uniform in height, though it can be irregular along the top to simulate the gentle swells of a distant mountain range. When you get to the sides, turn a *sharp* corner and switch to natural stones (if you weren't using them already). Use triangular wedges of rock (see Figure 47) whose attrac-

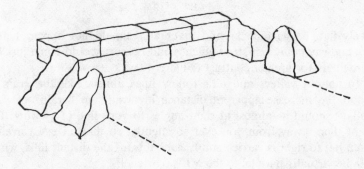

Figure 47

tive slopes can afford exposure. The height of these stones should diminish as they approach the front until they are level with—or even actually below—the ML's artificial front border.

Landscaping:

Basically, you now have an open "picture frame" of rock that, just like a Rockery, should be filled with well-rotted leafmold mixed with sand. (Extremely raw leafmold should be avoided, since it tends to decay even further after being packed and planted. The resulting sinkage can cause the collapse of banks and promentories.) Now the real fun begins! Dump your soil in eccentric heaps, and carve and tunnel it into hills, ravines, gulches, mountains, canyons, plateaus, and so forth.

It doesn't hurt to glean some inspiration from the *National Geographic* or from a book of Hiroshige's landscape prints, but a few basic rules will help you achieve more satisfying results. Measuring back from the forefront of the ML, the first foot or so should be rela-

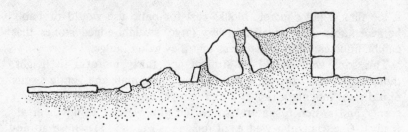

Figure 48

tively flat. Large hillocks and mountains should not appear before the midway point, but steep gulches and ravines should come just *before* them, for greater contrast (Figure 48).

In nature, valleys and hills follow lines almost like the grain in wood. To increase apparent distance involved, the "grain" of your valleys should be almost at right angles to your line of viewing. But slant them away from you ever so slightly, so that an eye traveling from left to right is carried subtly *back* toward the distant hills, which can be virtually parallel to the ML's rear wall.

Hills are basically mounds of soil fitted with rocks at the tops or sides for greater stability. Natural hills seldom have vertical rock faces, so use round rocks broken in half to suggest the exposed crowns or faces of glacier-scoured stone.

Valleys are simply troughs carved out of the basic soil mixture. Remember that *natural* valleys narrow and widen, their bottoms usually sloping upward to one end or the other. Valleys should always be a bit deeper than you might think right, because the plants will eventually soften their outlines just as would a moderate fall of snow. Within a valley, any rocky outcrops should face the ML's front. (There's no point in hiding a rock where it can't be seen.)

Mountains are nothing but a veneer of flat but rugged-looking stones fitted around a central core of soil. Once the soil has packed down over a year of rain and frost, the mountain's peak is ready to be planted with—preferably—a small prostrate evergreen that will cascade down the rock faces. The best planting sites are right *beneath* a rock face: seams of soil between facing stones can be fitted with smaller rocks (duplicating a mountain scree) and planted almost immediately.

Slopes wherever they occur, should always seem to have washed down from a higher elevation. Thus the higher a mountain, the steeper its slopes can be allowed to be. Smaller slopes on the sides of valleys should appear to be following the pattern of the underlying bedrock.

Ravines running from back to front, across the "grain" of the valleys, should imitate the eroded banks of stone originally carved out by an alpine river. For maximum effect, the ravine should fold back on itself several times in a flattened zigzag as seen from above. When seen from the normal viewing angle, these curves will appear to be coves, promontories, and small islands, all telescoped by ordinary perspective and making the entire display vastly more interesting.

The ravine should not bisect the ML at dead center, but should be placed slightly to the left or right, with a prominent mountain occupying the larger hunk of land. Such a ravine can have its "source" in a small background or foreground valley that suddenly widens into a full-scale gorge. Therefore, you should dig down as well as build up. Level off the "riverbed" bottom of the ravine so that it appears relatively flat. Then raise walls of rock on either side, and behind them, pack in good quantities of rich soil.

Once you're satisfied with the lay of your land, inlay its steeper slopes with rocks for greater stability. Rocks you select should be finely textured and fairly flat so that they can be used to "panel" the sides of steep slopes, leaving as much soil as possible behind them. If any of your rocks has a *perfectly* flat surface, that's the side that should be buried. Let the irregularities show.

Rock outcrops should appear mostly toward the foreground, since naturally exposed stone is seldom visible at a distance. All exposed rock faces should appear to be the individual outcrops of a single stratum. But when natural rock splits into flat planes, outcrops are usually so eroded by the elements that they never display straight lines. So rather than line up stones, stagger them. A stone with a vein of quartz running through it can be stood on end at the rear of the ravine to suggest a waterfall.

I'm often asked why I don't have real water running through my ravine. For one thing, that would mean sealing the bed with concrete or fiberglass and installing a fairly expensive pump system. But ironically, real water does not give the *effect* of a river as seen from a distance. So your final step is to install roundish pebbles that closely resemble the huge water-polished boulders that cram alpine streams. (Arrange the pebbles so that they protrude at least a quarter-inch above the bed's surface. This way you'll be able to walk in the center of the river without crushing the small plants that will eventually grow between them.) A meandering trail of crushed limestone will create a surprisingly effective rapids of "white water."

Planting:

Just as in a real landscape, introduce your trees before any other selections. Even in miniature, trees need the most root-room and can do the most to add or detract from the general design.

Many of the dwarf conifers mentioned in Chapter 14 can be effective in a ML. They're often sold as very small grafts or rooted cuttings, but eventually they'll grow out of scale and demand to be pruned back or moved to a new location. It makes better sense to begin with truly miniature plants.

I. The "Larger" Miniature Conifers

Unless mentioned otherwise, all of the following varieties top out at a foot or less after ten years of growth and are best for the very forefront of the ML. My personal favorites are marked.

*Abies balsamea, variety hudsonia: lovely balsam fir foliage. Plant needs some open pruning to show off properly.

A. b. nana: needles circle the twigs, as with a spruce.

Chamaecyparis lawsoniana 'Ellwood's Pygmy': an electric blue bun of juniper-like foliage. Open pruning is not always permanent, since exposed wood is quickly furred with new growth.

C. l. fletcheri nana: low, feathery blue-green bun.

C. l. forsteckensis: deeper green color and more feathery foliage borne in tight, broad fans. High-prune to expose the trunk.

*C. l. 'Green Globe': more attractive foliage than either of the above; tight, well-proportioned foliage suggests a much larger tree.

Chamaecyparis obtusa: hinoki cypress cultivars are particularly valuable for the ML, since their foliage mimicks that of a far larger tree.

C. o. nana: has attractive fans of foliage, borne in a low explosive bun like a miniature green thunderhead. High-pruning is a must, as with all of the larger hinokis.

C. o. 'Rigid Dwarf': a naturally fastigiate miniature, comparable to *nana* in growth rate but far more desirable because of its shape.

Chamaecyparis pisifera compacta: recurved branches of blue-green foliage.

C. p. nana aureovariegata: beautiful yellow-green billows of semi-prostrate foliage. Ideal as the crown to a small hill or to represent the forest of a mountain slope.

C. p. plumosa compressa: a very neat yellow-green ball of tight, erect foliage resembling a Korean boxwood in shape.

Chamaecyparis thyoides conica: gratifyingly slow-growing plant like an attenuated hinoki in habit, but with more prickly foliage.

C. t. contorta forms a neat pyramid of threadlike foliage unlike that of most hinokis.

Cryptomeria japonica vilmoriniana: a low, prickly cone of cryptomeria foliage.

Cupressus glabra compacta: a bit large for ML confines—15″ in ten years—but worth growing for its exquisite threadlike blue foliage.

Juniperus communis compressa: a miniaturized Irish juniper, with perfect full-scale proportions. One of the very few fastigiate dwarfs; a little over 1′ in five years.

Juniperus horizontalis glomerata: forms bright green tufts of foliage that suggest stands of far larger junipers. Good for imitating the drift of mists and clouds, this is the tree planted in the crest of the "mountain" illustrated in the Color Section.

Picea abies echiniformis: literally, "sea-urchin-like" Norway spruce with tight prickly growth never above 18″ high. High-prune to expose the trunk.

P. a. globosa nana: dependably low flattish bun, like a tiny bird's nest spruce.

P. a. gregoryana parsonii: similar to *globosa nana,* but forms greater irregularities, bumps, and billows as it gets older.

P. a. 'Mrs. Cessarini': fine-textured globe; not yet widely available.

P. a. nana: conical unlike most dwarfs, eventually getting up to 15".

*P. *a. pygmaea:* tight, rounded twigs that are extremely slow growing. The entire plant is far more upright than most *Picea abies* cultivars.

**Picea glauca echiniformis:* a tiny bluish cousin of Alberta spruce.

Picea mariana nana: tiny blue-green spruce with small needles.

Picea orientalis nana: a slow, dense bun that requires some open pruning.

Picea pungens nunnewelliana: the smallest of the blue spruces, fine-textured with good color.

Pinus contorta minima: twisted needles are striking, to 16".

Pinus strobus 'Hillside Gem': tight pyramidal growth, fine texture.

*Pinus strobus 'Hordsford's Dwarf': a delightful little bun of a white pine. The needles are reflexed so that each bundle of five is splayed outward like a small trumpet. To my mind, the loveliest of the *strobus* miniatures.

Pinus strobus minuta: more open and a bit faster-growing than 'Hordsford's'.

**Pinus sylvestris viridis compacta:* a pyramidal Scots pine with contorted needles of two different lengths; to 15".

Thuja occidentalis 'Hetz Midget': globose arborvitae, 15" high after twenty years.

**T. o.* 'Little Gem': foliage not as upright as in most other *Thuja* miniatures; plant is a deep green and resembles a semi-weeping hinoki cypress.

**T. o. minima:* small, tightly spherical plant with parallel upright foliage. Some open-pruning needed to keep it from looking like an ordinary suburban foundation planting.

**T. o. rheindiana globosa:* deeper green than *minuta,* with better winter color.

Thujopsis dolabrata nana: very dwarf yellow-green tree resembling a slightly contorted arborvitae.

Tsuga canadensis lewisii: compact sprays of congested foliage; dark green and extremely amenable to high-pruning.

II. Smaller Miniature Conifers

All of the following are tiny squat buns, never higher than 8″ even after many years of growth. All are supremely desirable.

Chamaecyparis obtusa caespitosa: a coral-like mound of absolutely beautiful mounded foliage. Ten-year plants are flat buns four inches across and barely three inches high. Protect from winter winds.

C. o. 'H.N.': an erect but very slow-growing hinoki.

C. o. *minima:* similar to *caespitosa,* only lower.

Chamaecyparis pisifera nana, also called *plumosa minima:* feathery scales on tightly packed sprays of branches.

C. p. *plumosa compressa:* a golden-yellow tree, absolutely symmetrical and apparently trimmed. Variously billed in catalogs as *c. p. adpressa, c. p. squarrosa aurea pygmaea,* and so forth, but is always described as the tiniest chamaecyparis that nurseries have to offer.

C. p. *squarrosa minima:* the slowest of the gray-green mounds; 8″ after ten years.

C. p. *squarrosa* 'Tsukumo': tiny prostrate false cypress that reaches a high 6″ after ten years.

Cryptomeria japonica spiralis: needles twisted sharply around the branches; distinctive and extremely compact, 5″ at ten years.

C. j. 'Yatabusa': allegedly the smallest of all cryptomerias, with sharp foliage like a tiny juniper.

Juniperus communis echiniformis: a tiny bristly mound of Irish juniper, 6″ at ten years

Juniperus procumbens nana: a prostrate form that grows quickly —up to a foot a year—but the upward growth is highly stunted, producing an irregular cushion of green that looks exactly like a forest seen from the air. Only occasional pruning is needed to keep the lateral growth from getting too straight and obvious.

Juniperus squamata 'Shimpaku': an extremely dwarf, low-spreading juniper.

Picea abies echiniformis: the smallest Norway spruce—3″ at ten years.

P. a. procumbens nana: another fine clump-forming prostrate tree; twigs are larger than the growth of *Juniperus procumbens nana.*

P. a. pygmaea: new growth of ½″ per year, plus upright habit seldom found in such small cultivars.

Picea alba 'Little Globe': very tight white spruce.

Picea pungens glauca 'Bacon Dwarf': impossibly tiny blue spruce, 2″ at ten years!

Pinus bandsiana nana 'Witch's Broom ⚹1': an absolutely minute Jack pine with needles barely ¾″ long and upright stature.

Pinus parviflora hillerii: extremely tiny, short-needled Japanese *goyumatsu.*

Pinus strobus 'Northway Broom': an extremely compact low flat cluster of branches, 5″ high in ten years.

Tsuga canadensis 'Jervis': pleasantly crowded needles eventually spreading into a tight ball.

T. c. minuta: utterly hardy little marshmallow of green. New growth is noticable only by color; the best miniature hemlock for multiple use.

T. c. pygmaea: is an extraordinary plant, suitable for the ML only in its extreme old age. Yearly growth is only ⅛″; five-year cuttings are only an inch tall. This tiniest of all hemlocks is said to grow to a venerable eight inches after twenty years or so, but until it attains noticable size, its almost geological slowness demands that you protect it from injury and neglect—either in a pot or in some highly sheltered spot where it won't be smothered by a fallen leaf.

Japanese gardeners create the illusion of greater space by situating larger plants toward the front of a garden and smaller ones toward the back. This works extremely well in ML situations, especially when you plant your hinoki cypresses and other larger Group I evergreens toward the front. To be consistent, however, this means relegating many of your gemlike Group II miniatures like *Tsuga canadensis minima* to the back of the ML, where they're effectively lost to close-up viewing.

But you needn't follow the miniatures-to-the-back rule *too* religiously. In nature, large trees are undergrown by smaller seedlings of the same species. So plant your extreme miniatures right beside taller plants. (Make sure that the larger one is high-pruned so that it doesn't overshadow the miniature.) The middle can be seeded with duplicates and less interesting varieties of Group II, planted more closely together to reinforce the illusion of distance.

Most nurseries root at least a few of their dwarf evergreens from cuttings. However, if you want pine and spruce miniatures, you'll have to tolerate grafts. If the dwarf scion is joined by a whip, splice, or inlay graft to a rootstock of the same diameter, the site will heal with only a small, knobby scar. But some nurseries find it quicker to effect a side graft, in which the scion protrudes at an unsightly angle and takes some years to match up to the larger stock. Plant side grafts so that the grafted scion *faces* the garden front; the later scar will be less obvious.

Never plant any tree *directly* atop a hill. In nature, the top of a hill usually has less soil and available moisture to support plants of any size. But for looks alone, any tree on a pronounced, symmetrical rise should be slightly off-center; in fact, larger trees should occupy the bottom of low valleys to reduce their stature as much as possible.

III. Broadleaf Plants

. . . are best grown in the very forefront of the ML, where they can contrast with the larger Group I conifers. All stay under 12″ unless noted.

*Buxus microphylla nana compacta: the smallest of the boxwoods, this forms a dense mound to 8″ after ten years and can easily be pruned smaller if desired.

*Cotoneaster apiculata 'Tom Thumb': like their larger counterparts, all miniature cotoneasters feature pink to white flowers and bright red berries. 'Tom Thumb' forms a low spreading mound rising to 5″ above the roots, and thus can be planted to create a hill by itself.

Cotoneaster horizontalis 'Little Gem': very long, straight branches need clipping to form a dense, well-filled bun.

Cotoneaster microphylla cooperi: tiny evergreen leaves on low, almost prostrate stems; a slow grower with bright red berries.

Ilex crenata 'Morris Dwarf': far tinier than the usual variety *hillerii* usually sold for foundation and bonsai work.

Kalmia poliifolia microphylla: short, thick, vertical stems with tiny pale green leaves; dark pink mountain laurel flowers in early spring.

Pieris japonica pygmaea (miniature Japanese andromeda): Leaves are about ½" long; plant forms a loose-branched bun. Start new plants in shade or weak sun until they develop a full-fledged root system.

Rhododendron includes a few species good for ML use. Their hybrids *may* be acceptable; but check the descriptions in catalogs.

Rhododendron camplogynum variety *myrtilloides:* extremely dwarf bun with minute flowers in varying shades of red.

R.   *chrysanthum:* mound-forming or creeping, large (to 3") leaves, yellow flowers.

R.   *forrestii:* prostrate habit never above 6", bright red flowers.

R.   *fragariflorum:* tiny leaves on a dense, creeping plant, flowers varying shades of purple.

R.   *impeditum* does classify as a true miniature, but I'd advise you to skip it. The flowers are of a deep bluish lavender that shows up poorly; the tiny leaves are oblong and hairy, not glossy, giving the plant the look of an outsize herb.

R.   *ludlowii:* loosely spreading prostrate twigs, spotted yellow flowers.

R.   *lowndesii:* dense, prostrate, spreading species with spotted yellow flowers.

R.   *pemakoense:* tiny habit and pink bloom.

R.   *pronum:* prostrate, compact growth; leaves to 2½", white, yellowish or pink flowers.

R.   *radicans:* utterly prostrate mats, leaves never over ¾" long, flowers in shades of purple.

R. sargentianum: very dense and compact, slow-growing; yellow to white flowers.

IV. "Shrubs"

These can be grown in either the foreground or middle range, depending on their size and how interesting you find them. While a number have quite beautiful flowers, their main asset is that they mimic the shape of full-scale shrubs, copses, briar patches, hedgerows, and so forth. Many can also be open-pruned to simulate a tiny grove of trees.

The miniature stature of these alpine species is at least partly the result of the lean, gravelly soil in which they're grown. Many times, the rich soil of my ML has coaxed miniatures to double or triple their size, and I've had to remove them to the Rockery or Low Garden. But the species and varieties listed here are all dependably tiny, even in robust health.

Acaena buchananii (New Zealand burr): sea-blue mats of 2″ foliage.

Acorus gramineus minimus: 1½″ mound of tiny foliage.

Armeria juniperifolia, or *setacea:* 3″ mounds of threadlike foliage; constant pinkish flowers spoil the illusion of a large grass tussock.

Artemisia mutellina: 2″ silver tussock; of the same genus as sagebrush.

A. splendens: 2″ mat of white foliage; yellow flowers.

Asplenium sarelli pekingense: 3″ Chinese spleenwort fern.

Calluna: I don't recommend the heathers for ML use, since they are susceptible to a summer fungus that eventually kills the plant. If you're willing to spray and open-prune, however, the following should be ideal:

*Calluna minima: 3″ tight clump; purple flowers.

C. vulgaris foxii nana

    C. *v.* 'Humpty Dumpty': mounds of bright green foliage

    C. *v.* 'Mrs. R. H. Gray': a prostrate heather.

Cassiope lycopodioides: scaly leaves like those of a cypress in a sprawling evergreen clump 3″ high and about 4″ across. Tiny pinkish bells bloom in April.

Cheilanthes tomentosa: a tiny fern whose fronds form a 3″ clump; relishes full sun.

Coprosma petriei: 4″ mound-forming evergreen shrub with tiny needle-like leaves on gray-barked stems. Likes to creep and may need some trimming back.

Draba bryoides imbricata: 2″ mound of tiny light-green foliage that finally grows to be 6″ in diameter; yellow flowers.

D. mollissima: 1″ mound

D. olympica: 2″ mat

D. repens: 2″

D. salamonii: 1″ cushion

Equisetum scirpoides: 3″ horsetail

Genista delphinensis: 3″ Scots broom

G. pilosa: 1″ prostrate Scots broom; yellow flowers

G. villarsii: 2″

Globularia bellidifolia: 1½″ shrub

Hutchinsia alpina: 3″ loose mounds of tiny pinnate leaves.

Lysimachia japonica minutissima: 1″ miniature moneywort; yellow flowers.

Penstemon menziesii 'Olympic Mountain Form': trailing 1″ stems like a miniature euonymous; purple flowers.

P. rupicola alba: 2″ shrub-like plant; white flowers.

Sedum: a very few species are small and slow-spreading enough to provide good accents among low groundcover.

S. brevifolium: tiny drop-shaped light-blue leaves on upright 1″ stalks. Colony resembles a miniature stand of blue spruce; white flowers.

S. nevii: flattened gray-green rosettes seldom over ½″, extremely slow-spreading, rarely flowers.

S. stahlii: deep green 1″ mats.

Selaginella remotifolia compacta: ½" arborvitae-like trailing branches. Likes a deep, rich soil and protection from afternoon heat.

S. sanguinoleutra compressa: thin, upright 1½" branches

S. sibirica: tight mat of small green leaflets

Thlaspi rotundifolium: tiny tussock of deep green tiny leaves, studded with proportionately tiny pinkish flowers. Resembles an infinitesimal rhododendron.

Vaccinium vitis-idaea minus: 1" creeping shrublet

In the distance of any real-life vista, you no longer distinguish any trees at all. Instead, trees blend into forest; forest blends into a series of rolling hills. Accordingly, at the very back of your ML, you should use prostrate, or mound- or hummock-forming plants whose flowers are insignificant or at least short-lived.

V. Groundcovers

You don't want your miniatures too closely crowded, of course, so there's still the problem of what to do with bare ground. Moss, the Lilliputian equivalent of Astroturf, might seem the best answer. But moss doesn't secure itself to the underlying soil. I've found moss dependable only in shady clefts where moisture's relatively assured, and where it's too much trouble for a bird to scratch it loose.

Antennaria (pussytoes) forms loose-spreading mats of prostrate silvery foliage. Unfortunately, most species have relatively large leaves, so that plants give a convincingly "miniature" effect only at a distance. The smallest types include *A. microphylla* and *A. minima rubra compacta*.

Arenaria verna (Irish moss): normally a 3" groundcover, has two desirable varieties: *A. aurea,* forming yellow-green mats about ½" tall, and *A. caespitosa,* of deep green and comparable size. Attractively tiny white flowers are borne at intervals all summer. However, *Arenaria* is sensitive to drought and too often becomes sparse and leggy. Plantings may often experience considerable winter dieback (*A. aurea* is particularly vulnerable to cold), and so fail to cover properly. Interplant with *Sagina* (see below).

Herniaria glabra (burstwort) has minute triangular leaves on stems. The plant grows loosely erect in part shade, but in full sun it settles down to prostrate trailing. New stems grow over one another like ivy until the entire colony is about 2″ deep. The resulting gently rounded mats have a wonderful texture and are thick enough to snuff all but the hardiest weeds.

Hypericum yakusimanum is a 2″ Japanese St. John's wort. Like burstwort, it trails over the ground and itself to form mats. The tiny orange-yellow flowers, contrasting with the shiny green oval leaves, are a definite plus. However, it can become sprawling and is not dependably hardy. *H. yakusimanum* seeds itself, but the young plants are tiny and slow to establish themselves.

Sagina (bird's-eye, pearlwort) is extremely similar to arenaria, forming a ½″ mat of tight, deep green. *S. procumbens* blooms all summer with small greenish flowers; other low-growing species include *S. normaniana*, *S. glabra* (which has an *aurea* form), and *S. sublata*—probably the best bet for ML purposes. Since most *Saginas* are indistinguishable from arenaria to all intents, try as many different of both genera as you can.

Thymus cimicinus is an utterly hardly, compact 1″ thyme with pink flowers. Best planted with *Hypericum,* which has a similar growth habit.

Viola nana, also called *yakusimana,* is an indispensable gem. The world's smallest violet, it produces ¼″ shiny green leaves in mats only 1″ tall. In May and June, perfectly formed white flowers ⅛″ across appear on ¾″ stalks. Although deciduous, *V. yakusimana* is dependably hardy and returns more lushly each spring.

Happily, *yakusimana* reproduces like a weed. In July, after the flowers have faded, the plant begins producing parthenogenic seedpods that—unlike such pods on larger violets—are attractive in themselves. New seedlings are absurdly tiny—six or seven leaves radiating from a hairlike white taproot. But no mater how poor their chosen location, I leave them where they are until late August. By then, the clumps are the size of a nickel and have thrown a root system that goes straight down as deeply as two or three inches.

When you begin a ML, it's tempting to get quick results with the large, faster-growing strains. But after you have experienced some of the really select miniatures whose ancient specimens huddle well under six inches, you'll find yourself seeking the very tiniest trees and perennials you can find.

Many such miniature plants tend to be expensive because they take so long to reach marketable size. It would take several hundred dollars to complete a miniature landscape properly in one season, but by judicious use of rocks, pebbles, and fast-spreading temporary groundcovers, you can at least cover the soil and achieve a respectable illusion.

Like a Rockery, a ML demands weeding until the groundcovers and perennials have *fully* covered its surface. You should pinch off weeds as soon as you recognize them so that their roots don't get established. But check any odd seedling carefully to be sure it's not an offspring of one of your desirable plants. Thereafter, Miniature Landscaping is largely a process of refinement. Once you find a variety that seems as small as you can get, a still tinier one will appear in the new listings of a miniature plant specialist. And this search for the "perfect" miniature offers a never-ending opportunity for discovery, artistry, experimentation, and delight.

At present, a high percentage of the best ML plants come from the American Rockies and Japan. Plant collectors continue to find hitherto unknown strains on mountain peaks, in temple gardens and specialized nurseries. But too many of these plants are still viewed as impractical curiosities; even the incomparable *Viola yakusimana* is still not available by mail! Far more good plants should be more widely available, and judicious hybridization could easily improve hardiness and proportions. But Miniature Landscaping is not yet a recognized garden hobby: it is, instead, a young art whose best examples—and true masters—have yet to emerge.

ORDERING PLANTS BY MAIL

Following is a list of nurseries that, taken together, offer most of the plants discussed in this book. But first, a few tips on ordering from these and other firms.

Be wary of catalogs that offer prizes, sweepstakes, or nonhorticultural giveaways. Any outfit with healthy, desirable stock doesn't need gimmicks to attract its customers. Catalog descriptions that begin, "Just imagine! Won't your friends be amazed when they see . . ." are usually exaggerated and inaccurate. Ignore nursery-coined names for plants such as "Miracle Beauty Bush," and don't buy *any* plant unless at least the Latin name of the genus is provided.

On the other hand, don't underestimate unillustrated, mimeographed price lists. Many firms that sell extremely rare and desirable plants are too busy grafting and propagating to bother with four-color layouts. A seemingly crude Xeroxed list often includes helpful cultural information and a wide variety of high-quality stock.

Accept no substitutes! When the order blank asks, "If your choice is sold out, may we substitute a variety of equal or greater value?" your answer should always be *No*. A nursery's substitutions are based on *cash* value, not on the color, size, or growth habit of your original choice. (I once ordered a white-flowered creeping perennial for the Low Garden; the "substitution" was a tall, upright pink-flowered strain—technically rarer, but utterly useless for my purposes!) Always request a credit or refund.

Too often, I've ordered plants with no forethought of where they'd look best, or what conditions they require. The result is haphazard, poorly planned garden design. Before ordering *anything,* decide exactly where you intend to plant it. Then write that site down, right beside the plant's description in the catalog, and mark the page for future reference. Most catalogs are mailed far in advance of the shipping season, so you may wait up to six months between the time of your order and the day the plants arrive.

When they do, the dormant bulbs, huddled seedlings, or bare roots seldom give you a clue as to what the eventual plant will look like— much less why you ordered them in the first place. Is this the loose-spreading blue flower for the Cultivated Meadow, or the clump-forming pink for the Rockery? But if your catalog is handy, you'll be able to recall exactly what's what and—most importantly—where it's supposed to go.

The catalogs of the firms listed below are rated as to general information and usefulness; those I give three stars are practically indispensable.

J. Herbert Alexander
Middleboro, ME 02346

**Alpines West Nursery
Route 2, Box 259
Spokane, WA 99207

**Appalachian Nurseries
Box 87
Waynesboro, PA 17268

Beaver Dam Creek Nursery
43 Davos Road
Brick Town, NJ 08723

**Blackthorne Gardens
48 Quincy Street
Holbrook, MA 02343

***Bluestone Perennials, Inc.
3500 Jackson Street
Mentor, OH 44060

Bovees Nursery
1737 S.W. Coronado Street
Portland, OR 97219

*Brand Peony Farm
Box 36
Faribault, MN 55021

**Breck's of Boston
(Dutch Bulb Catalog)
6523 North Galena Road
Peoria, IL 61632

*Brimfield Gardens Nursery
245 Brimfield Road
Wethersfield, CT 06109

**W. Atlee Burpee Company
Warminster, PA 18974

**Carroll Gardens
Westminster, MD 21157

*Common Fields Nursery
17 Spring Street
Ipswich, MA 01938

**The Cummins Garden
P.O. Box 125
Colts Neck, NJ 07722

***P. De Jager & Sons, Inc.
188 Asbury Street
South Hamilton, MA 01982

**Duncraft Wild Bird
Specialists
25 South Main Street
Penacook, NH 03301

**Far North Gardens
15621 Auburndale Avenue
Livonia, MI 48154

*Henry Field Seed & Nursery
Co.
Shenandoah, IA 51602

*Dean Foster Nurseries
Hartford, MI 49057

Garden Valley Nursery
Box 10
Bothell, WA 98011

***Greer Gardens
1280 Goodpasture Island
Road
Eugene, OR 97401

*Griffey's Nursery
Route 3, Box 17A
Marshall, NC 26753

Ruth Hardy's Red Cedar
Wildflower Nursery
U. S. Route 7
Falls Village, CT 06031

***Imperial Flower Garden
202 North 4th Street
Box 255
Cornell, IL 61319

**Inter-State Nurseries
Hamburg, IA 51644

**Island Gardens
701 Goodpasture Road
Eugene, OR 97401

**Jackson & Perkins Company,
Inc.
1 Rose Lane
Medford, OR 97501

**Jamieson Valley Gardens
Jamieson Road
Route 3
Spokane, WA 99203

***Kelly Brothers Nurseries,
Inc.
Dansville, NY 14437

*Joseph J. Kern Rose Nursery
Box 33
Mentor, OH 44060

**Krider's Nurseries, Inc.
Middlebury, IN 46540

***Lamb's Nurseries
East 101 Sharp Avenue
Spokane, WA 99202

*Lounsberry Gardens
Box 135
Oakford, IL 62673

*MacPherson Gardens
2920 Starr Avenue
Oregon, OH 43616

**J. E. Miller Nurseries, Inc.
Canandaigua, NY 14424

**Miniature Gardens
Box 757
Stony Plain
Alberta TOE 2G0, Canada

***Musser Forests, Inc.
Indiana, PA 15701

**Oliver Nurseries
1159 Bronson Road
Fairfield, CT 06430

***George W. Park Seed
Company, Inc.
Box 31
Greenwood, SC 29647

***Putney Nursery, Inc.
Putney, VT 05346

***Rakestraw's Perennial
Gardens & Nursery
G-3094 South Term Street
Burton, MI 48529

**Rainier Mountain Alpine
Gardens
2007 South 126th Street
Seattle, WA 98168

**Rhodoland Nursery
Vida, OR 97488

***Clyde Robin Seed Company,
Inc.
Box 2855
Castro Valley, CA 94546

**The Rock Garden
RFD #2
Litchfield, ME 04350

***John Scheepers, Inc.
63 Wall Street
New York, NY 10005

**Sperka's Woodland Acres
Nursery
Route 2
Crivitz, WI 54114

**Joel W. Spingarn
1535 Forest Avenue
Baldwin, NY 11510

**Spring Hill Nurseries
110 West Elm Street
Tipp City, OH 45371

**Star Mums and Star Roses
The Conrad-Pyle Company
West Grove, PA 19390

***Stark Brothers
Louisiana, MO 63353

**Stern's Nurseries
Geneva, NY 14456

*Stokes Seeds, Inc.
Box 548
Buffalo, NY 14240

*The Tingle Nursery
Pittsville, MD 21850

***Van Bourgondien Brothers
Box A
245 Farmingdale Road,
Route 109
Babylon, NY 11702

***Watnong Nursery
Morris Plains, NJ 07950

**White Flower Farm
Litchfield, CT 06759

***The Wild Garden
Box 487
Bothell, WA 98011

*Woodstream Nursery
Box 510
Jackson, NJ 08527

**Melvin E. Wyant
Rose Specialists, Inc.
Johnny Cake Ridge
Route 84
Mentor, OH 44060